Rape Culture Hysteria:

Fixing the Damage Done to Men and Women

by Wendy McElroy

Dedication

To my best friend, Brian Tomlinson.

Contents

Preface: Ain't I A Woman?

> If one believes women are more powerful than men because we own practically all of the vaginas, then women's power to withhold consent to sex is the greatest power there is. Which means the guy who can take away a woman's right to consent is basically a superhero. Right? – Kate Harding [1]

Introduction

There is no rape culture in North America. There is a rape culture hysteria that is not based on evidence, statistics or reason. In fact, the politically correct (PC) myth or lie of a rape culture flies in the face of all evidence, statistics and reason because it is ideologically motivated.

The rape culture is a wildly successful fiction created by PC feminists who wish to embed their vision of gender justice into society. Proponents may or may not be sincere in their beliefs. The important question is whether they are correct. A primary purpose of this book is to examine rape culture claims in order to ascertain their validity, if any. It is my experience, however, that those who stoke hysteria rarely do so because they have the backing of facts and logic. Hysteria is more often used to short circuit the critical thinking of listeners.

If advancing rape culture hysteria is a strategy, then it has been a successful one. The energy and urgency of hysteria is vital to imposing draconian measures on key areas of society, such as university campuses. There, the due process rights of male students accused of sexual misconduct are being

1

suspended in order to curb an *epidemic* of rape which does not exist. Without a righteous panic, however, these measures would encounter stiff resistance.

The ultimate goal of PC feminism is breathtaking in scope. It is nothing less than the deconstruction of the institutions, culture and values of Western society in order to reconstruct them anew according to a dramatically different blueprint of social justice. Innocent men who are devastated in the process are collateral damage and of no political consequence. So, too, are women who disagree with the blueprint.

Rape culture ideologues not only engender a climate of fear but also thrive upon it. Female students are afraid to walk across a campus in full daylight because they falsely believe they have a 1-in-5 or 1-in-4 chance of being raped. The anxiety created turns them into activists who tolerate no contradiction or questions from peers or experts. Professors watch as colleagues are terminated or slammed against a career wall for teaching incorrect ideas. They self-censor to avoid a similar fate, which means using only correct books, thoughts and words. Parents and the public do not question sensational headlines about rape on campus and so are outraged by the "epidemic"; they rush to endorse the passage of drastic laws. Critics who demand accurate data or freedom of speech are accused of being rape deniers or rape facilitators. The fear of slander and attack silences many.

Common sense can seem powerless against such crusading fear. More plausible findings on the rate of sexual assault are dismissed in favor of ones that cause a rush of righteous anger. Professors do not listen to logic but to the inner voice of caution about their own job security. It is useless to point out that *no* business or institution could survive if 20% of its customers were raped while using its services. Who would walk into Walmart if 1-in-4 shoppers would be sexually attacked in the aisles? But rape culture critics who raise such objections find that their characters become the topic of debate rather than the facts of rape.

I persist in objecting. I am female, a libertarian feminist, a victim of rape and domestic violence. I do not accept the existence of a rape culture in North America. And I have a question for PC feminists: Ain't I a Woman?

My Questions for PC Feminism

Ain't I a woman?

"Ain't I a Woman?" was an impromptu speech delivered in 1851 by the black ex-slave Sojourner Truth at an Ohio Women's Convention where woman's suffrage was being hotly debated. Sojourner's speech is one of most famous moments in American feminism but it is draped in lore, with several versions of the speech existing. The version preferred by history seems to be the one published in 1863 by Frances Dana Barker Gage. It came to be known as the "Ain't I a Woman?" speech because of how frequently that question occurs.

The scene of the speech also differs slightly from version to version but some facts seem clear. Men in the audience were openly critical of female suffrage due to what they believed was "woman's frailty." After listening to the comments from men, Sojourner stood up and walked with dignity to the stage and the podium. A hush fell. She stated her position simply but with conviction.

> That man over there says that women need to be helped into carriages, and lifted over ditches, and to have the best place everywhere. Nobody ever helps me into carriages, or over mud-puddles, or gives me any best place! And ain't I a woman?

> Look at me! Look at my arm! I have ploughed and planted, and gathered into barns, and no man could head me! And ain't I a woman?

> I could work as much and eat as much as a man - when I could get it - and bear the lash as well! And ain't I a woman?

> I have borne thirteen children, and seen most all sold off to slavery, and when I cried out with my mother's grief, none but Jesus heard me! And ain't I a woman? [2]

It is a bitter irony that contemporary women who reject gender politics must ask PC feminists, "ain't I a woman?" The answer is even more bitter. It reduces to, "no, you are not." If the woman is a rape victim, like me, then the answer can alter in essence to, "yes, you are...but not one who matters."

At the 19th century suffrage convention, privileged men heckled women who dared to dissent; privileged men told women they needed the protection of the opposite sex. Today, it is PC feminists who view dissenting women, like me, and dismiss them as mistaken, deluded or worse. At universities, such feminists occupy positions of elitism and power. From there, they survey the female population and conclude that wayward women need to be enlightened and guided by them. (Wayward women include conservatives, feminists from other traditions, the religious, those who embrace conventional marriage or sex roles...and the likes of me.) PC feminists assume the role once played by the privileged men at the convention. Today, they are the ones who silence, attack and revile women who disagree.

The dismissal can go so far as to define the rebels not merely out of feminism but also out of womanhood itself. Former feminist Dr. Elly Tams described being viciously attacked by her PC counterparts when she questioned the rape culture. Specifically, she objected to how badly the movement treated men based solely on their gender rather than upon their acts or character as individuals. In backlash, Tams was widely slandered. She was officially declared to be a man, and awarded an "honorary penis" in the form of a sculpture. [3] Tam claims to have housed it in a place of honor.

Despite the constant use of the word "diversity," the dominant voices in modern feminism demand ideological conformity and they do not tolerate intellectual differences. This one fact alone means they do not speak for women as a whole but only for a specific and narrow ideology: PC feminism.

Ain't I a feminist?

Ain't I a woman? With equal validity, I could ask, *"ain't I a feminist?"* I have been an individualist or libertarian feminist since the early 1980s when my first anthology, *Freedom, Feminism and the State,* was published by Cato Institute (1983). [4] For decades, I have been a dissenting voice within feminism, as evidenced by my 1995 book, *XXX: A Woman's Right to Pornography,* published by St. Martin's Press. [5] I've written or edited several other feminist books and written hundreds of articles on the topic. But the feminist tradition to which I belong is scorned by the politically correct, if they deign to notice it at all.

Individualist feminism in America arose from the anti-slavery movement called abolitionism, circa 1830. In fighting for the rights of slaves, abolitionist women asked themselves: "do we not have these rights as well?" The answer was a resounding, "no, we do not." The abolitionist Abby Kelley observed, "we have good cause to be grateful to the slave...in striving to strike his irons off, we found most surely that we were manacled ourselves." [6] What manacled them were laws that discriminated against women in a manner strikingly similar to how they discriminated against blacks.

In short, individualist feminists sought to destroy the institution of slavery and to embed equal rights for all into the law. They made no distinction between black or white, man or woman. They believed that a just system of law spoke only of human beings and aimed at a peaceful coexistence in which everyone enjoyed equal self-ownership. By self-ownership, they meant the rightful jurisdiction that every human being had over his or her own body and property. They meant the same natural rights as those expressed in the Bill of Rights. *That* was their revolutionary vision: genuine equality through which a natural respect between people had a chance to flourish.

It is my vision as well. No legal privileges due to race, gender or any other secondary characteristic. No legal disadvantages either. Simply by being human, everyone is entitled to identical protection and peaceful enjoyment of their person and property. In terms of the just distribution of wealth and power, my form of social justice is when people peacefully rise or fall through their own merit, not through state intervention. This is the opposite of elitism; it is a society in which the disadvantaged have an opportunity to advance through hard work and merit.

Ain't I a feminist? The PC answer is, "no, you are not." For one thing, individualists do not participate in the demonization of men or any other class of human being such as white or Christian. One of my favorite feminist quotes comes from the 19th century abolitionist Sarah Grimké, who declared, "men and women were CREATED EQUAL.... Whatever is right for a man to do, is right for woman....I seek no favors for my sex. I surrender not our claim to equality. All I ask of our brethren is that they will take their feet from off our necks and permit us to stand upright." [7]

PC feminists should take their feet off the necks of men and dissenting women. But doing so would involve abandoning the theory of patriarchy (white male culture) through which they view the wrongs of the world and conclude that women are always and everywhere oppressed by men. It would mean respecting opinions that differ from their own and abandoning orthodoxy. Reliquishing the theory of patriarchy and the demand for conformity will not happen. Until it does, men and uppity women will be lumped together and labeled as "anti-feminists."

Ain't I a victim of sexual violence?

The last question I have for PC feminists is the most awkward one for them. *Ain't I a victim of sexual violence?* As a teenager, I lived on the street for as short a period of time as possible; I experienced considerable violence, including a rape. In my twenties, I chose the wrong romantic partner and the mistake culminated in a domestic assault that was severe enough to leave me legally blind in my right eye. In each case, however, I was not attacked by *men* but by an individual *man,* and I hold those individuals responsible. I do not blame men per se. For one thing, most men I know now would put themselves in danger in order to defend me.

I recently stumbled across a poster, written anonymously, which expresses my feelings well.

> Four years ago, I was raped.
>
> I didn't ask for it. I didn't want it. I didn't deserve it.
>
> I also, however, didn't blame society.
>
> I blamed the man who raped me.
>
> The 'Patriarchy' did not assault me.
>
> 'Rape culture' did not slip sleeping pills into my drink.
>
> One man did.
>
> And he did it not because he was taught to.
>
> Not because society said he should.
>
> He raped me because he is a bad person and we should not be holding everyone accountable for bad people.
>
> Don't let rapists go free of responsibility by saying their choices are made for them by society.
>
> Bad people do bad things.
>
> Don't let them trick you into thinking that we are all to blame.

I learned brutal lessons from mistakes I made. And, no, I am not condemning myself for being harmed, for being a victim, but neither do I refuse to learn from experience. One lesson I've learned: I do not define myself as a victim because that would allow a rapist and a woman-beater to be an integral part of my self-definition. Who I am is not determined by what vicious people do **to** me but by the decisions I make, the person I choose to be. I refuse to become my victimhood.

And, yet, I make a point of mentioning I am a rape survivor. There are at least three reasons for doing so. First. I am *not* ashamed and I'm willing to speak about the attacks as long as it is in broad terms without personal details. Second, in a book about rape, having first-hand knowledge seems significant. It gives me a perspective that most women happily lack.

Third, by the standards of PC feminism, having been attacked gives me special credentials to speak out on the rape culture. My voice carries more weight – or, at least, it should according to the values of rape culture adherents. Anyone who has sat through a PC feminist gathering knows that a hushed silence falls over the group when a personal account of sexual violence is aired. After all, victims are the *raison d'etre* of gender and social justice warriors. Victims are the beating heart of the movements.

But victims like me are inconvenient. I've received the distinct impression that PC feminists would like to yank the victim-credential out from under women like me who both vindicate and debunk their ideology in the same breath. Some feminists actually grimace in anger when I speak of the violence I've experienced; the anger is directed at me and not at the men responsible. Their reason for doing so is simple. What I say about rape directly contradicts their vision of the rape culture, which has become core to their identity.

And so the PC answer to my question, *"ain't I a 'victim' of violence?,"* is a resounding silence interspersed with glares of rage.

As a woman, a feminist, and a survivor of sexual violence, I know the rape culture is a lie that harms women and victims of violence as well as men. It calls itself "justice" but the goal is to impose a specific ideology that legally disadvantages one class of people (white males) in order to benefit others. PC feminism calls itself "diverse" but it wages war upon true diversity which lives or dies in the ability of people to dissent and to make decisions about their own lives. The feminist movement once championed *human* rights while insisting that people shoulder responsibility for themselves. The current movement is a mockery of its past. If snapping my fingers could reverse the dogma and intolerance, my hands would be numb from overuse.

Real feminists still walk among us. Individualist and equity feminists – like Christina Hoff Sommers, Camille Paglia and Cathy Young – still work for real equality and respect between the sexes. But many more people need to speak out. In Hans Christian Andersen's tale, "The Emperor's New Clothes," the truth began with one child who believed the evidence of his eyes over what he was told. The crux of the story: swindling clothiers convince an Emperor that he is wearing fabulous garments which can be seen only by those who are worthy. Not wishing to appear *un*worthy, the Emperor parades proudly and publicly in the buff. None of his subjects have the honesty or courage to speak the truth of the Emperor's nakedness. Finally, a child calls out, "The Emperor is naked!" When he does, the reality quickly spreads and the Emperor's clothes are revealed as a scam. Truth is like that. Lies need to be enforced; the truth needs only to be spoken.

PC feminism sustains itself through government support and by silencing those who disagree on the ground that they are unworthy. Nevertheless, the Empress has no clothes.

> Stupid ideas spread when people who know better refuse to confront them. This would include college presidents and administrators terrified of challenging their academically deprived and anti-male women's studies departments, and it would include most of the mainstream news media, which have worked so hard to evade or botch coverage. –John Leo [8]

Overview of the Book

Rape Culture Hysteria is an introductory overview of the ideology, history, psychology and statistics that surround the rape culture. It argues passionately against the severe damage being inflicted upon women, men, victims of sexual violence and society in the name of social justice.

The book is written in a popular style because it addresses the bastion of gender sanity in North America: the average person whose intelligence and common sense are woefully underrated. The book has trappings of scholarship, such as footnotes, but they are provided only as a courtesy to readers who wish to pursue a point. The most onerous aspects of academia have been avoided because they seem designed to shut out civilians: the arcane jargon, incestuous references, bizarre math, and studies that are inaccessible even to the intelligent reader. Academia has become a closed club for elites who look down their noses at the average person. And, yet, it is the average person who must live under the laws that their "data" and activism facilitate.

Many aspects of the book will be controversial. For example, I believe women and men need to empower themselves by learning self-defense and taking common sense measures to reduce their chance of becoming a victim. Social justice warriors will call this victim-blaming and call me a rape denier. Their response only serves to obscure the real difference between advocating crime prevention and blaming victims.

Another controversial point: Contrary to political wisdom, I believer the rape culture deeply harms those who have been victimized by sexual violence. At its worst, the rape culture uses victims in an ideological high-stakes game of power. At its best, the rape culture unintentionally obstructs the ability of injured human beings to heal.

The book ends on a hopeful note, however, with positive recommendations to repair the damage and to return society to gender sanity. We can fix this.

Rape Culture Hysteria is divided into seven chapters.

Chapter One: The Fiction of the Rape Culture. Chapter One defines "the rape culture" and explains why the phenomenon does not exist in North America. Many of the concepts touched upon will be developed in later sections. For example, the real rate of rape in America is addressed even though the chapter on statistics examines the rate in detail. Chapter One also glances backward at the history of how the rape culture became embedded into society, especially into academia. Then it looks forward to an emerging and powerful trend within rape culture politics, which may deeply impact daily life in North America: microaggressions.

Chapter Two: Intellectual Framework and History of Rape Culture Myth. The myth of the rape culture did not arise in an intellectual or historical vacuum, and it is impossible to understand the concept without grasping the theoretical framework from which it draws meaning. In a straight-forward manner, Chapter Two explains the specific theories upon which the rape culture is based, including social construction, gender, the patriarchy, post-Marxism, and social justice. The chapter places particular emphasis on the seemingly innocuous slogan, "the personal is political." The history of the rape culture is traced from Susan Brownmiller's pivotal book *Against Our Will* to the current day. The chapter considers and rejects three of the rape culture's founding myths: rape is an essential part of patriarchy; men have created a mass psychology of rape; and, rape is a part of normal life.

Chapter Three: Dynamics of the Hysteria and Psychology of Rape Culture True Believers. The dynamics of the rape culture politics are laid bare through a presentation of the predictable strategies and behavior of rape culture adherents. A recent travesty is used to showcase those dynamics. On November 19, 2014, *Rolling Stone* accused members of a University of Virginia (U-Va) fraternity of gang-raping a female student. The accusation was quickly revealed to be a hoax or a delusion. The unraveling at U-Va. is a perfect vehicle to illustrate how rape culture dogma is maintained even when it is revealed to be untrue. An analysis of the rape culture mindset springboards off the U-Va story, as well as a discussion of effective tactics with which to handle confrontations.

Chapter Four: Data, False and True. The rape culture myth rests on a mixture of blatantly untrue and unfounded "facts," which have been repeatedly and meticulously refuted. And, yet, they lumber forward in academia, politics and the media. The dead facts walking among us are called zombie stats because they defy the refutation that would lay a normal lie to rest. They are kept alive by those to whom the lies are useful and so are repeated like a mantra that drowns out contradicting evidence. This chapter examines some of the more prevalent zombie stats:

- one in every 4 or 5 women will be raped in their lifetimes;

- only 2% of all rape accusations are false;

- one in 3 male students would rape if he could get away with it.

Where did the faux "facts" originate? What evidence, if any, supports them? Which stats better reflect reality and how are they derived?

Chapter Five: Comparative Studies and Surveys. This chapter compares and contrasts four of the most important, frequently cited studies and surveys on rape. The studies are: NCVS, National Crime Victimization Survey from Bureau of Justice Statistics; NISVS, National Intimate Partner and Sexual Violence Survey from Centers for Disease Control; CSAS, Campus Sexual Assault Study from National Institute for Justice; and, UCR, Uniform Crime Reporting Program from the FBI. The sources are analyzed independently but also compared to each other in terms of definitions, methodology, findings and the uses to which they have been put. Major strengths and problems with each are explored and compared. Lesser studies are also analyzed in passing.

Chapter Six: Harms of the Rape Culture. A gender war is fragmenting men and women into enemy camps, and destroying the recognition that we are all human beings with a shared humanity. Whatever diversity exists between the sexes and between individuals should be celebrated, not assaulted. The gender war must end. The myth of the rape culture is harming victims of sexual violence, women, men and the institutions of society, especially universities. Chapter Six offers in-depth perspective of the extreme damage being inflicted on innocent people, with emphasis on the damage done to victims of rape and to the value of academia. Victims are a focus because rape culture adherents claim to be their greatest champions; I believe the opposite is true in terms of the impact that rape culture warriors have upon victims. By contrast, the harm to men receives less attention in this chapter because it is highlighted throughout the book.

Chapter Seven: Solutions to Rape Culture Hysteria. Moving Toward Sanity. **We can fix this.** This is the ultimate message of the book. We can fix this. Undoing the specific damage wrought by the rape culture is not only possible but also within reach. The solutions offered in this chapter range from radical suggestions, such as abolishing the Department of Education, to more modest ones, such as repealing Title IX of the Education Act. Other remedies include privatizing higher education to provide the competition that offers freedom, and removing the power of the federal purse in academia. In addition, rape must be recognized as a criminal matter to be handled by police who are trained in forensics and investigation techniques.

Three Caveats

In addressing the rape culture, I make two omissions. One is a matter of self-respect; the other, a matter of regret.

Caveat #1. *The omission from self-respect.*

It is seems mandatory for a critic of the rape orthodoxy to preface herself with defensive remarks about how seriously she takes the issue of rape and how profoundly she empathizes with the pain of victims. No one who knows my history can doubt how seriously I take rape; no one can doubt that I empathize. The issue once devastated my life.

I refuse to provide the standard preface, however, and for two reasons.

First, no one has any business lecturing me or any rape victim on whether she understands the overwhelming impact of sexual violence. No one has the right to question my sincerity; it is an insult. And, yet, this is exactly what the preface mandated by PC voices entails. They demand that I defend my motives and character even before a discussion begins; this is is yet another way in which rape culture skeptics are silenced or diminished. For one thing, the demand assumes rape culture adherents are *the* ones who care passionately about sexual assault; they are the judge and juries of who else does. Not a single adherent with whom I've spoken or debated felt it necessary to open by reassuring the audience that she took the subject seriously or was sincere. Those motives were taken for granted. By contrast, the demand for a defensive preface assumes that skeptics are indifferent or callous toward victims. This is not a point on which I will tolerate the lecturing of others. I refuse to sanction insulting assumptions.

Why do rape culture proponents open discussion by calling the motives of dissenting women into quesiton? They derive great advantage from doing so. It allows PC feminists to claim the high ground of understanding and compassion. It means a woman who questions their position is questioning an intellectual and moral authority, and must rush to declare an equal depth of caring. It creates a rigged exchange in which, again, I refuse to participate.

A second dynamic is at work with the demand. Requiring me (or anyone) to assure an audience of my good intentions shifts the focus away from whether my statements are correct and toward an assessment of my motives or character. Frankly, it is offensive in the extreme to expect a victim of sexual assault to affirm her "right" to speak out by assuring an audience of her sincerity. It is an indirect form of ad hominem and a personal attack. Again, I refuse to participate.

Caveat #2. *The omission I regret.*

Except in passing, the book does not discuss male victims of sexual assault. I am aware of the extent and brutality of the sexual violence committed against men. Male rape is one of the most underreported and widely-dismissed crimes in society. Existing in the shadows, many male victims feel the same sort of shame and humiliation that was experienced by raped women in the 1950s, before liberal feminism lifted much of the stigma. There is no similar voice to champion sexualy abused males. And, yet, if the prison and military populations were included, the rates of male and female rape would probably be comparable. The male rate might even be higher.

My omission is not the result of indifference, although this is what male victims have come to expect. The standard dismissal was illustrated by a Q&A period at a speech I delivered; a comment was directed to me by a female student who angrily proclaimed, "women are overwhelmingly the victims of rape!" I shook my head from side-to-side.

"You disagree!" She seemed shocked.

"If you factor in military and prison rapes," I replied, "then I think the numbers of men and women may be roughly comparable."

"You can't include prison," she objected. "Those are totally different circumstances."

I asked if circumstances determined whether forced sex was rape. The student was smart enough to realize the intellectual precipice on which she stood. The evening had revolved around one assertion; namely, circumstances such as drunkness or the absence of protest had no revelance to whether or not a woman had been raped. If the questioner maintained that being imprisoned meant forced sex was not rape for a man, then I would have immediately replied, "which circumstances mean forced sex is not rape for a woman?" To the student's credit, she backed away. In my opinion, she did not do so not out of fairness to men but because her argument might have rebounded against women.

Other PC feminists display an explicit enjoyment of male pain, perhaps because they view it as some sort of payback. A popular saying on rape culture T-shirts, coffee mugs and posters is, "I bathe in male tears." Jessica Valenti's t-shirted photo boasting this slogan is easily found on the Internet.

In a 2014 *Slate* article, "The Rise of the Ironic Man-Hater," pop-feminist Amanda Hess explained [9] in all earnestness, "But man-hating is not just for fun: It's also a clever tactic for furthering the feminist agenda....[I]ronic misandry is typically paired with expressions of 'overt femininity, bordering on the exaggerated'." Expressions of hatred are viewed as clever politics, as a way to turn the tables on the patriarchy. Yet, when men make similar statements about women, their words are condemned as acts of violence and proof that the rape culture exists.

Other PC feminists *appear* to acknowledge male victims but they include men in such a manner as to actually ignore them. For example, they are mentioned in footnotes, in passing or through the use of neutral language that includes only women when any practical application arises. An example of the latter is California legislation SB-967 through which a "yes means yes" standard was imposed on California campuses in January 2015. The text of the bill uses gender neutral terms such as "student," "accused," and "complainant." [10] Once a perfunctory nod to male victims occurs, however, the campus focus snaps swiftly back to the narrative of "females as victims," "males as predators." Indeed, the neutral language may be nothing more than a way to sidestep problems with Title IX law which requires gender equity in tax-funded programs, including campus hearings on sexual violence.

Why then do I omit male victims of sexual assault? First and foremost, such an exposition demands a book of its own. It would be a fitting companion to *Rape Culture Hysteria* but the topic needs separate treatment. For example, exploring the reality of male rape would require an entirely different direction of research and analysis. Instead of exploring existing studies and statistics, it might require original research since very little data are now available on prison rape, for example. Finding solid statistics on male victims would be difficult. The NISVS is one of the most cited studies on sexual violence. Its approach illustrates just one problem with sorting out male rape victims. It states that *forcing* a male to penetrate another person – that is, compelling sexual coitus – is not considered to be rape. The NISVS explains [11],

"As an example of prevalence differences between the National Intimate Partner and Sexual Violence Survey and other surveys, the lifetime prevalence estimate of rape for men in this report is lower than what has been reported in other surveys (e.g., for forced sex more broadly) (Basile, Chen, Black, & Saltzman, 2007). This could be due in part to the National Intimate Partner and Sexual Violence Survey making a distinction between rape and being made to penetrate someone else. Being made to penetrate is a form of sexual victimization distinct from rape that is particularly unique to males and, to our knowledge, has not been explicitly measured in previous national studies. It is possible that rape questions in prior studies captured the experience of being made to penetrate someone else, resulting in higher prevalence estimates for male rape in those studies."

The tables offered [12] by the NISVS reveal that, if forced penetration is counted as rape, then the rate of rape for both sexes may be roughly equal: rapes for women are 13% (weighted); forced penetrations for men are 11% (weighted).

The NISVS is far from alone in refusing to classify sexual acts that may be forced upon men as sexual violence even though the identical acts are classified as such for women. Researcher Mary P. Koss, for example, commented [13] on methodologies for measuring rape in her 1993 paper, which is still used as a touchstone, "Detecting the Scope of Rape: A Review of Prevalence Research Methods."

Although consideration of male victims is within the scope of the legal statutes, it is important to restrict the term rape to instances where male victims were penetrated by offenders. It is inappropriate to consider as a rape victim a man who engages in unwanted sexual intercourse with a woman."

I vehemently disagree. But this book is not the proper venue in which to do so. This book's purpose is to confront and to refute the rape culture on its own terms. And, because the rape culture does not recognize males as sexual victims, they are not included in the narrative, except in the preface, except to point out what this cruel omission says about PC feminism.

Several links to discussions of male rape are included in the Notes below [14] to encourage readers to pursue the issue of sexual violence against men. To the extent males are viewed as victims in this book, however, the focus is upon the treatment of male students accused of sexual assault who are stripped of due process by campus sexual assault hearings.

Caveat #3. *This book has no academic pretensions.*

As mentioned earlier, end notes are provided to allow readers to follow-up on points of interest but they are provided for utility alone. Chapter Five on surveys offers rather dry exposition on and comparison of the most significant sources of rape data; the section is the closest to an academic presentation within the book but its focus is accessibility. The book is meant to be useful and it makes no apology for flaunting academic conventions that serve no reasonable purpose and interfere with readability.

Conclusion

Rape culture hysteria is devastating society, and it does so even as the rate of rape falls sharply.

Rape Culture Hysteria states, "The Empress has no clothes." The book presents a thorough overview of the destructive lie of the rape culture and of the social justice movement in general. It invites others to confront the absurd and vicious notion that North America is a rape culture.

The book also invites open discussion from rape culture adherents. Nothing is as important to the issue of rape and to freedom itself than open and vigorous debate. Sadly, PC feminism stifles individual women even as it claims to represent "women" as a class. PC feminism is now the political status quo with the power and funding to persecute heretics. And, yet, the ability of an individual to disagree with the status quo is where human freedom lives. The words, "I disagree," are the heart of liberty; the ability to act on that disagreement is liberty in motion. If PC feminists cannot tolerate uppity women who disagree, then I doubt their commitment to women and to diversity.

People have been politically Balkanized. But there is good news. We can fix this. People of benevolence and common sense can prevail. It happens all the time.

Notes

[1] Kate Harding, *Asking for It: The Alarming Rise of Rape Culture and What We Can Do about It.* https://www.amazon.ca/Asking-Alarming-Rise-Culture-about/dp/0738217026

[2] Sojourner Truth, "Ain't I a Woman?" text at http://www.emersonkent.com/speeches/ain_t_i_a_woman.htm. Retrieved

Sept. 20, 2015. The original, as reproduced by Frances Gage in *The History of Woman Suffrage (1881)*, volume 1 is also reprinted at the URL.

[3] Dr. Elly Tams, "Leaving the sisterhood: A recovering feminist speaks," *A Voice for Men*, Aug. 13, 2012.
http://www.avoiceformen.com/feminism/leaving-the-sisterhood-a-recovering-feminist-speaks/ Retrieved Sept. 20, 2015.

[4] *Freedom, Feminism and the State,* ed. Wendy McElroy (Washington DC, Cato, 1983; 2nd ed., Holmes & Meier, 1991). See also Wendy McElroy, "How the history and theory of individualist feminism differs, especially re: equality, justice and class," June 3, 2008.
http://www.wendymcelroy.com/plugins/content/content.php?content.116 Retrieved Sept. 20, 2015.

[5] McElroy, *XXX: A Woman's Right to Pornography* (New York: St. Martin's Press), 1995.

[6] Abby Kelley in *An Anti-Slavery Album, or Contributions from Friends of Freedom,* Western Anti-Slavery Society Collection, Library of Congress, p.100.

[7] Sarah Grimké, *Letters on the Equality of the Sexes and the Condition of Woman Addressed to Mary S. Parker,* 1838.
https://archive.org/stream/lettersonequalit00grimrich/lettersonequalit00gr imrich_djvu.txt Retrieved Sept. 20, 2015

[8] John Leo, "Let's Challenge the 'Rape Culture' Warriors," *Minding the Campus*, Dec. 11, 2013.
http://www.mindingthecampus.com/2013/12/lets_challenge_the_rape_cul tur_1/ Retrieved Sept. 20, 2015.

[9] Amanda Hess, "The Rise of the Ironic Man-Hater," *Slate*, Aug. 8, 2014.
http://www.slate.com/blogs/xx_factor/2014/08/08/ironic_misandry_why _feminists_joke_about_drinking_male_tears_and_banning.html Retrieved Sept. 20, 2015

[10] SB-967, Approved by Governor, September 28, 2014. Filed with Secretary of State, September 28, 2014.
https://leginfo.legislature.ca.gov/faces/billNavClient.xhtml? bill_id=201320140SB967 Retrieved Sept. 20, 2015.

[11] "The National Intimate Partner and Sexual Violence Survey: 2010 Summary Report," Centers for Disease Control, p. 84.
http://www.cdc.gov/ViolencePrevention/pdf/NISVS_Report2010-a.pdf Retrieved Sept. 20, 2015.

[12] "E-lert: Hidden Victims: Men Who are Forced to Penetrate," *Stop Abusive and Violent Environments*, March 11, 2014. http://www.saveservices.org/2014/03/e-lert-hidden-victims-men-who-are-forced-to-penetrate/ From NIPSV, pp. 18-19 Retrieved Sept. 20, 2015.

[13] Mary Koss, "Detecting the Scope of Rape: A Review of Prevalence Research Methods," *Journal of Interpersonal Violence*, Vol 8 #2, June, 1993, pp. 206-107. http://jiv.sagepub.com/content/8/2/198.full.pdf+html Retrieved Sept. 20, 2015.

[14] The following links provide a range of information on male rape:

- Nathaniel Penn, "Son, Men Don't Get Raped," *GQ*. On male rape in the military. http://www.gq.com/long-form/male-military-rape Retrieved Sept. 20, 2015.

- Anonymous, "Rethinking Gender and Assault: a male perspective," *The Stanford Daily*, Jan. 11, 2015. A male rape on campus. http://www.stanforddaily.com/2015/01/11/rethinking-gender-and-sexual-assault-policy-my-story/ Retrieved Sept. 20, 2015.

- Staff Reporter, "More men are raped in the US than women, figures on prison assaults reveal." *The Daily Mail*, Oct. 8, 2013. On male rape in prison. http://www.dailymail.co.uk/news/article-2449454/More-men-raped-US-women-including-prison-sexual-abuse.html Retrieved Sept. 20, 2015.

- "Let's look at male rape, shall we?" From the website Don't Need Feminism. A general overview of male rape in the United States. http://dontneedfeminism.com/post/71293039484/lets-look-at-male-rape-shall-we Retrieved Sept. 20, 2015.

Chapter One: The Fiction of the Rape Culture

Introduction to Rape Culture Hysteria

> It [rape] is nothing more than a conscious process of intimidation by which *all* men keep *all* women in a state of fear. [Emphasis added] –Susan Brownmiller [1]

No matter how loudly it is proclaimed by PC feminists, the rape culture is not a real crisis but a manufactured one.

The rape culture is a social construct that derives from the concept of "the patriarchy" – a system of oppression by which women as a class are said to be victimized by men as a class through the omnipresent threat of sexual violence. A social construct is the perception of an individual or a group that is presented as reality. The concept assumes the status of fact by spreading through a culture and convincing a sufficient number of people to accept it as real.

The "reality" of the rape culture has been created by the incessant broadcasting of politically correct perceptions over the past few decades. PC ideologues have hammered out theory and fabricated data to lend support to the construct. Through their dominance in academia, PC feminists have reinterpreted gender, politics, history, literature, science and the minutia of human behavior to validate their ideological beliefs.

The rape culture is a particularly vicious fiction because it brands half the human race – males, and especially white males – as rapists or rape facilitators. This slander would be denounced as hate speech if it were directed at any other class of human being, such as blacks, gays or women. But slandering men is tolerated or applauded because the falsehood is dressed up as justice. Gender justice is supposed to mean equal treatment and equal respect for the sexes. In practice, it has become a demand for women to be privileged while men are disadvantaged and demeaned. In practice, it is gender injustice.

How doublethink drives hysteria

> DOUBLETHINK means the power of holding two contradictory beliefs in one's mind simultaneously, and accepting both of them.... DOUBLETHINK lies at the very heart of Ingsoc [a totalitarian government], since the essential act of the Party is to use conscious deception while retaining the firmness of purpose that goes with complete honesty. To tell deliberate lies while genuinely believing in them, to forget any fact that has become inconvenient, and then, when it becomes necessary again, to draw it back from oblivion for just so long as it is needed, to deny the existence of objective reality and all the while to take account of the reality which one denies– all this is indispensably necessary. –George Orwell, *Nineteen Eighty-four* [2]

A Big Lie is a deceit so brazen and massive that people swallow it whole because they do not believe anyone would abuse the truth so outrageously. People are accustomed to telling small white lies. But they find it difficult to accept that anyone would lie consistently on a grand scale without there being some basis in fact. The deceit is also believed by those who have an emotional attachment to or vested interest in the content of the fabrication. Sometimes such people can repeat the lie as though it were God's honest truth without becoming liars themselves because they genuinely believe what they say.

The most effective lies are outlandish ones with content and presentation that strongly appeals to listeners. If a lie can inspire a sharp emotional reaction, such as rage or guilt, then it can bypass the normal filters of skepticism with which most people approach daily life. Sometimes the falsehood is surrounded by conveniently flawed data and statistics. Often it is accompanied by hyperbolic rhetoric. But it is stated with a straight face as though it were a matter of established fact with which no honest or reasonable person could disagree.

In a debate on the rape culture with PC feminist Jessica Valenti at Brown University (November 18, 2014), I saw this tactic in action. I spoke first. My presentation was a prepared argument against the very concept, into which I shoehorned as much evidence as my limited time allowed. Valenti stood up and declared herself to be "exhausted" by the continuing demand to defend the existence of a rape culture. "The work has been done," Valenti stated adamantly. [3] She proceeded as though the paradigm were self-evidently true, as though no counter-evidence or arguments had been uttered. It was the Big Lie in progress.

The following are some of the components that allow notorious falsehoods to succeed. (The dynamics are detailed in Chapter Three where a specific Big Lie – the U-Va./"Jackie" scandal – is dissected.)

1   *The Big Lie must be brash and colossal.* An example is the claim that men and women are separate political classes – almost separate species – who have antagonistic interests. In fact, men and women are full and equal members of the same species who benefit identically from human rights such as freedom of speech and freedom of conscience. There is no natural conflict of interests between peaceful individuals whose person and property are equally protected. Political conflict arises when rights are not equally protected, when one sex (or class of people) enjoys legal privileges at the expense of others. Rape culture adherents and legal privileges create separate antagonistic classes.

2   *The falsehood should make the average person ask, "Who would make up such a thing?"* People assume that women do not or would not lie about rape. Victims would not vent false trauma or accuse innocent men of terrible crimes. Feminists would not cry out against an epidemic of rape unless one existed. And, yet, people lie all the time. Men lie, women lie, feminists lie. This is particularly true when some personal or political advantage adheres to the lie.

3   *The Big Lie is constantly repeated because many people believe whatever they hear often enough or from many sources.* Rape culture warriors incessantly interpret all of society through the lens of sexual violence. Then they feed it back as loudly as possible over social megaphones. From such trivial matters as a man's casual glance of sexual interest to cataclysmic scenarios of war, the rape

culture is the omnipresent explanation. It saturates society through academia, mainstream media, literature, politics, activism...

4 *The fiction must be maintained by force, by law or other state action.* In the free market of ideas, truth has a strong tendency to prevail. And, so, political fictions must advance themselves through a combination of censorship and endorsement by authority. *Censorship* means "incorrect" ideas or words are stifled and punished. For example, the idea that women bear some responsibility for their own self-defense is treated as victim-hating. *Endorsement by authority* means legal or other state support for specific ideas, often in the form of funding them. For example, to receive federal funds, universities comply with Department of Education requirements on how to handle the alleged epidemic of rape on campus, including suspension of due process for those who are accused.

5 *The Big Lie must deeply impact people's emotions.* Few images elicit as much emotion as those of women – especially young daughters – being savagely raped. The specter of sexual violence elicits protectiveness from men, fear from women, and rage from both sexes.

6 *A significant number of people must want to believe the lie.* A significant number of women believe they are oppressed by men and are flooded with anger. Anger is the appropriate emotion if real oppression or violence occurs. But today's oppression is everywhere and in everything; it arises from political analysis rather than true disadvantage. Hearing the constant mantra of victimization, too many women have rooted their identity in their status as victims. They want to believe in a rape culture because they have internalized it as part of their identity.

7 *The falsehood is expressed in moral outrage and in pursuit of a righteous goal.* Thus, a rape culture adherent stakes out the moral high ground which is half outrage and half self-righteousness; skeptics are accused of assaulting justice rather than merely questioning facts. The moral outrage is stoked by accounts from raped or otherwise abused women; the discrediting of dissenters or questioners is achieved by depicting them as raping the victims over again.

8 *Anyone who opposes the Big Lie is vilified unmercifully.* To criticize rape culture ideology is equated with trivializing rape or denying its

existence. Focus shifts from statistics or factual claims and onto the character of the questioner. When a debate centers on whether one of the parties is a decent human being, the debate is over and the witch hunt is afoot.

But why are average people, who are not ideologues, willing to buy into the lie?

The dynamics of psychopathology

In 1841, the Scottish author Charles Mackay published a remarkable book that became a classic within sociology, economics, politics and psychology. In *Extraordinary Popular Delusions and the Madness of Crowds*, Mackay described a peculiar crowd psychology that seems to erupt from time to time within human history and drives widespread delusions or Big Lies. These included the tulip mania (circa 1637) as well as the witch hunts of the 16th and 17th centuries. Mackay's book is divided into three sections: "National Delusions," "Peculiar Follies" and "Psychological Delusions."

Mackay prefaced his work with the explanation [4], "In reading the history of nations, we find that, like individuals, they have their whims and their peculiarities; their seasons of excitement and recklessness, when they care not what they do. We find that whole communities suddenly fix their minds upon one object, and go mad in its pursuit; that millions of people become simultaneously impressed with one delusion, and run after it, till their attention is caught by some new folly more captivating than the first....Some delusions...have subsisted for ages, flourishing as widely among civilised and polished nations as among the early barbarians with whom they originated."

Making specific reference to Mackay's book, the iconic 20th century speculator Bernard Baruch expressed the same concept in different terms [5]. "Have you ever seen in some wood, on a sunny quiet day, a cloud of flying midges – thousands of them – hovering, apparently motionless, in a sunbeam? ...Yes? ...Well, did you ever see the whole flight – each mite apparently preserving its distance from all others – suddenly move, say three feet, to one side or the other? Well, what made them do that? A breeze? I said a quiet day. But try to recall – did you ever see them move directly back again in the same unison? Well, what made them do that? Great human mass movements are slower of inception but much more effective."

Some examples of past Big Lies that once dominated society are:

- Sociological: Blacks are not fully human. This appealed to the sense of superiority of slave-owners as well as to their economic self-interest. It also calmed pangs of conscience that might arise over owning another person.

- Religious: God hates gays. Building a religious basis for homophobia allows people to feel righteous and guilt-free while experiencing their prejudice.

- Political: Men and women are separate and antagonistic classes.

Crowd psychology has a dynamic that encourages the Big Lie. For one thing, a crowd tends to stifle voices of dissent in its midst; it turns on critics who stand in its path. Those who study mob psychology point out two defining characteristics. First, members lose their sense of individual responsibility and collectively act in a manner they would never entertain if they were acting alone. Second, a mob demands homogeneous behavior and tolerates no dissent or attempt to rein in its energy.

The rape culture is a popular delusion, a madness of the crowd. But it is important not to ignore a Big Lie. A popular delusion can inflict great harm upon individuals and society unless it is vigorously opposed. The most effective weapons are to make individuals shoulder responsibility for their own acts – to break up the mob – and to persist in the reasoned dissent that exposes truth. Ask questions of those who spread rape hysteria and include a demand for evidence at every turn.

What is the Rape Culture?

> Rape culture is a concept of unknown origin and of uncertain definition; yet it has made its way into everyday vocabulary and is assumed to be commonly understood. The award-winning documentary film *Rape Culture* made by Margaret Lazarus in 1975 takes credit for first defining the concept. –Prof. Joyce E. Williams [6]

The rape culture is a social construct created by pairing the two words "rape" and "culture." PC feminists mean something specific by each word and their definitions differ from normal discourse. For example, rape is seen as a political act committed collectively by men against women rather than as a crime committed by one individual against another. But it is useful to present the popular definitions of "rape" and of "culture" before exploring the ideological ones. (Chapter Three extensively addresses the PC definitions.)

The definition of rape currently used by the Federal Bureau of Investigation is "[t]he penetration, no matter how slight, of the vagina or anus with any body part or object, or oral penetration by a sex organ of another person, without the consent of the victim." [7] Few people would disagree with this definition although some would expand it. This makes the FBI usage a good base upon which to build.

A standard definition of culture is "the totality of socially transmitted behavior patterns, arts, beliefs, institutions, and all other products of human activity and thought." Culture is the collective identity of a society or a group, which distinguishes it from other societies or groups. Typical characteristics of a culture are its assumptions, code of courtesy, rituals, religious or ethnic make-up, and the vehicles through which everyday life is expressed, such as the cuisine. The institutions of a society are particularly important because they embody and administer the rules of the culture. Commonly cited examples of institutions are the family, the church and schools.

When a single adjective like "rape" is used to define a culture, it means the adjective captures a dominant, if not *the* dominant, attitudes and behavior of the society.

Some argue that applying any one word to North American culture is meaningless because the population is too large and varied to be captured by an adjective. But there is precedent for applying an overarching description to a large population. During World War II, America was accurately called a "war culture." Government-mandated rationing and price controls, as well as wage restrictions, were administered nationwide. Corporations and factories reconfigured themselves to meet the needs of the War Production Board and military agencies; pulpits preached love of country along with love of God. News media conformed to government demands; radio and film flooded the public with tales of patriotism and heroism in battle. Personal earnings or savings were diverted into War Bonds that were hawked by celebrities and financial institutions as paper evidence of patriotism. Most families had relatives in the military, which made them feel an intimate connection with the conflict. From minutia such as relabeling sauerkraut to "liberty cabbage" to massive events such as establishing internment camps for Japanese-Americans, the war *was* society. It became *the* defining factor in politics, economics, media, family life, career paths... America was a war culture because war had the institutional, state, public and private backing that embedded it into every aspect of daily life. This is the level of participation that allows one word to define a culture.

PC feminists claim that rape, like war during the 1940s, is *the* defining characteristic of our society. Does that claim seem true? Does government mandate policies and laws to encourage rape rather than to prevent or punish it? Are the news media, radio and films cooperating to applaud rape and provide rapists with a moral justification similar to what they provided to the military during WWII? Do churches preach the sanctity of sexually attacking others? Are people urged to buy sexual assault bonds or otherwise finance rape? Do most families have relatives who are rapists? The questions sound absurd but rape culture adherents would answer "yes"...at least, they would argue that the foregoing circumstances exist politically, if not literally expressed.

A standard PC definition of the rape culture was offered by Emilie Buchwald in her influential anthology *Transforming a Rape Culture* (1993). [8] She called it "a complex set of beliefs that encourage male sexual aggression and supports violence against women. It is a society where violence is seen as sexy and sexuality as violent." If people are unaware of the rape culture, she argued, this only proves it is omnipresent; that is, the rape culture is as common as air and taken as much for granted.

Buchwald reasoned in a circle. If a person accepted the existence of a rape culture, then that constituted proof of it. If a person denied its existence, then that constituted proof of it. A circular reasoning permits no contradictory evidence and so the rape culture becomes impossible to disprove.

Buchwald claimed that most women were well aware of the rape culture on some level, however. "In a rape culture, women perceive a continuum of threatened violence that ranges from sexual remarks to sexual touching to rape itself. A rape culture condones physical and emotional terrorism against women as the norm... In a rape culture both men and women assume that sexual violence is a fact of life, inevitable... However...much of what we accept as inevitable is in fact the expression of values and attitudes that can change." In simpler terms, a rape culture is a pervasive environment that reinforces sexual assault as the norm; it blames women for being victims and encourages men to sexually degrade women as a way to maintain their own power. PC feminists contend that rape, like war during WWII, has been institutionalized into culture as *the* defining characteristic. Women are victims; men are victimizers.

(Note: The attitude toward men has shifted somewhat in recent years. Males from marginalized groups, such as blacks, are increasingly exempt from being viewed as oppressors. The preceding addresses the roots of the rape culture rather than the intricacies of its current evolution.)

Backlash against rape culture deniers

Adherents of the rape culture decry what they see as a particularly objectionable behavior in critics: victim-blaming, which is the accusation thrown at anyone who questions a report of victimization. Victim-blaming consists of saying that a raped woman somehow brought the violence upon herself. For example, she walked down a dark alley at midnight or wore provocative clothing.

Victim-blaming has gone full circle. Decades ago, assaulted women were hideously attacked by those who should have helped them – the police, the courts, the media, society itself. In the 1960s, however, liberal feminism changed social attitudes toward raped women. The attacker was properly viewed as the *one* person responsible for the crime. The victim was properly viewed as just that – a victim. There are no circumstances under which a person deserves to be raped any more than than a person deserves to be murdered or mugged.

But the PC feminist backlash against victim-blaming has taken a bizarre turn. Even supportive statements and practical advice are now branded as victim-blaming. For example, teaching women self-defense is condemned as making them responsible for their own safety and blaming them for being defenseless when the focus should be on the guilt of the attackers. (Chapter 6 offers expanded discussion of the difference between victim-blaming and crime prevention.)

The iconoclastic feminist Camille Paglia came close to being burnt at the stake by PC feminists due to a passage on rape in her book, *Sex, Art, and American Culture: Essays.* [9] Paglia commented on female students who bought into the rape culture with its hyper-taboo of victim-blaming. She characterized them as saying, "'Well, I should be able to get drunk at a fraternity party and go upstairs without anything happening.' And I say, 'Oh really?' And when you drive your car in New York City, do you leave your keys on the hood? My point is that if your car is stolen after you do something like that, yes, the police should pursue the thief and he should be punished. But at the same time, the police – and I – have the right to say to you, 'You stupid idiot, what the hell were you thinking'?"

This is a harsh response but it should be considered in context of the arguments to which it is reacting. PC feminists demand that no one question the wisdom or propriety of a victim's behavior. It doesn't matter if the questioner acknowledges that criminal and moral responsibility lies entirely with the aggressor, as it properly does. It doesn't matter if she calls for summary execution of the attacker. It is politically verboten to hint at the imprudence of a woman passing out drunk in a stranger's apartment or to call any female behavior "dangerous." To do so is to become a "rape enabler." To question any actions of an attacked woman, rape culture zealots claim, is to exonerate the attacker and justify the woman's victimization. It is to rape her anew.

This is nonsense on stilts. To repeat: The attacker is 100% legally and morally responsible for the assault. But to advise a woman to act carefully while moving through a dangerous world is **not** to blame her for being attacked. The cautioner *wants* her to be safe and shows the woman enough respect to treat her as an adult who is capable of protecting herself – if not physically then through prudence. Yet, as Ashe Schow observed in the *Washington Examiner* [10], "Nowadays, you can't suggest that a woman watch her drink, avoid getting blackout drunk or to walk in well-lit areas without being accused of victim-blaming."

I remember a young woman who stood up in a feminist meeting to testify about her oppression under patriarchy. The specific oppression? The young woman's mother gave her taxi money whenever she went out for the evening so she would never be trapped in a situation without having a way home. To the young woman, this meant her mother was accommodating the patriarchy by shifting responsibility for a safe return onto her shoulders. I was gobsmacked. I wondered if the swaddled speaker had a clue about real oppression. I wondered if she knew how someone who had lived on the street, as I did, would have traded almost anything for a parent who cared so deeply. Yet a mother's love was aired as evidence of subjugation. Victim-blaming continues to be a stock accusation hurled at anyone who cares enough to suggest that women practice safe behavior in public in the same manner as they practice safe sex in private.

Summary statement of the rape culture

Rape culture arguments face a more basic problem, however. A rape culture does *not* exist in North America. This becomes clear when North America is contrasted with societies in which a rape culture *does* exist. In Afghanistan, for example, many females are forced into marriage by the age of 16, and they are often sold off – literally! – to much older husbands; young girls are bartered into marriage to repay family debts or to settle a dispute. It is common for women to be kidnapped and raped; when this occurs, it is the victim who is shamed and sometimes arrested. Honor killings threaten girls or women who assert themselves sexually through such offenses as marrying for love or having an affair. Few women are literate and many are widowed, with the average age of a widow in Afghanistan being 35 years old; these widows often turn to prostitution as the only way to support themselves and their children.

Afghanistan is a rape culture. North America is not.

In a *National Post* article entitled "'Rape culture' fanatics don't know what a culture is," journalist Barbara Kay commented [11] on how it is clear "that those who speak of a rape culture don't understand what the word 'culture' actually means. To define a culture, a phenomenon must be widely accepted as the *norm*. It is culturally normal in some countries for women to be virtual chattels, governed by patriarchal standards of honor; to be married against their will; to meet blame from their kinsmen and indifference or even hostility at law enforcement and court levels when reporting sexual assault; to be shunned as unmarriageable – or worse – for the 'shame' of having been raped, to have no employment options, and so forth. There we can legitimately speak of a 'rape culture'."

In North America, women and men are legally and socially equal. In a *Time* article entitled "Stop Fem-Splaining: What 'Women Against Feminism' Gets Right," equity feminist Cathy Young commented [12], "they [anti-feminist women] make a strong argument that a 'patriarchy' that lets women vote, work, attend college, get divorced, run for political office and own businesses on the same terms as men isn't quite living up to its label. They also raise valid questions about politicizing personal violence along gender lines; research shows that surprisingly high numbers of men may have been raped sometimes by women." (Women Against Feminism is a loose coalition of women who oppose PC feminism and are most prominent on tumblr.) [13]

It is a slap in the face of every rape victim and of every woman in a real rape culture for PC feminists to compare their lives of privilege to the terrible suffering of the truly oppressed. It is especially objectionable on the part of female students at major universities who enjoy an education that is denied to most women in the world. It also unfair to men who are cast as social villains and rapists. The opposite of a rape culture exists in North America. It is a rape hysteria culture.

The Rate of Rape in America

The 1-in-4 or 1-in-5 figure for the rate of sexual assault is a bastion stat of the rape culture. The rate is covered in Chapter Four and Chapter Five but a brief discussion is required here because it is difficult to proceed without touching upon an essential claim. The rape culture lives or dies on the prevalence of sexual violence. If rape is omnipresent, then the rape culture has traction and must be addressed as a burning concern. If it is no more common than other crimes, then the rape culture collapses and is revealed as hysteria; after all, we do not speak of America as a burglary culture or a murder culture. The prevalence is key.

The rate at which women are raped has fallen dramatically over the past several years. According to both the U.S. Department of Justice National Crime Victimization Survey 2008-2012 and the Rape, Abuse, Incest National Network (RAINN) – the largest anti-sexual assault organization in America – rape has decreased by more than 50% in recent years. [14]

Mark J. Perry, a professor of economics at the University of Michigan's Flint campus, offered an overview entitled, "My top ten gender charts of the year for 2014." [15] The first chart expressed the FBI findings on U.S. crime statistics for 2013 with reference to the rate of rape per 100,000 inhabitants; it compared the 2013 rate with other years since 1973. Perry observed, "the rape rate fell to a 40-year low in 2013 at 25.2 cases per 100,000 persons (about 1 for every 4,000 persons) – the lowest rate since 1973, and more than 40% below the peak rate of 42.8 rapes per 100,000 persons in 1992."

Perry asked, "How much media attention did the decline in the US rape rate to a 40-year low in 2013 generate? If you answered 'none', that would almost be an overstatement." A Google search on the term "falling U.S. rape rate" did not return a single hit. "Falling rape rate" returned four results. By contrast, "rising rape rate" rendered 5,000 hits, "rape epidemic" more than 100,000.

Why are PC feminists not celebrating the steady decline in sexual violence? They should be cheering from the rooftops. Why is society now hearing much *more,* not less, about the rape culture from media, politicians and PC zealots? Reasons vary. The media wants sensationalism. Politicians want to take a popular stand; or, at least, to avoid one that risks their being called "rape apologists." Rape culture adherents *need* a high rate of assault to justify a political agenda that is driven by fear. To them, the decline is bad news because it calls into question the validity of their world view and, for some, it threatens their livelihood.

The rape hysteria focuses on university campuses where young female students are said to be victimized at an alarming and undiminished rate. This is smart strategy. Campuses are strongholds of PC feminism. There, the orthodoxy is rarely challenged because it is institutionalized within the academic structure and it has powerful political support. For example, in January 2014, President Obama established a special White House Task

Force to Protect Students From Sexual Assault. He stated [16], "It is estimated that one in five women on college campuses has been sexually assaulted during their time there. ... It's totally unacceptable." It is also totally untrue.

On December 11, the Bureau of Justice Statistics (BJS) released its report, "Rape and Sexual Assault Among College-Age Females, 1995-2013." [17] The report's findings contradicted the claims of the White House and of rape culture zealots. For one thing, it indicated that campuses were not the most sexually dangerous places for women. The BJS found, "[t]he rate of rape and sexual assault was 1.2 times higher for nonstudents (7.6 per 1,000) than for students (6.1 per 1,000)....The rate of completed rape for nonstudents (3.1 per 1,000) was 1.5 times higher than for students (2.0 per 1,000)."

The claim that 20% of female students would be raped on campus was also debunked. Female students from 18 to 24 years old experienced 6.1 rapes and sexual assaults per year per 1,000 students. This is 0.61 percent and it reflects the *mean*; that is, 0.61 percent is the average of all numbers for the years 1995 to 2013.

As noted, the general rate of rape fell to a 40-year low in 2013. As a percentage, it fell even more sharply over the last several years. According to the BJS report, if you view the years between 2010-2013, then the mean rate was 4.75 per 1,000 per year for females students aged 18 to 24. Assuming a female student attends university for four years, then multiplying 4.75 by four approximates her overall risk between 2010-2013. That number is about 20 per 1,000 or approximately one in 50. More accurately, it is 1-in-52.6, not 1-in-4 or 1-in-5.

Of these sexual assaults, the BJS stated that 1-in-3 was a completed rape. Dividing by 3 gives a sense of the yearly risk that a female student will experience a completed rape: 1.6 per 1,000 female students, or 0.16 percent. Again, the overall risk of a completed rape over 4 years requires multiplying by four. The result: 6.3 per 1,000 or 0.63 percent.

Perry restated the BJS findings in slightly different terms. "For women attending college, the rate of rape/sexual assault has **fallen by more than 50%** over the last several decades, from 9.2 incidents per 1,000 women in 1997 to 4.4 cases per 1,000 in 2013.... According to the media, politicians and gender activists, there is supposed to be a college 'rape epidemic' when in fact, the rate of college female victimization has been trending downward for almost 20 years." [Emphasis in the original]

Perry continued,

> "What might be the most important statistic in the December DOJ report...is that the data reveal that only about **1 in 41 women were victims of rape or sexual assault** (threatened, completed and attempted; and reported and unreported) while in college for four years during the entire period investigated from 1995 to 2013, based on this analysis: 6.1 women per 1,000 = '1 in 163.9 women' per year, and over four years attending college would then be = '**1 in 41 women' while in college.** Because the victimization rate has been trending downward, that same analysis using data from the last four years (2010 to 2013) reveals that **1 in 52.6 women have been sexually assaulted or raped in recent years (see table above).**" [Emphasis in original, follow footnote link to access the referenced table.]

Rape culture exponents react to the BJS's awkward data in predictable ways. Some ignore it and continue to quote the same selective, validating sources; they repeat the 1-in-4 or 1-in-5 statistic as a mantra because 1-in-50 is 10 times less effective in achieving their goals and maintaining funding. Other exponents acknowledge the BJS report only to springboard into an attack on the character or morality of those who use it to argue for a realistic view of the rate of rape.

The 1-in-5 rate of rape on campus meme will continue, and for several reasons. The media wants sensational stories and shock-value statistics; both are good for ratings. Politicians with liberal and female voting bases have a vested interest in being PC; they want to be re-elected. Universities are both bribed and threatened by the federal government to embrace rape culture policies if they wish to access federal funding. And, then, there are the academics and administrators who rely upon a PC framework for their positions, prestige and salaries. The idea of a rape culture has been institutionalized, which makes it difficult to uproot.

The 1-in-5 meme will also retain traction because it speaks to a parent's worst fear of what could happen to a daughter who leaves the nest and ventures onto campus. The statistic sparks fear in young women, which cycles into anger. Ironically, the meme also draws upon whatever remains of chivalry within men, which makes them bristle protectively at the prospect of violence against women. In short, the meme is emotionally powerful.

But facts are facts. The rate of rape in society has been falling steadily; the rate on campus is falling as well, and even more quickly.

The Short Version of How We Got Here

Brendan O'Neill, editor of the social commentary site *Spiked*, observed [18], "The first rule of the politics of fear is that if you want to make something sound scarier than it actually is, you add the word 'culture' at the end of it." Doing so creates the impression of a crisis so dire and widespread that people are willing to take extreme measures to prevent the awful consequences. People surrender freedom and justice for security.

It has become the new c-word: culture. Depending on the political agenda of the alarmist *du jour*, we are said to live in a rape culture, a greed culture, a gun culture, an entitlement culture, an abortion culture, a divorce culture, a culture of racism, a culture of fear, a hook-up culture, etc. The descriptions are catchy but inaccurate. A culture does not rape, feel greed, buy guns, enjoy entitlements, abort, divorce, express racism, feel fear or have casual sex. Individuals do. And for rape to be a defining aspect of our culture, it must be the normal experience of average men and women. Individual men en masse must be constantly raping or threatening to rape women in daily life. This situation does not exist in North America. If it did, women could not walk down the street without packing a gun or being escorted by an armed guard.

The driving force behind the fear mongering is not reality but ideology. The goal of rape culture ideologues is to deconstruct the institutions of society and reconstruct them according to a radically different vision. Blaming individuals does *not* achieve that agenda. If individual criminals are to blame for rape, then arresting and prosecuting them would be the solution. There would be no need for a *systemic* change in how society approaches sex, gender, the law, the family, language and every other aspect of the so-called power structure.

Blaming the culture, however, facilitates the demand for a complete overhaul of society. What would such a reconstructed society look like?

What gender justice looks like

Anne Marie Goetz, as the chief advisor at the United Nations's UNIFEM agency Governance Peace and Security, defined the term "gender justice" in a manner that has become standard. The International Development Research Center (IDRC) rendered Goetz's definition as [19], "the ending of, and the provision of redress for, inequalities between women and men that result in women's subordination to men. Seeing gender justice as outcome and as process helps differentiate between what is to be achieved and how it is to be achieved."

Added to the IDRC definition is the need for social institutions "to dispense justice." This means current institutions, such as the legal system or the family must be reconstructed to provide redress for women. In practical terms, gender justice uses state muscle to impose policies and law in order to create or revolutionize institutions in order to favor women. Everything from language to media, from the religion to education must dispense gender justice. (Chapter Two explores the concept in detail.)

The personal is political

Most people are too preoccupied with the business of living to worry about reconstructing society. Nevertheless, if a new vision is to succeed, then the cooperation or passive acceptance of average people is necessary.

One way to secure it is to change the assumptions of society so as to favor a rape culture interpretation of reality. This shift has been going on for decades and it is captured by one phrase: the personal is political. PC feminist Susan Moller Okin explained [20] the origins of the slogan in her influential book *Justice, Gender, and the Family* (1989). "The earliest claims that the personal is political came from those gender feminists of the 1960s and 1970s who argued that, since the [traditional] family was at the root of women's oppression, it must be 'smashed'."

More specifically, the slogan came from the New Left which was a loose coalition of left-wing or Marxist educators and agitators who focused on "social justice" through specific issues such as gender, gay rights, and abortion. Carol Hanisch popularized the slogan "the personal is political" in the title of a brief essay, dated February 1969, which was published by the radical feminist group Redstockings. [21] The "Redstockings Manifesto" stated [22], "Because we have lived so intimately with our oppressors, in isolation from each other, we have been kept from seeing our personal suffering as a political condition. This creates the illusion that a woman's relationship with her man is a matter of interplay between two unique personalities, and can be worked out individually. In reality, every such relationship is a class relationship, and the conflicts between individual men and women are political conflicts that can only be solved collectively."

The underlying meaning of "the personal is political" is that all actions and attitudes, however personal or peaceful they may seem, are actually political and must be addressed as such. Why? Because a person's private actions and attitudes impact all other individuals and society itself. For example, my decision to join a conservative church may "harm" gays who feel disrespected by its teachings. Therefore, my freedom of religion is not actually an individual choice or right but a political one that injures others. It violates their alleged right to social justice, and the violation occurs even if I privately pursue my beliefs. Thus, society and marginalized groups have a defensive right to "encourage" me to think and to act in a manner that is *not* harmful, through use of law if necessary.

The preceding is a loose description of political correctness itself, which rests upon "the personal is political." In practice, the principle eliminates the personal realm altogether so that nothing but the political remains.

The stripped-down flow of PC logic:

- Nothing is truly personal because everything affects society.

- All things formerly in the private sphere – from sexuality to child-raising, from speech to religious belief – are the proper subjects of political reaction.

- Objectionable acts and attitudes should be politically discouraged; correct ones should be encouraged. In short, social control for a collective good.

How does this approach impact the issue of rape? Before the 1970s, rape was viewed as a crime that individuals committed against other individuals and it was addressed through the court system. Rape was an experience that differed from the reality of every day; it was a violation of normal life.
Rape's journey from being a crime to becoming the *rape culture* began innocuously enough. In the 1960s, liberal feminists shredded the lie that only bad girls were raped. They erased the vicious notion that women had been "asking" for it, and the myth that rapists were seedy men in back alleys. Feminism replaced bias with facts, and offered practical help for women in pain. The first U.S. rape crisis line opened in 1971.

In the '60s and early '70s, liberal feminism was the dominant voice of the movement and it accomplished worthwhile goals. For example, sexual freedom blossomed. But a different intellectual current was also active. Radical or PC feminists did not aim for reform but for revolution. Society needed to be upended. The old system had to be deconstructed and new structures built on the cleared ground. The revolutionary feminism stressed an integrated philosophy and politics of gender rather than focusing on more specific issues like birth control. The integration included a reinterpretation of history, science, literature, language and all things political. PC feminism wanted a new *culture* to create a new world.

The new approach drew upon Marxism, which caused some radical feminists to call themselves "Marxist feminists."[23] Catherine MacKinnon, a main architect of PC feminism, wrote the highly influential essay, "Feminism, Marxism, Method, and the State: Toward Feminist Jurisprudence" (1983). [24] The sexual exploitation and subjugation of women as a class by men as a class was the beating heart of the PC feminist world view. The act that captured its essence was rape. A time line for rape culture theory developed.

Kate Millett's *Sexual Politics* (1968) [25] argued that women had been "confined to the cultural level of animal life" by men who used them as sexual objects and breeding stock. A series of works expanded on Millett's theories. For example, in *Psychoanalysis and Feminism: Freud, Reich, Laing and Women* (1974) [26], Juliet Mitchell dovetailed the traditions of feminism, Marxism and psychoanalysis. Linda Gordon's pivotal *Woman's Body, Woman's Right: A Social History of Birth Control in America* (1976) [27] provided a history of birth control and reinvented the issue within a radical feminist context; many feminist issues were reinvented in a similar manner. Susan Brownmiller's wildly successful book, *Against Our Will: Men, Women and Rape* (1975) [28], "gave rape its history" – a history in which men were natural and sadistic rapists. The rape culture was born.

By the late 1980s, rape had been thoroughly politicized. Rape described the *zeitgeist* or "spirit" of gender relations and every act, every word, every attitude was viewed through its filter.

The triumph of ideology over fact

PC feminism is not evidence-driven but ideological. It is futile to point out that, if prison populations are included, the rate at which men are raped may well be greater than women. Some rape culture zealots will respond with an outright denial that men *can* be raped.

It is equally futile to argue that innocent men have been destroyed by false accusations. Over decades, I have brought up news articles such as the one I read this morning, "False Rape Accusation Leads To Alaska Man's Beating Death." [29] The woman admitted to making a false rape accusation in order to conceal an affair; as a result, an innocent man was beaten to death. At the mention of such articles, the PC response I encounter is a blank expression or a flash of anger; the anger is directed at me, not the false accuser. Then the mantra resumes: "We must believe the woman, every woman must be believed," as though a woman's admission of lying is not relevant. The accusation is believed while the retraction is ignored because a rape culture adherent will believe only what is useful to her world view.

Women who demand evidence and refuse to automatically accept an accusation are often called self-haters or gender traitors. In a *New York Observer* article, "Women Against Womyn: First Wave, Second Wave, Third Wave, and Now Three Steps Back," [30] Nina Burleigh – a prominent PC feminist and White House correspondent under President Bill Clinton – expressed a common sentiment toward women skeptics. "[T]here's another new club for self-effacing female enablers of angry white men. Women Against Feminism had, last time I checked, 16,013 followers on Facebook." Jessica Valenti's attitude, expressed in a *Guardian* article [31], is also typical. "When women come out against gender justice, it feels worse....a betrayal....Anti-feminist organizing is based on a deep hypocrisy and selfishness – an ideology built to assure conservative women that as long as *they* are doing just fine, other women will make do. And they're putting up roadblocks to progress right in the middle of a renewed feminist awakening."

The hostility toward dissenting women is growing because they are becoming a threat. If women reject the rape culture, then skepticism about the concept cannot be called a *male* phenomenon. Moreover, the disagreement of an increasing number of women means that PC feminists speak for themselves rather than for an entire class. Women are not a single political class but a collection of individuals with varying interests and beliefs.

The PC response to this heresy is to harden its positions.

The definition of rape hardens

The definition of rape has been revolutionized and it keeps expanding.

As far back as 2008, Heather McDonald commented [32] on the elasticity with which rape is defined. "The [rape] crisis doesn't exist. During the 1980s, feminist researchers committed to the rape-culture theory had discovered that asking women directly if they had been raped yielded disappointing results– very few women said that they had been. So *Ms.* commissioned University of Arizona public health professor Mary Koss...to develop a different way of measuring the prevalence of rape. Rather than asking female students about rape per se, Koss asked them if they had experienced actions that she then classified as rape. Koss's method produced the 25 percent rate, which *Ms.* then published....[T]he most powerful refutation of Koss's research came from her own subjects: 73 percent of the women whom she characterized as rape victims said that they hadn't been raped. Further– though it is inconceivable that a raped woman would voluntarily have sex again with the fiend who attacked her– 42 percent of Koss's supposed victims had intercourse again with their alleged assailants."

Koss's report (published in 1987) created a firestorm because it was touted as the first national study on rape. And its results were sensational. It became the engine behind the statistical claim that 1-in-4 or 1-in-5 female students would be raped on campus. (See Chapter Five for a more comprehensive critique of Koss's study.) Suddenly, the cry of "rape epidemic" was taken seriously by non-ideologues, like concerned parents. The definition of rape expanded to include any time a woman was manipulated into sex or had negative feelings, either during or after sex. It included acts that the "victim" herself did not consider to be rape.

Some of the early campus reforms that resulted were reasonable. An example is the Clery Act (1990), which was named after the 19-year-old freshman Jeanne Clery who was raped and murdered at Lehigh University in 1986. Universities that access federal funds are now required to disclose information about crimes on or near their campuses.

Other reforms were a bellwether for the conflicts ravaging many campuses where sexual violence is defined in an overly broad and vague manner. In some cases, the definition makes it difficult to imagine sex that doesn't qualify as rape. This is the case with the latest trend in the expanding definition of rape – "yes means yes" or affirmative consent policies. The revolutionary redefinition has been a long time in coming.

In 1991, Antioch College (Ohio) became the first university in North America to adopt sexual consent requirements similar to the "yes means yes" standard that is becoming popular today. Typical features of the standard are:

- Explicit consent is required every time there is sexual activity

- Consent is required regardless of the parties' prior sexual history

- Each new level of sexual activity requires clear consent; for example, moving from an agreed upon kiss to an embrace requires a new explicit agreement

- Forms of communication such as gestures or safe words are acceptable but they must be agreed upon beforehand

- Without prior agreement, body movements and non-verbal responses, such as returning a kiss, are not consent

- Silence is not consent

- Although the policies are often gender neutral in language, the male is almost always considered to be the default offender

The Antioch standard was widely ridiculed in 1991 but it is now the cutting edge of rape policy and it slices deep. (More on affirmative consent in Chapter Six.)

Microaggression: The Next Rape Culture Frontier

At the same moment, another expansion is occurring. Microaggression is a PC campaign launched by students who are running out of even vaguely real things to complain about. A microaggression is a minor act of discrimination against a person who belongs to a marginalized group, such as female, gay or a racial minority. It does not matter if the discriminating person meant no offense and acted with good will. All that matters is how the person in the disadvantaged group reacted.

Coined in 1970 by Harvard professor Chester M. Pierce, the term "microaggression" first described the unconscious racial insults delivered by whites to minorities. An example is a white teacher who asks a black student whether he needs help with a math problem; if the student feels his math ability is being questioned because he is black, then the inquiry becomes a microaggression. According to the *New York Times* [33], "The recent surge in popularity for the term can be attributed, in part, to an academic article by Derald Wing Sue. Sue, a psychology professor at Columbia University, published in 2007 in which he broke down microaggressions into microassaults, microinsults and microinvalidations. Dr. Sue literally wrote the book on the subject, called *Microaggressions in Everyday Life: Race, Gender, and Sexual Orientation.*" [34]

Microaggression consists of three basic acts. A *microassault* is a conscious act of discrimination, such as telling a racially insensitive joke. A *microinsult* is verbal or nonverbal communication that makes someone feel demeaned due to his or her identity. An example is asking an Asian coworker where she comes from because the question may suggest she is a foreigner and not an authentic American. A *microinvalidation* is verbal or nonverbal communication that negates the feelings of a marginalized person. An example is not responding to comments made by a female participant in a group discussion.

According to Sue, microaggressions are an especially egregious form of discrimination. Writing of race, Sue claimed, "The person of color is caught in a Catch-22: If she confronts the perpetrator, the perpetrator will deny it." The denial may be sincere but this only deepens the harm. The person of color, Sue contended, is victimized anew by being left in a state of confusion, anger and "an overall sapping of energy."

These microaggressive behaviors lead to *microinequities* – a term coined by MIT economist Mary Rowe. She is also credited with stretching Pierce's original term to cover discrimination against women, which makes it a handmaiden of the rape culture. Microaggressions and microinequities have the incredible PC advantage of being everywhere and all the time because they exist in the eye of the beholder, the ear of the listener. They are communicated by facial expressions, gestures, tone, word choice, nuance and syntax. Or by silence, a person's absence or his unwillingness to meet another's eyes. Rowe described microinequities [35] as, "apparently small events which are often ephemeral and hard-to-prove, events which are covert, often unintentional, frequently unrecognized by the perpetrator, which occur wherever people are perceived to be 'different'." *Psychology Today* offered examples:

- checking emails or texting during a face-to-face conversation

- interrupting a person

- making eye-contact only with males while talking to a group with both males and females

- taking more questions from men than women

- rolling your eyes

- sighing loudly

- mentioning the achievements of some people but not others whose achievements are equally relevant

- consistently ignoring a person's emails

- only reading half of a person's email and then asking her about the content later [35]

As with so many expressions of PC zeal, the crusade against microaggressions took root at universities and quickly lost any connection to common sense or common decency. In 2013, Prof. Van Rust was fired from UCLA due to his microaggression against black students. Susan Kruth, Program Officer of the Foundation for Individual Rights in Education's Defense Program, reported [36], "Rust's alleged offenses comprise his seemingly typical feedback on students' work. As [protest] demonstration leader ... Kenjus Watson argued, Rust created a hostile climate in his class by, among other things, correcting 'perceived grammatical choices that in actuality reflect ideologies'. Another of the alleged microaggressions appears to be that Rust required students to use *The Chicago Manual of Style* ..." In other words, he wanted university students to use the standard spelling and grammar they would need in professional life.

Microaggressions are an accelerating political trend. On December 5, 2014, Princeton University students set up a "Tiger Microaggressions" service through which students could anonymously report the slightest offense, sexual or racial. [37] The online page referred to the discrimination as "paper cuts of oppression" that are "small but slice deep." The *National Review* quoted the service operators as saying [38], "microaggressions are all around us." Literally anything can qualify because "there are no objective definitions to [the] words and phrases" that might cause offense.

A columnist for the *Miami Herald* commented [39], "So if I write, The sky is blue you are perfectly within your rights to assume that what I actually meant is, 'Everybody but white guys should writhe in Hell for all eternity'. Because, really, who's to say?" The example is extreme ... but no *reductio ad absurdum* is possible with political correctness. If the subjective listener is "to say," then anything can be a microaggression.

The discovery of oppression in the most trivial matters was clear in a *Guardian* column by rape culture zealot Jessica Valenti. [40] She claimed to love everything about Christmas. Well, except one thing. Due to gender oppression, she was responsible for wrapping presents for her family, child and other loved ones. While African women are being trafficked, Afghan girls are raped or killed for honor and Indian woman deal with the horror of acid in their faces, Western women are traumatized by wrapping Christmas presents for loved ones. Her family's oppressive expectation, in Valenti's own words, made Christmas into "a goddamn clusterfuck."

Madness is loose on the land. Microaggression is a blank check for rape culture adherents and the politically correct. It justifies the censorship of every word and the social control of all behavior.

Conclusion

The claim that America is a rape culture is a particularly vicious lie for at least four reasons. It brands all men as rapists or rape facilitators. It reverses the glaring truth that women are a legally and socially protected class with privileges, such as affirmative action. It obstructs the truth about rape and so prevents the healing of individuals as well as the ability of society to address the crime. It shuts down real discussion of a burning issue.

Notes

[1] Susan Brownmiller, *Against Our Will: Men, Women and Rape,* (New York: Simon & Schuster, 1975).

[2] George Orwell, *Nineteen Eighty-four,* (London: Secker Warburg, 1949). As quoted in online edition, Univ. of Adelaide, 2014. Chapter Nine. https://ebooks.adelaide.edu.au/o/orwell/george/o79n/chapter2.9.html Retrieved Sept. 16, 2015.

[3] Wendy McElroy, Jessica Valenti, Debate: How Should Colleges Handle Sexual Assault?, Brown University, November 18, 2014. https://www.youtube.com/watch?v=jBsk1WzEdCA Retrieved Sept. 16, 2015.

[4] Charles Mackay, *Extraordinary Popular Delusions and the Madness of Crowds,* (London: Richard Bentley, 1841). http://www.gutenberg.org/files/24518/24518-h/dvi.html#preface Retrieved Sept. 16, 2015.

[5] Bernard Baruch as quoted by Michael J. Kosares, "Extraordinary delusions or the madness of machines," *USAGold*, April-May, 2012. http://www.usagold.com/publications/specialreportdelusions.html Retrieved Sept. 16, 2015.

[6] Joyce E. Williams, *Blackwell Encyclopedia of Sociology*, 2007. Online. http://www.webcitation.org/6GOcYWDeS Retrieved Sept. 16, 2015.

[7] Federal Bureau of Investigation, National Press Release, "Attorney General Eric Holder Announces Revisions to the Uniform Crime Report's Definition of Rape," Jan. 06, 2012. http://www.fbi.gov/news/pressrel/press-releases/attorney-general-eric-holder-announces-revisions-to-the-uniform-crime-reports-definition-of-rape Retrieved Sept. 16, 2015.

[8] Emilie Buchwald as quoted at Women Against Violence Against Women website, "What is Rape Culture?" http://www.wavaw.ca/what-is-rape-culture/ Retrieved Sept. 16, 2015.

[9] Camille Paglia, *Sex, Art, and American Culture: Essays,* (New York: Vintage Books, 1992), p. 57.

[10] Ashe Schow, "When Its Okay To Blame The Victim," *The Washington Examiner,* Jan. 15, 2015. http://www.washingtonexaminer.com/when-its-okay-to-blame-the-victim/article/2558670 Retrieved Sept. 16, 2015.

[11] Barbara Kay, "'Rape culture' fanatics don't know what a culture is," *National Post*, March 8, 2014. http://fullcomment.nationalpost.com/2014/03/08/barbara-kay-rape-culture-fanatics-dont-know-what-a-culture-is/ Retrieved Sept. 16, 2015.

[12] Cathy Young, "Stop Fem-Splaining: What 'Women Against Feminism' Gets Right," *Time,* July 24, 2014. http://time.com/3028827/women-against-feminism-gets-it-right/ Retrieved Sept. 16, 2015.

[13] Wikipedia on Women Against Feminism. "[A]lso known as #WomenAgainstFeminism, is Twitter hashtag, Tumblr blog, and social media campaign on Facebook, YouTube, and other Internet media in which women post pictures of themselves, some in 'selfie' style, holding up handmade placards stating reasons why they disapprove of modern feminism. Most of the posts begin with the statement, 'I don't need feminism because', followed by their reason(s)." http://en.wikipedia.org/wiki/Women_Against_Feminism Retrieved Sept. 16, 2015.

[14] From Rape, Abuse, Incest National Network, "How often does sexual assault occur?" https://www.rainn.org/get-information/statistics/frequency-of-sexual-assault. Retrieved Sept. 16, 2015. Note: RAINN is not a conservative source but a liberal one.

[15] Mark J. Perry, "My top ten gender charts of the year for 2014,"American Enterprise Institute, Jan. 9, 2015. http://www.aei.org/publication/top-ten-gender-charts-year-2014/ Retrieved Sept. 16, 2015.

[16] "Remarks by the President and Vice President at an Event for the Council on Women and Girls," White House Press Release, Jan. 22, 2014 http://www.whitehouse.gov/the-press-office/2014/01/22/remarks-president-and-vice-president-event-council-women-and-girls Retrieved Sept. 16, 2015.

[17] "Rape and Sexual Assault Among College-Age Females, 1995-2013," The Bureau of Justice, Dec.11, 2014. http://www.bjs.gov/index.cfm?ty=pbdetail&iid=5176 Retrieved Sept. 16, 2015.

[18] Brendan O'Neill, "Why I am pro-choice: Read the speech Brendan O'Neill was banned from making at Oxford University," *Spiked*, Nov. 20,

2014. http://www.spiked-online.com/newsite/article/why-i-am-pro-choice/16221#.VK0M1c6m1Ss Retrieved Sept. 16, 2015.

[19] Anne Marie Goetz, "Gender Justice, Citizenship and Entitlements *Core Concepts, Central Debates and New Directions for Research*," International Development Research Center. http://www.idrc.ca/EN/Resources/Publications/openebooks/339-3/index.html Retrieved Sept. 16, 2015.

[20] Susan Moller Okin, *Justice, Gender, and the Family,* (Basic Books, New York, 1989.)

[21] Carol Hanisch, "The Personal is Political," Redstockings journals, February 1968. http://www.carolhanisch.org/CHwritings/PIP.html Retrieved Sept. 16, 2015.

[22] "Redstockings Manifesto," 1968. http://www.redstockings.org/index.php/consciousness-raising-papers-1968-72?id=76 Retrieved Sept. 16, 2015.

[23] It is an error to equate radical or PC feminism with Marxism. It is more accurate to view the movement as critiquing gender with a Marxist lens and critiquing Marxism with a PC one. There are important differences between the two traditions. For example, Marx did not credit what PC feminists view as the "oppression of women" – e.g. her responsibility for child-raising – as a class issue.

[24] Catharine A. MacKinnon, "*Feminism, Marxism, Method, and the State: Toward Feminist Jurisprudence,*" *Signs* Vol. 8, No. 4 (Summer, 1983), the University of Chicago Press.

[25] Kate Millett, *Sexual Politics*, (New England Free Press, Boston, 1968.) In republished editions, the book became a best-seller and has been called "the first book of academic feminist literary criticism."

[26] Juliet Mitchell, *Psychoanalysis and Feminism: Freud, Reich, Laing and Women,* (New York: Pantheon Books, 1974).

[27] Linda Gordon, *Woman's Body, Woman's Right. A Social History of Birth Control in America* (New York: Grossman/Viking, 1976).

[28] Brownmiller, op.cit.

[29] Chuck Ross, "False Rape Accusation Leads To Alaska Man's Beating Death," *The Daily Caller*, Jan. 8, 2015. http://dailycaller.com/2015/01/08/false-rape-accusation-leads-to-alaska-mans-beating-death/ Retrieved Sept. 16, 2015.

[30] Nina Burleigh, "Women Against Womyn: First Wave, Second Wave, Third Wave, and Now Three Steps Back," *New York Observer*, July 30, 2014. http://observer.com/2014/07/women-against-womyn-first-wave-second-wave-third-wave-and-now-three-steps-back/ Retrieved Sept. 16, 2015.

[31] Jessica Valenti, "Punching Gloria Steinem: inside the bizarre world of anti-feminist women," *The Guardian*, July 7, 2014. http://www.theguardian.com/commentisfree/2014/jul/07/anti-feminist-women-hobby-lobby-decision-great?CMP=twt_gu Retrieved Sept. 16, 2015.

[32] Heather MacDonald, "The Campus Rape Myth. The reality: bogus statistics, feminist victimology, and university-approved sex toys," *City Journal*, Winter 2008. http://www.city-journal.org/2008/18_1_campus_rape.html Retrieved Sept. 16, 2015.

[33] Tanzina Vega, "Students See Many Slights as Racial 'Microaggressions'," *The New York Times*, March 22, 2014. http://www.nytimes.com/2014/03/22/us/as-diversity-increases-slights-get-subtler-but-still-sting.html Retrieved Sept. 16, 2015.

[34] Derald Wing Sue, *Microaggressions in Everyday Life: Race, Gender, and Sexual Orientation* (New York: Wiley, 2010).

[35] Berit Brogaard, "Micro-Inequities: 40 Years Later," *Psychology Today*, April 2013. https://www.psychologytoday.com/blog/the-superhuman-mind/201304/micro-inequities-40-years-later Retrieved Sept. 16, 2015.

[36] Susan Kruth, "UCLA Report Suggests Chilling Speech Is the Answer to Offensive 'Microaggressions'," The Foundation for Individual Rights in Education, Jan. 8, 2014. http://www.thefire.org/ucla-report-suggests-chilling-speech-is-the-answer-to-offensive-microaggressions/ Retrieved Sept. 16, 2015.

[37] The Tiger Microaggressions Community on Facebook https://www.facebook.com/pumicroaggression Note: Checked Sept. 16, 2015. Page no longer available.

[38] Katherine Timpf, "Princeton Students Set Up Micro-Aggression-Reporting Service," *National Review*, Dec. 11, 2014. http://www.nationalreview.com/article/394461/princeton-students-set-microaggression-reporting-service-katherine-timpf Retrieved Sept. 16, 2015.

[39] Glenn Garvin, "It's a mad, mad, mad, mad world!," *Miami Herald*, Dec. 29, 2014. http://www.miamiherald.com/opinion/op-ed/article5144901.html_ Retrieved Sept. 16, 2015.

[40] Jessica Valenti, "No, I will NOT wrap all the presents. Why are women still responsible for the holiday joy?" *The Guardian*, Dec. 10, 2014. http://www.theguardian.com/commentisfree/2014/dec/10/wrap-presents-women-holiday-chores Retrieved Sept. 16, 2015.

Chapter Two: Intellectual Framework and History of Rape Culture Myth

Intellectual Framework
- The social construction of human beings and gender
- Gender fluidity, nature v. nurture
- The concept of patriarchy
- Post-Marxism
- Social justice

History of the Rape Culture
- Myth One: rape is an essential part of patriarchy
- Myth Two: men have created a "mass psychology" of rape
- Myth Three: rape is a part of normal life.

Additional Myths About Rape
Conclusion
Notes

> Rape culture is a concept of unknown origin and of uncertain definition; yet it has made its way into everyday vocabulary and is assumed to be commonly understood. The award-winning documentary film Rape Culture made by Margaret Lazarus in 1975 takes credit for first defining the concept. –Prof Joyce E Williams [1]

Intellectual Framework

Like "rape culture," terms such as "social construction" are used without being precisely defined. Social construction refers to far more than merely deconstructing an idea or a social institution, such as the court system, and then reconstructing it to serve a different vision; it is more than tearing down a post office to erect a co-op. As with other rape culture concepts, many people have only a superficial grasp of what social construction means. Why would they? Once you walk off campus, the theory has little real-world value.

But it is necessary to grasp the underlying theories in order to understand how PC feminism and the rape culture are trying to change the world in which we live. Otherwise, they may succeed.

The social construction of human beings and gender

Social construction theory has evolved since its introduction into American feminism decades ago but its basics remain the same. The theory reaches back to post-modern French philosophy, which developed in the 1940s and blossomed in the 1960s. Of the post-modernists, Michel Foucault arguably had the deepest impact on PC feminism in America. Foucault's popularity peaked in the late '60s and early '70s when political correctness ideologically overwhelmed the broader feminist movement. His impact came despite the fact that he has little discussion of gender or women's issues in his books. What did Foucault discuss and why was it so influential within the feminist movement?

In 1989, Beth B. Hess and Myra Marx Ferree, editors of *Analyzing Gender*, wrote [2], "Feminist scholars, many drawing on the insights offered by Michel Foucault, have urged us to develop new ways of thinking and speaking" in these specific areas: sex and the body, identity and subject, power and politics. In 1992, Helen Crowley and Susan Himmelweit, editors of *Knowing Women: Feminism and Knowledge,* explained the presence of extensive quotes from Foucault within their text. [3] "Foucault's discourse theory and the 'post-structuralist' methods of analysis which depend on it have become very influential within feminist studies." Foucault's presence in feminism has faded since his death in 1984. The decline is exemplified by the scholarly anthology *After Foucault* [4] which contains two chapters that face off against each other on the question "Is Foucaldian feminism a contradiction in terms?" [5] But his legacy is immense.

The aspect of feminism on which Foucault exerted the most influence is called "identity politics." This is a focus on the shared interests and perceptions of a defined group, such as blacks or women. It includes analysis of the manner in which society has shaped the identity of the group and continues to do so. For example, the identity politics of blacks includes the history of slavery and an analysis of current racism.

Foucault focused on the identity politics of sexuality and the manner in which it was defined by the culture. In the *Internet Encyclopedia*, Aurelia Armstrong explained [6], "Foucault's claim here is that the relationship between power and sexuality is misrepresented when sexuality is viewed as an unruly natural force that power simply opposes, represses or constrains. Rather, the phenomenon of sexuality should be understood as constructed through the exercise of power relations."

Translation: Foucault believed sex or gender was not primarily a biological force that was controlled through manipulation by the powers that be. It was a social construct defined by the people in power. Otherwise phrased, it was not an a priori condition; it was created by the dominant culture. Foucault claimed the dominant culture *defined* a person's sexuality in a literal sense. In other words, a person's sexuality was not biologically determined; it was established by those in control of the culture.

Foucault's landmark book is *Les mots et les choses: Une archéologie des sciences humaines* (1966); in English, the title is *Words and Things: An Archaeology of the Human Sciences.* Foucault laid out a theory of social construction. He presented what he considered to be two fundamental facts about knowledge: it is power; and, no absolute knowledge exists. Knowledge is subjective, and reality is whatever a dominant group is able to construct as truth. The powerful group does not need to be a majority. It must only be dominant and its truth must be accepted by a sufficient number of people, even on a passive level.

Consider an example. If the constructed knowledge is in the area of medicine, then the power group, such as state-licensed medical doctors and other medical interests, can define what is the truth about the human body, including sexuality.

But truth changes through time as dominant groups rise and fall. This means the truth of human biology changes through time. This is not a statement of Darwinian evolution. The "facts" of human biology have no hard or a priori existence because truth is subjective; human biology evolves because it is recreated by a new dominant faction. Otherwise stated, if knowledge seems to increase, it is not because people better understand an objective reality but because those who dominate have *constructed* a more satisfying truth. Power can be reduced to the creation and control of knowledge within society as manifested in the flow of culture.

The foregoing is counter-intuitive to people who are used to truth being objective, which means rephrasing the human biology example may be useful. Most people assume there is a pre-cultural human body; that is, they assume the flow of culture does not alter the truth of human biology. But, for Foucault, the human body is constructed, not objective. He wrote [7], "We believe...that the body obeys the exclusive laws of physiology and that it escapes the influence of history, this too is false. The body is molded by a great many distinct regimes; it is broken down by the rhythms of work, rest, and holidays; it is poisoned by food or values, through eating habits and moral laws; it constructs resistance."

In his treatise, *The Birth of the Clinic: An Archaeology of Medical Perception,* Foucault presented what he called the "medical gaze." Through the medical gaze, the body was objectified into a 'thing' that medicine sought to control. The medical gaze of the 18th century differed from that of the twentieth century, however, and the body itself was redefined by each culture that gazed at it.

The idea that truth is constructed underlies the entire PC feminist approach to sexuality and gender; its importance is difficult to overstate. The theory explains why PC feminists consider sexuality and gender to be fluid and not fixed by biology. They believe gender is infinite, which is evident in how many new forms of gender identity have emerged in recent years. Facebook now offers users the opportunity to define their own gender, with more than 50 options available. One is "neutrois." According to *The Daily Beast* [8] this is "an umbrella term within the bigger umbrella terms of transgender or genderqueer." It includes "people who do not identify within the binary gender system (i.e., man/woman)." The social construction of truth also makes sense of the PC rebellion against traditional sex roles, such as those of a nuclear family, because the truth of those roles are defined by the dominant white-male culture.

To Foucault and the PC mind, the texts of society are the most important factor in controlling the power that is knowledge. The texts create truth and power. To grasp this point, consider the Victorian epoch of repressed sexuality in the nineteenth century. A common approach is to view its plays and literature, its songs and newspapers – its texts – and to conclude that they reflect a sexually repressed culture. PC feminists reverse the cause and effect. Society or culture has been created by the texts, which are the source of the power enjoyed by the dominant group. The texts do not reflect the culture; they create it. The culture creates what is truth.

Words and texts, as much or more than acts, are the keys to power because they determine reality. This is why PC feminists require everyone to use only politically-correct language; words create reality. Social construction motivates crusades for the inclusion of gay characters in children's literature and for the exclusion of traditional families. It causes universities to censor the use of innocuous words. Obsession with the texts and narratives of society underlies the drive to re-write history books and ban classical literature from courses. The goal is to control the narratives of society.

A left-leaning grad student named Fredrik deBoer addressed the overwhelming importance that PC feminists place on uttering only proper thoughts through sanitized syllables. DeBoer lamented [9],

I have seen, with my own two eyes, a 19-year-old white woman–smart, well-meaning, passionate– literally run crying from a classroom because she was so ruthlessly brow-beaten for using the word "disabled." Not repeatedly. Not with malice. Not because of privilege. She used the word once and was excoriated for it. She never came back. I watched that happen.

I have seen, with my own two eyes, a 33-year-old Hispanic man, an Iraq war veteran who had served three tours and had become an outspoken critic of our presence there, be lectured about patriarchy by an affluent 22-year-old white liberal arts college student, because he had said that other vets have to 'man up' and speak out about the war. Because apparently we have to pretend that we don't know how metaphorical language works or else we're bad people. I watched his eyes glaze over as this woman with $300 shoes berated him. I saw that. Myself.

To understand the insistence on "correct" language, it is useful to backtrack to Foucault's denial that the human body objectively existed apart from the culture. In the preface of *Les mots et les choses,* he claimed [10], "man...is probably no more than a kind of rift in the order of things...[I]t is comforting, however, and a source of profound relief, to think that man is only as recent invention, a figure not yet two centuries old, a new wrinkle in our knowledge." The truth of mankind's biology and sexuality is up for grabs for Foucauldian relativists and PC feminists.

The latter add a twist. "If there is no objective man," they argue, "then there is no objective woman." They reject what is called "sexual essentialism," which is the belief that there is a biological base to deeply-held urges such as motherhood and the disposition toward heterosexuality or homosexuality. (More on this topic later in the chapter.) PC feminists insist instead that body identity and power relationships are based on the culture with no objective reality outside of texts and narratives. That's why an overriding ideological goal is to control the texts and narrative.

Doing so requires using the state or other force because many people will refuse to be silent or to obediently repeat the approved text. Translated into PC terms: the dominant group will not relinquish control of the texts because that is the source of their power. In her book, *Gender Outlaw: On Men, Women and the Rest of Us,* the former heterosexual male Kate Bornstein explained [11], "[M]en couldn't have privilege if there were no males. Women couldn't be oppressed if there was no such thing as 'women'. Doing away with gender is key to the doing away with patriarchy. The struggle for women's rights (and to a lesser degree for men's rights) is a vital stopgap measure until we do away with the system....Gender fluidity is the ability to freely and knowingly become one or many of a limitless number of genders, for any length of time."

Gender fluidity, nature v. nurture

The concept of gender fluidity plays a central role in framing the rape culture.

The term "gender fluidity" was coined by the postmodern philosopher Judith Butler, who was the main conduit of Foucauldian thought into North American feminism. In her essay, "Performative Acts and Gender Constitution: An Essay in Phenomenology and Feminist Theory," Butler wrote [12], "When Simone de Beauvoir claims, 'one is not born, but, rather, *becomes* woman,' she is appropriating and reinterpreting this doctrine of constituting acts from the phenomenological tradition. In this sense, gender is in no way a stable identity or locus of agency from which various acts proceed; rather, it is an identity tenuously constituted in time–an identity instituted through a *stylized repetition of acts*." [Emphasis in the original] The formula for "gender transformation" was to break the "subversive repetition of that style."

Translation: gender is not pre-defined but open-ended. It is created by the surrounding culture unless the individual creates her own gender through the "subversive repetition" of a style that is chosen rather than reflective. Fixed categories of gender such as male and female are an "illusion" that individuals "come to believe and to perform." But transformation is within reach.

The preceding view constitutes one extreme of the nurture versus nature debate. In this context, the disagreement is whether sexual identity comes from socialization or biology. Of course, most people acknowledge the importance of both in the development and expression of sexuality. For them, the true debate revolves around which factor is the most important. By contrast, rape culture adherents believe gender is constructed...period.

PC feminism's unshakable commitment to gender fluidity can be judged by a renowned medical experiment. It began at roughly the same time as social construction theory gained traction in feminist circles. The work of Dr. John Money at Johns Hopkins argued that gender choices were open-ended and could be constructed by a combination of socialization and medical therapies. Specifically, he studied the psychosexual flexibility of babies and young children; he experimented on the possibility of altering an infant's sex of birth. The ensuing debacle illustrates the tragic harm to innocents that can be inflicted by rejecting the power of biology in sexual identity. Even if biology is not the only defining force, it demands deep respect.

In 1965, identical twin boys named Bruce and Brian were born to the Reimer family. At 8 months old, Bruce's penis was destroyed in a botched circumcision; reconstructive surgery was not then sufficiently advanced to restore the organ. The frantic parents took their son to Money, a well-respected psychologist in the area of gender transformation. He espoused the theory of "Gender Neutrality" and was a pioneer in the controversial surgery known as "sex re-assignment." In short, he argued for gender fluidity. Gender identity, he insisted, was the result of socialization at a very early age. Money recommended that the Reimers raise Bruce as "Brenda," never revealing his original sex of birth to him. Bruce was to be converted to a female identity through surgical, hormonal, and psychological treatments. Money did *not* reveal to the parents, however, that his procedures were still experimental.

Having identical twins as patients must have seemed like a dream experiment to Money, for several reasons. The Reimers rendered consent for what would have otherwise been an illegal human experiment; with parental consent, Money could publish his work and gain recognition for his theories. The intact brother acted as a control for Bruce/Brenda, which boosted the scientific credibility of the experiment. Bruce/Brenda was also young enough to fit nicely into Money's theory of gender malleability through early socialization.

The "John/Joan" case, as Money labelled the venture, had pathbreaking implications. It was widely viewed as the first gender reassignment of a male infant which had not been required by a biological abnormality at birth. John/Joan provided a near perfect case to promote Money's theory that newborns were psychosexually neutral and gender identity could be reduced to socialization. The experiment became a touchstone to justify medical gender assignment for infants with atypical sex anatomies.

What happened? When Bruce/Brenda was 22 months old, Money performed a surgical castration. Hormone therapy was introduced when Bruce/Brenda neared puberty. The socialization imposed by the well-meaning parents was absolute, with Bruce/Brenda being raised as a girl in every way, including the clothes she wore and the toys with which she played. Nevertheless, Bruce/Brenda strongly resisted the socialization, tearing up her dresses and becoming a pain-racked misfit. She moved from school to school, from psychiatrist to social worker.

Meanwhile, both Reimer children endured years of follow-up visits with Money during which he put them through odd procedures, such as playing-out mock sex acts in which Bruce/Brenda was told to take the traditional role of female. According to John Colapinto [13], an award-winning journalist who later authored a book-length exposé of the Reimer case, Money justified the orchestration of sexual activity on the grounds that "childhood 'sexual rehearsal play'" was important for a "healthy adult gender identity."

Money's response to Bruce/Brenda's resistance? Babette Francis of the Population Research Institute wrote [14], "Despite all the indications that the experiment was a massive failure...in December 1972, Dr. Money unveiled his famous twins' case. In a two-day series devoted to 'Sex Role Learning in Childhood and Adolescence' at the annual meeting of the American Association for the Advancement of Science in Washington D.C., Money's paper was delivered to a capacity crowd of over one thousand scientists, feminists, students and reporters.... From his description the case was a great success..."

The faux results from the John/Joan case were also trumpeted in Money's book, *Gender Identity from Conception to Maturity* (1972), co-authored with psychiatrist Anke A. Ehrhardt. A subsequent book, *Sexual Signatures on Being a Man or a Woman* (1976), co-authored with reporter Patricia Tucker, popularized the case. But, when Money pressured the Reimers to bring Bruce/Brenda into Johns Hopkins for surgery to construct a vagina, the child threatened suicide and visits to Money ceased. Nevertheless, the John/Joan case remained widely accepted in the medical field and applauded by the politically correct.

In 1980, Bruce/Brenda finally learned the truth from his/her father. Bruce responded [15], "Suddenly it all made sense why I felt the way I did. I wasn't some sort of weirdo. I wasn't crazy." He reportedly had only one question: "What was my name?" He later assumed the name David and eventually reversed the gender reassignment through successful phalloplasty operations, a double mastectomy and male hormone injections. In 1990, he married and became a stepfather to three children.

Meanwhile, Francis noted [16], "Money's views on the malleability of gender identity was the established wisdom of the scientific community and particularly of the feminist movement.... Until David Reimer spoke publicly about his ordeal, the medical establishment was reluctant to admit the dangers of current practice in treating intersex babies, their reluctance no doubt underpinned by their deference to the feminist movement, which, still stuck in a time warp, believes that one can produce an androgynous society by adopting 'counter-sexist' educational practices."

David spoke out because a storm of publicity was poised to descend on the John/Joan case, which would have stripped him of anonymity. In 1997, a paper, "Sex Reassignment at Birth: A Long Term Review and Clinical Implications," co-authored by Dr. Milton Diamond and Dr. H. Keith Sigmundson, appeared in the *Archives of Pediatrics and Adolescent Medicine.* [17] Sigmundson had been a supervisor on the John/Joan case. With Sigmundson's assistance, Diamond was able to track down David Reimer and discover the reality behind the hype of John/Joan. Several documentaries and popular articles further stripped Money's work of credibility.

The lamentable episode ended tragically. In 2002, David's twin brother committed suicide. Two years later, the 38-year-old David shot himself in the head with a sawed-off shotgun. Yet even the tragedy of Bruce/Brenda does not cause PC voices to doubt the validity of the John/Joan case. To do so means doubting the theory of gender fluidity.

The concept of patriarchy

(Note: This book addresses the origin of PC terms and their popular dynamics. But it would be negligent to ignore the fact that some concepts have evolved in meaning. It would be confusing to present the debates and divisions on usage in a book intended as an introduction, however. Instead, the differences are acknowledged in passing, often in footnotes, to allow readers to follow up.)

"Patriarchy" is a term under debate. Discussion in some PC circles hinges on whether *all* men benefit from the so-called rape culture or whether *some* men are victimized as well. The classic example of men victimized by hierarchal power are slaves in the pre-bellum south. It is difficult to argue that a black male slave was privileged in relationship to a white female owner. The emerging belief that some men are also victims comes from approaching patriarchy as a system of interconnected social structures through which individuals can be subjugated regardless of gender. No concept is as closely associated with PC feminism, however, as patriarchy in its original meaning. That is the focus here.

The word "patriarchy" is Greek and means "rule of the father." Adrienne Rich – a key philosopher of early PC ideology – advanced what became a standard definition of patriarchy in her book, *Of Woman Born: Motherhood as Experience and Institution* (1976) [18].

Patriarchy is the power of the fathers: a familial-social, ideological, political system in which men – by force, direct pressure or through ritual, tradition, law, and language, customs, etiquette, education, and the division of labor, determine what part women should or shall not play, and in which the female is everywhere subsumed under the male....The power of the fathers had been difficult to grasp, because it permeates everything, even the language in which we try to describe it. It is diffuse and concrete; symbolic and literal; universal, and expressed with local variations which obscure its universality.

Patriarchy as the system by which all men subjugate all women is a basic concept from which PC feminism evolved. The concept is a key ideological line that divided Second Wave liberal feminism from its subsequent PC counterpart. The latter may seem to be a continuation of the '60s movement, partly because some of the same women were prominent in both. But many of the founding mothers of liberal feminism, including the pivotal Betty Friedan, were critics of the PC version. Friedan pleaded [19] for feminism to transcend "sexual politics and anger against men to express a new vision of family and community." She urged, "We must go from wallowing in the victim's state to mobilizing the new power of women and men for a larger political agenda on the priorities of life. We're at a dangerous time."

In the '60s and '70s, the Second Wave embraced sexual liberation and rejected the sexual constraints that had shackled their mothers. A constellation of factors broke down social and sexual mores. The Vietnam War prompted a political backlash that led to the wide questioning of social values; sexuality was redefined by birth control and greater access to abortion. Women openly attended classes on masturbation; they consumed pornography in increasing numbers; couples lived together without shame; lesbians marched arm in arm down the street; single motherhood became an acceptable option. It was the era of sexual liberation.

Somewhere along the line, however, the streak of rebellious joy was replaced with accusatory rage. Somewhere along the line, patriarchy happened. Instead of celebrating the freedom and joy of sex, PC voices barraged women with its perils: rape, domestic violence, harassment. Helen Reddy's song lyrics, "I am strong, I am invincible, I am woman," became the anthem of '60s feminism. But PC feminism defined woman as the perpetual victim of man – a victim for whom "I am weak, I am subjugated, I am woman" seemed more appropriate. A go-to-hell spirit gave way to a society-is-hell attitude.

'60s feminism was liberal and basically reformist, with a focus on specific issues such as the Equal Rights Amendment (ERA), birth control and abortion. '90s feminism was revolutionary and hammered out an ideology of oppression that subsumed all issues under one label: patriarchy. From date rape to the alleged wage gap, from housework to pornography...all of woman's ills had but a single root – patriarchy. Because men controlled the texts and institutions of society, they controlled the reality of women. The two genders became class enemies, and feminism's relationship to men was entirely politicized.

Susan Brownmiller, Andrea Dworkin and a surge of extreme-PC figures pointed to the one male tactic that defined patriarchy and how it maintained power over women: rape. They declared *all* men to be rapists with the goal of subjugating *all* women. It did not matter whether men were conscious of the goal or the benefit they received. Even men who had never raped were branded as oppressors because the male privilege they were said to enjoy flowed to them from a rape culture. They may not be rapists themselves but, as men, they were rape facilitators or rape beneficiaries.

In her legendary essay, "Rape: The All-American Crime," [20] the eco-feminist Susan Griffin opened, "I have never been free of the fear of rape. From a very early age I, like most women, have thought of rape as a part of my natural environment– something to be feared and prayed against like fire or lightning. I never asked why men raped; I simply thought it one of the many mysteries of human nature." She concluded, "Indeed, the existence of rape in any form is beneficial to the ruling class of white males. For rape is a kind of terrorism which severely limits the freedom of women and makes women dependent on men....This oppressive attitude towards women finds its institutionalization in the traditional family."

Just as all men were rapists or rape beneficiaries so, too, were all women rape victims. Rape was a political crime of one class against another. The opening paragraph of the *New York Radical Feminists Manifesto of Shared Rape* [21] maintained that "rape is not a personal misfortune but an experience shared by all women in one form or another. When more than two people have suffered the same oppression the problem is no longer personal but political– and rape is a political matter....The act of rape is the logical expression of the essential relationship now existing between men and women."

Post-Marxism

PC feminism is sometimes called Marxist feminism, especially by critics who oppose the ideology. The term "Marxist feminism" is both accurate and not. PC feminist theory has drawn significantly from Marxism but the movement has more correctly been called the "post-marxist feminism of social transformation" by the ultimate gender feminist Catharine A. MacKinnon in her book *Toward a Feminist Theory of the State* (1989). [22]

What is the *post* in post-Marxism? PC feminism disagrees with Marxism on a fundamental concept that defines both ideologies: class theory.

Before identifying the deviation, it is useful to ask, "what is a class?" A class is a conscious, subjective grouping of things that share common characteristics. It is *conscious* because the person doing the grouping does so for her or his own purpose. A researcher studying drug addiction, for example, might break research subjects into two classes: heroin users and non. It is *subjective* because the division serves the purpose of the classifier and the person can use any dividing-line characteristic, from hair color to deodorant use.

Generally speaking, political class analysis divides society into separate groups in order to explain conflicts that exist within society. The focus is on politics, economics, sociology or some combination thereof.

The basic Marxist divide in society arises from a person's relationship to the means of production. Those who own or profit from the means of production, such as factory owners, are capitalists. Those who labor for the means of production, such as factory workers, are the working class or proletariat. Capitalists are said to exploit workers which leaves the two classes inevitably and irreconcilably in conflict.

Arguably, the *lumpenproletariat* is a third category. These are workers or peasants with no class consciousness, no interest in revolution. The lumpenproletariat are either political nonentities or political impediments to Marxist goals.

A key feature of Marxist class analysis is its predictive value – that is, it predicts the behavior of individuals based on their class affiliation and interests. Each class has a different approach to facts and to logic. Accordingly, what is true for one class is not necessarily true for another. Indeed, since the two are locked in irresolvable conflict, it makes sense that what they view as true conflicts as well. In other words, a capitalist is expected to think with bourgeois logic and act in his own interests; the same is true of a worker. What is reasonable and evidence-based for one could be nonsense to the other. This allows a Marxist to draw conclusions without the need for thought or the analysis of evidence; all that is necessary is a knowledge of the other person's class affiliation. (The parallel to PC feminism's stress on male versus female logic, male versus female science, male versus female justice, etc. is remarkable.)

PC feminism veers sharply away from Marxism on the issue of class. Marxism views economic relationships as *the* factor in defining a class. PC feminism sees the dividing line as gender; is the individual male or female? Feminist class analysis claims that men share political and social interests that are in direct and necessary conflict with those of women and other marginalized groups who, like the workers in Marxist theory, live in class oppression. Arguably, females with no class consciousness or interest in overthrowing the patriarchy form a third class. They could be called the *lumpengender*.

For PC feminism, there is a thorny problem with Marxism. Namely, it has no place for gender. In Marxism, a capitalist and a worker can be either male or female, which makes gender a side-issue at best. PC feminism redefines a class so that the dividing line is no longer economic but a person's relationship to male privilege – in short, gender.

As with Marxism, the classes have entirely separate and antagonistic interests. Men oppress women. They have done so throughout history, they will do so in the future. Why? Because oppression is in their class interest. What must be removed is the basis of maleness itself.

PC feminist class analysis shares another trait with Marxism. Being male becomes a significant predictive factor in determining how members of that class will think and behave. The character or intentions of individual men does not matter; their class affiliation does. That's why PC feminists can level accusations of "rapist" or "rapist facilitator" at all men. (Note: as mentioned, an increasingly common wrinkle in this presentation of class theory has been to excoriate only *white* men along with lumpengender women.)

Yet another similarity exists. Both revile capitalism. To PC feminists, capitalism provides institutional support for patriarchy. Other institutions cluster under its umbrella: the free market, the traditional family, religion... Consider the PC approach to the free market as a parallel to Marxism. Historically, Americans have viewed the free market as a coordinating mechanism that functions spontaneously to balance supply with demand and to express the economic preferences of everyone involved; for example, people buy when the price is right and sell for the same reason. But PC feminists assess all functions of society in terms of the social justice they provide. (The term "social justice" is defined extensively in the next section.) They view the free market as an expression of privilege, as an oppressive mechanism of patriarchal control over women and other marginalized people.

The feminist sociologist Joan Acker explained [23] this perspective in writing of comparable worth – the policy of forcing businesses to pay workers identical wages for performing what is judged to be the same work. "Comparable worth takes issue with the theory that wages are set by the unseen hand of the market, or by genderless return to human capital. These theories are major ideological justifications for the contemporary class structure. Comparable worth has the potential to expose such theories as ideology." In other words, the free market is a matter of ideology and class conflict. True to the PC preference to use state force, Acker became a member of the legislative task force responsible for a study on mandated pay equity in Oregon.

Or consider the PC feminist approach to the traditional family in light of the movement's connection to Marxism. The family is depicted as a less obvious vehicle by which capitalism oppresses women. It is a bastion and breeding ground of private property, the class structure, and the means of production.

Kate Millett, a founding mother of gender theory, was fond of quoting Friedrich Engels, who co-authored the *Communist Manifesto*. Millett's groundbreaking book, *Sexual Politics* (1970), allocates 19 pages to a discussion of Engels's *The Origin of the Family, Private Property and the State* (1884). Unlike Marx, Engels addressed the plight of women as a sex. He believed their oppression sprang from the nuclear family and he was contemptuous of the then-popular notion that the family had subordinated women throughout history. Instead, he blamed capitalism because its development destroyed the prestige women once enjoyed within the family. Engels wrote [24], "That woman was the slave of man at the commencement of society is one of the most absurd notions....Women were not only free, but they held a highly respected position in the early stages of civilization and were the great power among the clans." In primitive society, woman was the equal of man or his superior. The PC conclusion: The traditional family was a product of capitalism and should be deconstructed. (Of course, their analysis is far fuller.)

Confusing post-Marxist or PC feminism with Marxism proper is understandable but not quite accurate. PC feminism accepts much of the Marxist context but it rejects the central claim that economic relationships determine class affiliation. *Gender* does. Gender is also key to the concept of social justice.

Social justice

> Circumstances such as where a person is born, where they live or their gender and ethnicity should never determine their income or their opportunities for quality education, basic healthcare, decent work, adequate shelter, access to drinking water, political participation or living free from threatened, or actual, physical violence. – UN Secretary-General Ban Ki-moon, 2014 World Day of Social Justice [25]

News stories and broadcasts increasingly employ the term "social justice." What does it mean?

The definition is fluid but the term generally refers to an equitable distribution of power across society. "Equitable" means a just share of wealth and opportunity. A "just share" means that marginalized groups are provided with more advantages or privileges than white males in order to compensate them for oppression that may have occurred centuries ago. Individuals are granted access to advantages based on their class affiliation which is based, in turn, on skin color, gender and other factors by which they are included in a marginalized group. The institutions of society – from government to the private sphere – are expected to facilitate equal or preferred access to benefits such as health care, education and employment. If the advantages do not flow voluntarily, then force should be used to pry them loose from the privileged. Examples of social justice policies are progressive taxation, affirmative action, hate-speech laws, and other forms of "positive" discrimination.

The term "social justice" dates back to the mid-19th century when it was coined by the Jesuit priest and scholar Luigi Taparelli. Taparelli believed law should serve morality because unrestrained freedom harmed the cohesiveness of society, even if the expression of freedom was nonviolent. A virtuous society required law that did not merely or primarily protect person and property but protected morality by imposing it. Justice comes down to enforcing a code of morality.

This approach can be seen in the rape culture campaigns on campuses today, especially in the campus misconduct hearings that are so common. (Chapter Three deals with the hearings in detail.) Rape culture adherents speak of "justice" but the word does not signify what it does within traditional Western jurisprudence, which hinges on safeguards such as due process. Indeed, the social justice usage runs counter to it. The columnist Ezra Klein illustrated this [26] schism when he endorsed a common social justice sentiment in an article entitled "SB 697, California's 'Yes Means Yes' law, is a terrible bill. But it's a necessary one." Klein admitted that male students would be devastated and expelled even though they were innocent of accusations against them. He not only accepted the inevitability but also declared it to be a positive thing.

First, Klein offered a capsule explanation of SB 697. "It tries to change, through brute legislative force, the most private and intimate of adult acts. It is sweeping in its redefinition of acceptable consent; two college seniors who've been in a loving relationship since they met during the first week of their freshman years, and who, with the ease of the committed, slip naturally from cuddling to sex, could fail its test."

Then Klein nodded in approval at the act of expelling an innocent male accused of sexual assault. "Critics worry that colleges will fill with cases in which campus boards convict young men (and, occasionally, young women) of sexual assault for genuinely ambiguous situations. Sadly, that's necessary for the law's success. It's those cases – particularly the ones that feel genuinely unclear and maybe even unfair, the ones that become lore in frats and cautionary tales that fathers e-mail to their sons – that will convince men that they better Be Pretty D–n Sure." The disconnect between social justice and real justice is clear. It does not matter if the innocent are punished. All that matters is the social impact of the punishment.

A spin-off term has entered the popular vocabulary: Social Justice Warrior (SJW). SJWs express an aggressive political correctness by which peaceful but incorrect acts and ideas are suppressed, by force if necessary. Correct acts and ideas are promoted, often in the form of tax-funding, legal privilege or other state support.

The SJW seeks to impose a uniformity of far-left expression upon society. The art of argumentation – that is, the exchange of opinions with the goal of reaching truth – is seen as destructive. The truth of social justice is to be accepted absolutely, like dogma, and dissent is equivalent to immorality. Criticism is defined as hate speech or an act of oppression. Remember, truth is constructed and it is relative rather than objective. The class affiliation of the critic is what is important rather than the argument or evidence he presents. After all, the argument and evidence are determined by his class or gender interest.

Thus, SJWs do not deal in argument or evidence when engaging others. They address the perceived power structure inherent in the exchange. Their first response is not to reason or persuade but to launch an offensive aimed at silencing the dissenter and assuming the power of the narrative. This is true in the most trivial of exchanges. For example, a common SJW tactic is to swarm or to dogpile a website at which someone has posted an unPC sentiment; a man might joke about his spouse in a manner that would occasion no notice if the joke were made by a woman about her boyfriend. Using social media sites, like Tumblr or Twitter, members of a group dedicated to swarming will be notified and a coordinated SJW attack is launched. The purpose is to overwhelm, intimidate and abuse the joke-maker into silence or retreat.

A guest lecturer at a university will be shouted down by SJWs in the audience or she will be uninvited. Julie Bindel self-identifies as a radical feminist but she is also an outspoken critic of the SJW movement. Bindel described [27] her own experience of speaking on campuses.

> Any time I'm invited to an event or a talk, as soon as the privileged PhD-seeking Foucauldian types hear about it, then I get threatened with a picket, and the organisers get harassed, harangued and threatened relentlessly. And, eventually, it just doesn't seem worth it for the organisers to go ahead. If the organisers are a student body, for example, they face the threat of having their funding withdrawn....They [the SJWs] think they've won, but they haven't. They love censorship, because they want to shut up the voices of dissent so that they sound reasonable... That's because they're such idiots that if they don't shut up the voices of reason they will come across as exactly what they are.

The political theme unifying SJWs is a demand for "equality" by which they mean "equity" or the just distribution of power. To some, the goal may ring with fairness but it is profoundly flawed and unjust. For example, there is no end-point; there is no measurement or definition of when equity is attained. This is an inevitable by-product of the SJW approach. They sift selectively back through centuries of history in order to assess the collective and timeless social debt owed to marginalized groups by whites or white males. Fresh generations who have done nothing wrong, blameless individuals are pronounced "guilty" of and liable for the acts of their predecessors from centuries ago. SJWs become remedial historians who impose the cost of historical wrongs, such as slavery, on individuals who share the skin color or gender of the people who committed them.

One reason for the lack of an end point: There is no downside for SJWs in having the restitution, retribution process continue indefinitely. Indeed, there are massive advantages.

History of the Rape Culture

> Feminism keeps saying the sexes are the same. It keeps telling
> women they can do anything, go anywhere, say anything, wear
> anything. No, they can't. Women will always be in sexual
> danger...feminism, with its pie-in-the-sky fantasies about the perfect
> world, keeps young women from seeing life as it is. –Camille Paglia
> [28]

Rape culture ideology consists of the preceding concepts of social
construction, gender-fluidity, the patriarchy, post-Marxism and social
justice. The concepts require a disconnect from practical reality. Myths now
surround the issue of rape, and they are accepted as a matter of faith on
college campuses today. What are some of the most common and venerated
myths?

In 1975, a pivot point occurred within PC feminism on rape. The book
Against Our Will: Men, Women and Rape by Susan Brownmiller appeared. In
its pages, Brownmiller attempted to chart the history of rape from the
Neanderthal through to modern man, placing great emphasis on periods of
war and crisis. *Against Our Will* reportedly gave rape its history. It became a
founding document of the rape culture, which further propelled the
feminist movement from liberalism to political correctness.

Brownmiller maintained [29] that rape is the primary mechanism through
which men subjugate women. "Man's discovery that his genitalia could
serve as a weapon to generate fear must rank as one of the most important
discoveries of prehistoric times, along with the use of fire, and the first
crude stone ax. From prehistoric times to the present, I believe, rape has
played a critical function. It is nothing more or less than a conscious process
of intimidation by which *all* men keep *all* women in a state of fear."

Brownmiller cemented some of today's most prevalent myths about rape
into the culture. In particular, Brownmiller presented three interrelated
fictions:

1. Rape is an essential part of patriarchy;

2. Men have created a mass psychology of rape; and,

3. Rape is a part of normal life.

Myth One: Rape is an essential part of patriarchy

Rape culture adherents who contend that rape is essential to white male
culture need to ignore many facts. For example, according to most statistics,

women and men experience sexual violence at similar rates. Women and men are victimized by domestic violence at virtually the same rate. Men constitute the vast majority of prisoners; and, if prison populations are included in data on rape, then men probably experience the crime more frequently than women. Moreover, there is no evidence whatsoever that white men commit more sexual violence than minorities.

If patriarchy is not the source of rape, then what is?

Several decades ago, researchers were closer to explaining the causes of sexual violence than they are today. One of the first casualties of political correctness was impartial research in the social sciences, which was usually conducted by universities or other facilities funded by tax dollars. This made researchers vulnerable to political influence. Studies on the multiple causes of rape have almost entirely dried up because only *one* cause is now permitted to enter the narrative: patriarchy.

During the heyday of liberal feminism and sexual freedom, research was far more sophisticated. In their book, *The Crime and Consequences of Rape* (1982), Charles W. Dean and Mary de Bruyn-Kops reported [30], "The Kinsey study, begun in the 1950s and completed after Kinsey's death by Gebhard and associates, classified seven types of rapists: assaultive, amoral, drunken, explosive, double-standard, mental defective and psychotic..." Kinsey has fallen into disrepute but a fact remains: the approach to rape used to be more nuanced and informative than it is today.

People murder for money, for love, in the name of religion, to defend a loved one, out of jealousy, in a rage, under the influence, and even out of patriotism. The motives of violent individuals are as diverse as human beings are themselves. Men *and women* rape because of miscommunication, sexual hunger, a need to prove themselves, a desire for revenge, socio-pathology, hatred of the other sex, impaired judgment, peer pressure, in the presence of extreme circumstances such as war, or as a political strategy. Men *and women* rape from a multitude of complicated motives, all of which become further blurred when alcohol or drugs are involved.

But it is no longer politically expedient to suggest the possibility of many motives for rape. Other explanations are defined out of existence in order to maintain the myth that one thing and one thing alone is responsible for the rape of women: the patriarchy.

Fortunately, this myth is starting to crack. The Rape, Abuse & Incest National Network (RAINN) is not only the largest anti-sexual violence network in America, it also tends toward the PC. On February 28, 2014, RAINN sent a 16-page letter to a new White House Task Force on sexual assault on campus. The letter caused a furor in rape culture circles because it called for emphasis to be placed on individuals who assault rather than on ideological explanations. RAINN stated [32], "There has been an unfortunate trend towards blaming 'rape culture' for the extensive problem of sexual violence on campus.... [I]t is important not to lose sight of a simple fact: rape is caused not by cultural factors but by the conscious decisions of a small percentage of the community to commit a violent crime." A focus on the rape culture, RAINN argued, made it "harder to stop sexual violence since it removed the focus from the individual at fault, and seemingly mitigates personal responsibility."

It is time to return to investigating the motives of rapists, both male and female. It is time to impartially analyze "the conscious decisions of a small percentage of the community" who chose "to commit a violent crime."

Myth Two: Men have created a "mass psychology" of rape.

Brownmiller's second myth: Men have created a mass psychology of rape, which is now known as the rape culture. Throughout her book, Brownmiller dips in and out of history, selecting whatever evidence supports that statement. Some references, such as passages from novels, are fiction with little standing in reality; the sources cannot not be taken seriously by anyone who values actual data. Brownmiller also points to historical events that are difficult to credit. When she writes of prehistoric times as the point at which man began to use "his genitalia...as a weapon," for example, the reader is left wondering where she acquired her amazing knowledge of Neanderthals and their sexual attitudes. Interviews? Diaries? Anecdotal accounts? The questions are sarcastic but they highlight an immense problem with her evidence; namely, where does it come from? Many statements are impossible to verify. And, yet, rape culture adherents swallow Brownmiller's pronouncements whole.

Contradictory evidence is casually dismissed in passing, if it is mentioned at all. Yet, even after carefully cherry-picking from fiction and history, Brownmiller cannot support the conclusion that rape "is nothing more or less than a conscious process of intimidation by which *all* men keep *all* women in a state of fear." To punch up the claim, she introduces dubious statistics. (For a refutation of PC data, especially the 1-in-4 or 1-in-5 stats on the chance of a woman being raped, see Chapters Four and Five.)

For the sake of argument, however, let's accept Brownmiller's inflated 1-in-4 statistic at face value. Even assuming a one-to-one correlation between rapists and victims – that is, assuming no serial rapists or serial victims –

Brownmiller's claim means that 75% of men will *never* rape, 75% of women will *not* be raped. Indeed, from personal experience, I know many men would defend an attacked woman. I believe most would. And I always bring extra skepticism to statistics that run counter to my personal experience of life.

Brownmiller's claims invite a political question. What other class of people in our society could be collectively demonized for the actions of some members without occasioning a backlash of outrage? If *all* blacks were accused of being criminals or of benefiting from crime because *some* of them do, SJWs would howl in protest. Yet, with the demonization of white males, SJWs are the accusers.

And lest a single man escape the accusation of "rapist" by pleading that he had never so much as contemplated the act, Brownmiller explains how good intentions, behavior and character do not exonerate him. "Once we accept as basic truth that rape is not a crime of irrational, impulsive, uncontrollable lust, but is a deliberate, hostile, violent act of degradation and possession on the part of a would-be conqueror, designed to intimidate and inspire fear, we must look toward those elements in our culture that promote and propagandize these attitudes, which offer men...the ideology and psychological encouragement to commit their acts of aggression *without awareness, for the most part, that they have committed a punishable crime,* let alone a moral wrong." [Italics in original]

Brownmiller is correct. If we accept her premise "as basic truth," then her conclusions follow. But one of the main purposes of discussing ideas is to establish which premises are supported by evidence. If a person opens a discussion with an unquestionable truth, such as "Zeus exists," then many conclusions naturally follow. Few of the conclusions are likely to true or valid because they follow from a false statement. Thus, Brownmiller makes her reasoning immune to evidence. There is no possibility for a man to escape the charge of rape because accepting the "basic truth" of her statement makes the charge axiomatically and ideologically true.

Myth Three: Rape is a part of normal life

Brownmiller's third myth: Rape is part of normal life. To reach this conclusion, Brownmiller makes great leaps of logic.

Chapter after chapter of *Against Our Will* dwells on rape during times of war and severe social turmoil. Because men are prone to rape in such times, she argues that rape is a part of normal life. But the contexts Brownmiller presents are the opposite of normal; otherwise, calling them "times of crisis" would make no sense. During war and other upheavals, the frequency of *all* violence increases, including the murder of civilians which would be prosecuted in times of peace. In other words, Brownmiller's examples prove the opposite of what she contends. The soaring violence during social turmoil is an indication that *normal* life has been abandoned for savagery. The pervasive violence is a characteristic of social crisis, not of everyday life. The circumstances graphically highlighted by Brownmiller do not describe normal life but its breakdown. Yet, arguing from facts that prove the opposite, Brownmiller draws conclusions about the normal.

Against Our Will arrives at its myths by way of ideology, not empirical research. Although the book is sometimes taken for a chronicle of historical fact, a glaring political slant underlies the presentation of its cherry-picked data. Consider Brownmiller's opinion of private property: "Concepts of hierarchy, slavery and private property flowed from, and could only be predicated upon, the initial subjugation of woman." These are not the words of an unbiased historian who has no ideological filter.

In her book *Sexual Personae* [32], the dissident feminist Camille Paglia offers a more plausible relationship between society and rape. Paglia writes, "Generation after generation, men must be educated, refined, and ethically persuaded away from their tendency toward anarchy and brutishness. Society is not the enemy, as feminism ignorantly claims. Society is woman's protection against rape." Translation: A woman is safer in a room full of socialized men if only because the majority of them have been conditioned to protect women and to behave with fairness.

Additional Myths About Rape

Since *Against Our Will*, myths about rape and a rape culture have proliferated. On the Oxford University Press blog, Helen Reece authored the scholarly essay "Rape Myths: Is Elite Opinion Right and Popular Opinion Wrong?" [34] Her answer? The commonsense public is correct. According to Reece, legal reformers have created "myths about myths, or myth myths," which makes the crafting and execution of effective law extraordinarily difficult. Reformers have done so for a variety of reasons. Some truly believe in the rape culture; others are ambitious; many comply with the loudest social demand in their ears.

Reece listed seven myths over which she stumbles. All of them are common within the Western legal system and each represents an obstacle to approaching the crime of rape in a reasonable manner.

1. Myth: *The rate of the conviction for rape is unusually low because the crime of rape is underreported.* Reece wrote, "Throughout the criminal justice system, the proportion of offenders who end up convicted is tiny – higher than rape for some crimes, lower than rape for other crimes. There is not good evidence that people are less likely to acknowledge or report rape than other crimes." (Supporting link embedded in her essay.)

2. Myth: *Surveys prove that most people support beliefs that rape culture adherents consider to be myths.* Reece questioned the objectivity of current research that "tends to define rape myths as ethically wrong rather than factually false." Thus, even factually-based views are listed as myths if they are "ethically wrong." What the rape researchers are actually proving is "lots of people have views that are accurate but different from the researchers. We now have the oxymoronic 'true myth'."

3. Myth: *Most people believe real rape has to be violent and the woman has to be injured for a rape to have occurred.* Reece asked, "What does this even mean? Does it mean that people believe 'real rape' is the only sort of rape, the most common sort of rape, or the most serious type of rape?" The only hard evidence for the myth, she claimed, is that violent rapes are more likely to result in a conviction at trial. But this is more likely because the jurors have solid evidence rather than a he said/she said scenario.

4. Myth: *Most people think women cry rape when, in fact, they do not.* Reece referenced a recent rape awareness campaign in England that was entitled "We Believe You" and urged people to automatically believe an accuser. Reece observed, "There isn't good evidence that people are less believing of rape complainants than other complainants." The mere questioning of a rape accusation was being confused with disbelieving it, she suggested. Yet entertaining the possibility of false accusations was nothing more than legal prudence.

5. Myth: *Women are presumed to render consent through their behavior, such as having a drink with a man.* This is a more difficult myth because it also contains truth. Clearly, many behaviors cannot and must not be equated with consent. Other behaviors are more difficult to judge because consent in our culture is often rendered in a non-verbal manner. If a woman sits in a man's lap, for example, he may reasonably conclude she wishes to be kissed. Reece argued, "Sometimes rape myth reformers' real objection seems to be to a traditional construction of heterosexuality in which men pursue women. There are many good reasons to challenge this gendered binary, but it can't be done by creating a code cracker for sexual consent. A different sexual vision needs to be argued for openly, not smuggled in..."

6. Myth: *Jurors scrutinize such factors as how the alleged victim was dressed in arriving at a judgment.* To this contention, Reece answered, "yes, and they should." The myth here is not that jurors scrutinize the facts; they do. The myth is believing they are wrong to do so. Jurors are trying to assess the reality behind a murky situation. Such details as conversation between the two parties and how each of them behaved are proper topics of scrutiny. If the man's behavior and demeanor is fair game in evaluating his guilt, then the woman's behavior and demeanor is also on the table. Just law recognizes no double standard.

7. Myth: *People blame an accuser even if they believe her.* There is no good evidence for this claim. Indeed, anyone who even doubts an accuser is publicly excoriated these days, which makes it difficult to believe the claim.

So many myths about rape have entered politics, the law, history and the other social sciences that it is difficult to list them. But most rest on the three key myths argued for and largely established by *Against Our Will*.

Conclusion

Myths about rape harm men, women and the victims of sexual assault, both male and female. Goodwill between the sexes has been displaced by rage or resentment, and for no productive purpose. Rape is not a tool of patriarchy; like all crime, it is a lamentable choice that some people make for their own individual reasons. Men, as a class, are *not* the enemy and they have not created a mass psychology of rape; PC feminists have created a mass fear about rape. Rape is not a part of "normal" life; in normal life, men and women do not assault each other.

Hysteria must be replaced by reason.

Notes

[1] Prof Joyce E. Williams, *Blackwell Encyclopedia Of Sociology* (2007) http://www.blackwellreference.com/public/tocnode?id=g9781405124331_yr2012_chunk_g978140512433124_ss1-19 Retrieved Sept. 13, 2015.

[2] *Analyzing Gender: A Handbook of Social Science Research*, eds. Beth B. Hess and Myra Marx Ferree (NewburyPark: Sage Publications, 1989), p.519.

[3] *Knowing Women: Feminism and Knowledge,* eds. Helen Crowley and Susan Himmelweit (Cambridge: Polity Press, 1992) p.65.

[4] *After Foucault*, ed. Jonathan Arac (New Brunswick: Rutgers University Press), 1988.

[5] Ibid, p.161.

[6] Aurelia Armstrong, *The Internet Encyclopedia of Philosophy*, http://www.iep.utm.edu/foucfem/ Retrieved Sept 13, 2015. By focusing on Foucault, I do not mean to diminish the influence of other post-modern or post-structuralist philosophers, such as Jacques Derrida. My purpose is merely to present the basics of ideas underlying feminism as clearly as possible.

[7] As quoted in *Gender and Power in Contemporary Spirituality: Ethnographic Approaches,* ed. Anna Fedele and Kim E. Knibbe (New York and Routledge, 2012) p.118.

[8] Debby Herbenick and Aleta Baldwin, "What Each of Facebook's 51 New Gender Options Means," *The Daily Beast*, Feb. 15, 2014. http://www.thedailybeast.com/articles/2014/02/15/the-complete-glossary-of-facebook-s-51-gender-options.html Retrieved Sept. 13, 2015.

[9] Fredrik deBoer, "I'm fed up with political correctness, and the idea that everyone should already be perfect," *Quartz,* Jan. 29, 2015. http://qz.com/335941/im-fed-up-with-political-correctness-and-the-idea-that-everyone-should-already-be-perfect/ Retrieved Sept. 13, 2015.

[10] As quoted by François Dosse, "Foucault Sells Like Hot Cakes," *History of Structuralism: The rising sign, 1945-1966*, (University of Minnesota, 1997), p.333.

[11] Kate Bornestein, *Gender Outlaw: On Men, Women and the Rest of Us,* (New York: Rutledge), p.115.

[12] Judith Butler, *Gender Trouble: Feminism and the Subversion of Identity,* (New York: Routledge, 1990). http://en.wikipedia.org/wiki/Gender_Trouble Retrieved Sept. 13, 2015. Quotation from the essay, "Performative Acts and Gender Constitution: An Essay in Phenomenology and Feminist Theory," *Theatre Journal.* Vol. 40, No. 4, pp. 519-531, December 1988.

[13] John Colapinto, *As Nature Made Him: The Boy who was Raised as a Girl,* (New York: HarperCollins, 2000). Revised, 2006.

[14] Babette Francis, "The Deconstruction of Gender," Population Research Institute, May 1, 2002. http://pop.org/content/deconstruction-of-gender-1798 Retrieved Sept. 13, 2015.

[15] Colapinto, op.cit.

[16] Francis, op.cit.

[17] Dr. Milton Diamond and Dr. H. Keith Sigmundson, "Sex Reassignment at Birth: A Long Term Review and Clinical Implications," *Archives of Pediatrics and Adolescent Medicine.* No. 151 (March 1997). http://hawaii.edu/PCSS/biblio/articles/1961to1999/1997-sex-reassignment.html Retrieved Sept. 13, 2015.

[18] Adrienne Rich, *Of Woman Born: Motherhood as Experience and Institution,* (New York: Norton, 1976), pp.40-41.

[19] as quoted by Nancy Gibbs, "The War Against Feminism," *Time*, June 24, 2001. http://content.time.com/time/magazine/article/0,9171,159157,00.html Retrieved Sept. 13, 2015.

[20] Susan Griffin, "Rape: The all-American crime," *Ramparts,* Vol. 10, No. 3, Sept. 1971. http://www.unz.org/Pub/Ramparts-1971sep-00026 Retrieved Sept. 13, 2015.

[21] As quoted in *Rape: the First Sourcebook for Women by New York Radical Feminists,* ed. Noreen Connell and Cassandra Wilson, (New York: New American Library, 1974.) https://web.viu.ca/davies/H323Vietnam/Manifesto.SharedRape.1971.htm Retrieved Sept. 13, 2015.

[22] Catharine A. MacKinnon, *Toward a Feminist Theory of the State,* (Harvard University Press, 1989). http://fair-use.org/catharine-mackinnon/toward-a-feminist-theory-of-the-state/chapter-8 Retrieved Sept. 13, 2015.

[23] Joan Acker, *Doing Comparable Worth: Gender, Class, and Pay Equity* (Temple University, 1989), p.22.

[24] Frederick Engels, *The Origin of the Family, Private Property and the State,* (Resistance Marxist Library, 2004), p.60.

[25] Ban Ki-moon, "Secretary-General's message for the World Day of Social Justice," the United Nations, Feb. 20, 2014. http://www.un.org/sg/STATEMENTS/index.asp?nid=7470 Retrieved Sept. 13, 2015.

[26] Ezra Klein, "SB 697, California's 'Yes Means Yes' law, is a terrible bill. But it's a necessary one," *Vox*, Oct. 13, 2014 (updated).

http://www.vox.com/2014/10/13/6966847/yes-means-yes-is-a-terrible-bill-and-i-completely-support-it Retrieved Sept. 13, 2015.

[27] As quoted by by Tim Black, "Julie Bindel vs 'the stupid little bellends'," *Spiked*, Feb. 6, 2015. http://www.spiked-online.com/newsite/article/julie-bindel-vs-the-stupid-little-bellends/16673 Retrieved Sept. 13, 2015.

[28] Camille Paglia, *Sex, Art, and American Culture: Essays*, (New York: Vintage Books, 1992), p.50.

[29] Susan Brownmiller, *Against Our Will: Men, Women and Rape*, (New York: Simon and Schuster, 1975).

[30] Charles W. Dean and Mary deBruyn-Kops, *The Crime and Consequences of Rape*, (Springfield, Illinois: Charles C. Thomas, 1982).

[31] The Rape, Abuse & Incest National Network, Feb. 28, 2014. https://rainn.org/images/03-2014/WH-Task-Force-RAINN-Recommendations.pdf Retrieved Sept. 13, 2015.

[32] Camille Paglia, *Sexual Personae: Art and Decadence from Nefertiti to Emily Dickinson, Volume 1*, (New York: Vintage Books, 1992), p.23.

[33] Helen Reece, "Myths about rape myths," Oxford University Press Blog, July 22, 2013. http://blog.oup.com/2013/07/myths-about-rape-myths/ Retrieved Sept. 13, 2015.

Chapter Three: Dynamics of the Hysteria and Psychology of Rape Culture True Believers

Introduction

Chapter One offered the defining characteristics of rape culture hysteria and the reasons why people credit it on some level. Again, the core myth in question is the existence of a rape culture itself.

How does the rape culture meme get embedded into society? The people who buy into the myth is only half of the equation. The other half is the ideologues who *sell* the fiction. Promoting the rape culture hysteria involves at least two interrelated factors: the dynamics of how the myth permeates the general culture; and, the specific psychology of ideologues who deal in dogma.

A recent event captured the dynamics of the rape culture and the tactics used to embed the myth. In the last gasp of 2014, the fraternity Phi Kappa Psi at the University of Virginia (U-Va.) experienced a 21st century lynch mob. The mob consisted of university officials, student activists, politicians, media and opinion makers...all of whom were led by PC feminists. "Gang-rape!" was the shrill banner they hoisted. "Believe the women!" was the incessant mantra. They sought nothing short of the destruction of the fraternity system. In the wake of what is now is known as the "gang-rape hoax," the U-Va. narrative is a real-life illustration of how the rape culture hysteria functions.

Background of the U-Va. Gang-Rape Myth

The article, "A Rape on Campus: A Brutal Assault and Struggle for Justice at UVA," appeared in the December 2014 issue of *Rolling Stone*. The capsule description provided by the magazine [1]: "Jackie was just starting her freshman year at the University of Virginia when she was brutally assaulted by seven men at a frat party. When she tried to hold them accountable, a whole new kind of abuse began." The "new kind of abuse" was the dismissive manner in which the university allegedly handled Jackie's report of rape.

In the *Rolling Stone* article, well-known journalist and contributor Sabrina Rubin Erdely graphically depicted the 2012 gang rape. The details were so gruesome that the story blew past the barriers of skepticism with which most people filter daily life. It elicited the same sickened but riveted revulsion as torture porn. Unfortunately, the sensational details also made the story irresistible to the ratings-driven media, which uncritically broadcast the account.

Erdely wrote of Jackie:

> She remembers every moment of the next three hours of agony, during which, she says, seven men took turns raping her, while two more – her date, Drew, and another man – gave instruction and encouragement. She remembers how the spectators swigged beers, and how they called each other nicknames like Armpit and Blanket. She remembers the men's heft and their sour reek of alcohol mixed with the pungency of marijuana. Most of all, Jackie remembers the pain and the pounding that went on and on.

> As the last man sank onto her, Jackie was startled to recognize him: He attended her tiny anthropology discussion group. He looked like he was going to cry or puke as he told the crowd he couldn't get it up. "Pussy!" the other men jeered. "What, she's not hot enough for you?"

"A Rape on Campus" appeared in *Rolling Stone* on Wednesday, November 19th. That same day, U-Va. President Teresa Sullivan issued a campus-wide letter in which she referred to Jackie's story as "an alleged sexual assault" and promised a full investigation. [2] Sullivan was resoundingly criticized for calling the sexual assault "alleged" because the word was said to cast doubt upon Jackie's veracity. On Thursday afternoon, nearly 1,000 members of the university community rallied at a "Stand Up Against Rape Culture" event in the campus Amphitheatre. [3] On Friday, Sullivan received a petition signed by more than 1,000 students and faculty members. The petition's demands included the immediate and permanent closure of Phi Kappa Psi, punishment of those identified as rapists and a thorough reform of how the university handled sexual assault reports. The university was admonished to be more supportive of accusers. [4]

Meanwhile, *Rolling Stone* issued a second article [5] that suggested Jackie's experience was far from being an isolated one: "Rape at U.Va.: Readers Say Jackie Wasn't Alone." The article offered a capsule description. "Rolling Stone's investigation into sexual assault on the University of Virginia campus elicits intense personal stories." The stories of rape and assault were offered and reprinted under signatures such as "Sadly," "Hibiscus Oil 'Hoo," and "Guest D." The anonymity made it impossible to verify accuracy.

On Saturday the 22nd, Sullivan circulated a follow-up letter [6] to the campus community in which she took a much harder stand in favor of Jackie. The subject line in the second letter changed from the initial one of "Sexual Misconduct" to "Sexual Violence." The word "alleged" did not appear; instead, Sullivan addressed "[t]he wrongs described in *Rolling Stone* which were 'appalling'." Rather than speak of an upcoming investigation, Sullivan took immediate action. All fraternities, sororities and other Greek organizations – not just Phi Kappa Psi – were suspended until Spring semester. The suspension reportedly affected 31 fraternities in the Inter-Fraternity Council, 16 sororities and 15 minority-oriented Greek-letter organizations that functioned under other councils. Approximately 3,500 students were affected, with traditional holiday dances, parties and charity fund raisers canceled. Sullivan also vowed to revamp U-Va.'s sexual misconduct policies and procedures to make them more welcoming to accusers.

At an emergency meeting of U-Va.'s governing board, the U-Va. Rector George Keith Martin expressed [7] the shared response of administration and faculty. He publicly apologized to Jackie and to her parents, stating, "The status quo will no longer be acceptable. I am appalled, simply appalled."

Response swelled and spilled outside the campus. The Charlottesville police began an investigation into the gang-rape, even though it had not been officially reported to them. State Attorney General Mark Herring announced plans to appoint an independent counsel to review U-Va.'s procedures regarding sexual assault. Elected officials, including Gov. Terry McAuliffe (D) and Sen. Mark R. Warner (D), swiftly mounted podiums to express outrage and profound concern. McAuliffe made the uncontroversial declaration [8], "Sexual violence is a nationwide problem, and it is critical that our schools acknowledge that this is a pervasive issue and take bold action to end it." The media's prurient obsession with the U-Va. gang-rape has been too well explored to deserve more discussion.

The foregoing occurred even though no one had been formally accused of rape, no one had been charged with a crime or had been fully identified. The witch hunt was based entirely on anonymous accounts by which an entire category of people were indicted: frat boys.

Fortunately, lone voices asked awkward questions. The first mainstream voice was   Richard Bradley, editor-in-chief of *Worth* magazine. In a November 24 blog post [9], "Is the Rolling Stone Story True?," Bradley wrote, "I'm not convinced that this gang rape actually happened. Something about this story doesn't feel right."

One red flag? Earlier in his career, veteran reporter Bradley had developed a principle by which to evaluate journalistic accounts. "One must be most critical about stories that play into existing biases," he wrote. The U-Va. story nourished a lot of existing biases – against fraternities, against men, against the South. It played into a strong protective bias toward naive young women, especially young Southern women, and a horror at their rape. The story supported a belief in the existence – indeed, the prevalence – of a rape culture. And the story raised hostility toward the university bureaucracies that "allowed" sexual assault to run rampant on campuses.

Other red flags were more circumstantial, more specific to the U-Va. story. For one thing, Jackie was never identified, which meant the entire account rested on one unnamed source. Most details were impossible to verify. Moreover, some seemed counter-intuitive or hyperbolic. Bradley wrote, "Jackie, for example, alleges that one out of three women who go to U.Va. has been raped. This is silly." The figure was unbelievable and over the top.

The Jackie story quickly unraveled and was exposed as an incredible invention with which rape culture adherents, administrators, politicians and the media had chosen to run, each for their own benefit. Some believers expressed genuine outrage, with many appearing to feel an odd sort of high from the adrenaline of rage. Other believers swallowed the story whole because it fit their preconceptions of rape and fraternities. Still others used the hysteria to facilitate goals such as reform and the acquisition of power within the university system.

How U-Va. Expressed the Rape Culture Myth Dynamics

The purpose here is *not* to chart the facts or time line of an unraveling hoax. Rather, it is to analyze the dynamics of the rape culture myth, and how the myth has become so powerful. The analysis reveals factors that are common in the dynamics of a long-series of *faux* "rape culture" scandals, from the Duke Lacrosse case of 2006 to the Columbia University rape hoax that occupied so much media attention in 2015. The latter crime was alleged by "Emma Sulkowicz– famous for carrying her mattress on campus as a symbol of her burden as a victim and a protest against Columbia's failure to expel the man she calls her 'rapist' who has become the face of the college rape survivors' movement." [10] Sulkowicz's face is that of a liar.

The common dynamics of U-Va. include:

The myth plays into existing biases

> For much of their [male] lives, they've looked forward to the hedonistic fun of college, bearing every expectation of booze and no-strings sex. A rape heralds the uncomfortable idea that all that harmless mayhem may not be so harmless after all. Easier, then, to assume the girl is lying, even though studies indicate that false rape reports account for, at most, eight percent of reports. –Sabrina Rubin Erdely, "A Rape on Campus." [11]

The comedian Stephen Colbert coined the term "truthiness" to refer to an argument or claim that is made or accepted on the basis of a gut feeling rather than on evidence or reason. "Truthiness" was declared to be 2005's Word of the Year by the American Dialect Society; it was among the Words of the Year 2006, which were chosen by Merriam-Webster. The word achieved immediate acceptance because it captured a phenomenon that is rampant in the socio-political discussions of our day: the misuse of emotional appeals and prejudices which substitute for evidence and reasoned arguments.

In expressing his early doubts about Jackie's story, Bradley outlined several biases that fed a widespread willingness to believe the account, and to do so without reflection. The biases included a hostility toward fraternities, toward men, and against the South. The most prevalent bias is probably the anti-fraternity one, especially against Phi Kappa Psi at U-Va., which was viewed as a white Southern boys' club on a wealthy campus. The anti-frat bias was palpable in many articles that picked up the Jackie story like a football near the end zone; the touchdown many wanted was nothing less than eliminating the entire fraternity structure.

Colin Downes, a third-year law student at U-Va., wrote an article for *Slate,* "Greek Gangs. States should treat rogue fraternities as criminal organizations and seize their assets." [12] Downes commented, "Seizing a fraternity's house emphasizes the institutional character of the problem. Moreover, as a civil action, the commonwealth would only need to prove its case by preponderance of the evidence– a 'more likely than not' standard. By contrast, criminal prosecution is held to the higher 'beyond reasonable doubt' standard." Downes typified an approach favored by rape culture adherents. The high standards of proof required by criminal courts are side-stepped in approaching the crime of rape; instead, punishment is based on the extremely diluted criterion of civil courts. In short, rape culture adherents have repurposed the low standards employed by traffic courts in adjudicating parking offenses and are using them in campus hearings on rape.

The faculty and administration of U.Va. also expressed deep antipathy toward fraternities. U.Va. English Professor Allison Booth was widely quoted as declaring to an administrative meeting that "the whole [fraternity] culture is sick." [13]

Public opinion joined the general backlash. A *Bloomberg* article, "Dean Wormer's Favorite Editorial," [14] packed a great many anti-frat assumptions into very few words. It accused frats of abusing alcohol, and pointed to hazing deaths from pledge rituals. No one denies that the latter need to be prevented but the *excesses* of fraternities were not identified as such; they were portrayed as defining characteristics of the typical frat house. The article accused frats of anti-intellectualism and used "Animal House" as an example, as though an over-the-top comedy was a documentary that constituted real world evidence.

The article ended with a statement of purpose, "Too often, fraternities are at odds with the mission of a college or university. Focusing on that mission may be the best way for colleges and universities to see their way clear to the reform and, when necessary, abolition of campus fraternities." *At odds with the mission of a college or university.* That means the fraternities contradict what is now the "mission" of universities – to impose PC values and constraints.

Many people *wanted* to believe Phi Kappa Psi was guilty of gang rape because it fed into a bias and an agenda.

The myth allows for no contradiction

> Ultimately, the costs of wrongly disbelieving a survivor far outweigh the costs of calling someone a rapist. Even if Jackie fabricated her account, U-Va. should have taken her word for it during the period while they endeavored to prove or disprove the accusation....The accused would have a rough period....The cost of disbelieving women, on the other hand, is far steeper. –Zerlina Maxwell [15]

Rape culture zealots repeat the word "believe!" as a mantra. "Always *believe* the accuser, always *believe* the victim." They eschew such words as "alleged victim" or "accuser," and attack anyone who has the accuracy to prefer to use such words prior to an adjudication of guilt. Accuracy does not matter to those who *believe*. They do not need an investigation, evidence, testimony from the other side or a legal process. The woman is telling the truth...period. In a bizarre twist this means PC feminists would have sided with Mayella Ewell, the young white woman in the 1960 novel, *To Kill A Mockingbird,* who falsely accused a black man of rape. They would have supported the cry of rape from every prebellum white woman against every black man. They would have joined the lynch mobs that sought to exact justice without requiring the nicety of a trial before finding the man "guilty." Rape culture zealots would have done so in the name of gender justice, which requires them to accept the woman's word without question.

The demand runs counter to justice and to common sense, which require the recognition of two simple facts: people lie; and, people can be mistaken.

Lies. The average person lies occasionally, but some people do so pathologically. Generally speaking, people are more likely to lie when there is some advantage to doing so, such as making money, securing child custody, gaining attention, or exacting revenge. The list of possible advantages is long and varied. When someone makes an accusation, it is not possible to know whether she or he is an occasional liar or a pathological one. It is not clear if the accuser is pursuing a vested interest rather than justice. The fact that either circumstance is possible makes an unbiased investigation necessary.

Mistakes. Quite a few convicted rapists have been exonerated by DNA testing after spending years in prison. Good people can make bad mistakes without meaning harm. Misidentification of an accused becomes more likely if alcohol or drugs were involved. Unless an accusation is weighed objectively, a mistake can destroy the life of an innocent person. This becomes all the more important in cases, like sexual assault, that often devolve to "he said, she said" scenarios.

Due process rights are common sense protections for an accused against lies and mistakes. For example, a defendant has the right to confront an accuser and remove the anonymity or psychological distance that makes lying much easier. The accuser must look the accused in the eye and be willing to lie to his or her face. The right to cross-examine a witness allows inaccuracies to be spotlighted and rebutted by the defense. The right to an attorney means the defense will be conducted by someone who is skilled and sophisticated in the law. In criminal cases, the "beyond a reasonable doubt" standard applies so that other feasible explanations are not lightly dismissed. After all, being found "guilty" of a criminal offense can have life-shattering consequences.

The main due process protection, however, is the presumption of innocence. A person is presumed innocent until proven guilty, with the burden of proof resting on the accuser, not on the accused. The accuser assumes the burden for several reasons. One is the difficulty of proving a negative. For example, an accused rapist or murderer can rarely provide clear evidence of the lack of a crime. By its nature, the lack of a crime involves a lack of evidence. In logic and in law, therefore, the person stating that something happened assumes the task of proving evidence.

A long string of false accusations against male students highlights the extreme need for due process. The 2006 Duke Lacrosse case was one of the first media storms surrounding an alleged gang-rape on campus. The accusations were remarkably similar to those in the recent gang-rape lie at U-Va. I addressed the former In a *FOX News* editorial (Sept. 19, 2006) [16].

> The Duke Lacrosse case, in which three white male students are accused of raping a black woman last March...has become a litmus test for the American justice system. I believe the accused are blatantly innocent....In this case, I believe the legal system is the enemy of justice, and nakedly so. How naked? Consider one of the suspects, Reade Seligmann. He is scheduled to be tried on three felony charges despite overwhelming evidence of his innocence: exculpatory DNA tests, a corroborated alibi, a string of

contradictory statements by his accuser and an irredeemably tainted I.D.

The assumption of innocence has been reversed by the demand to always believe the accuser. This means the accused is presumed "guilty" and must prove his innocence. It actually means more than that. If the woman is always believed, then it is impossible for the man to ever prove his innocence. No matter how much evidence the accused produces, the demand to believe the accuser will prevail. That's what the *always* command devolves to. Despite factors such as exonerating evidence or contradicting witnesses, the woman's accusation must be *always* believed. It becomes a logical impossibility for an accused to prove his innocence before a rape culture court.

In fact, when taken to its logical conclusion, the demand to always believe an accusation removes any need for investigation or adjudication. Simply by being uttered, every accusation of rape is true and tantamount to proof that the accused is guilty. What purpose does an investigation serve if the accusation must be true?

Campus hearings have not progressed quite as far as obsoleting themselves. Nevertheless, they no longer afford the accused a reasonable or fair chance to establish his innocence. (See Chapter Six, Harms of the Rape Culture.) The situation is especially disturbing because universities throw enormous financial resources and personnel behind hearings. Moreover, they have the extreme advantage of discretionary power over the life of an accused.

The extreme pro-accuser bias was evident in U-Va.'s treatment of Phi Kappa Psi. The fraternity's innocence has been so thoroughly established at this point that the first accuser – *Rolling Stone* – publicly apologized. The university has not; indeed, the opposite of an apology occurred. The fraternity's suspension continued, and punitive measures were imposed through through a unilateral change to the Fraternal Organization Agreement, which fraternities are required to sign in order to be reinstated.

In the anti-PC ezine, *Spiked*, Sean Collins commented [17] on the political implications of U-Va.'s victimization of the innocent. "[T]oday's attack on fraternities should be seen as part of a wider cultural onslaught on private associations, especially male-only groups, which are viewed as inherently suspect. The ability to associate privately is a key freedom, one which sits alongside the freedom of speech and assembly. This includes the freedom to form associations limited to one sex. In their own defense, fraternities emphasize how they encourage leadership, community service and philanthropy. That's fine, but it is also okay if they, and other groups, simply get together to have fun. Outsiders have no right to demand that fraternities justify their existence."

Whether or not male students or male groups are vindicated, they lose. Whether or not they are proven innocent, they are guilty. Rape culture justice is a "heads I win, tails I win" proposition in which the outcome is predetermined. Justice, men, and freedom lose.

The myth allows for no negotiation

On January 12, U-Va. announced that Phi Kappa Psi had been reinstated on campus. The act of apparent largesse occurred only after the fraternity signed a new and unreasonable addendum to the University's former Fraternal Organization Agreement. [18] One aspect of the addendum's unreasonableness: it unilaterally violated a prior agreement on the process through which revisions were to occur.

Other provisions dictated the manner in which future frat parties were to be conducted, making demands that were both expensive and insulting. On January 8, a headline in *The Chronicle of Higher Education* asked, "Could You Plan a Fraternity Party Under U.Va.'s New Rules?" A check list allowed readers to assess how arduous compliance would be. Some of the rules – such as the provision of a guest list to approved security guards who were posted at the entry point – seemed designed to establish a prosecutable list of attendees. [19] No discussion, no negotiation was permitted. Despite being exonerated and having grounds for a lawsuit against the university, Phi Kappa Psi signed.

Other fraternities refused and released statements. Kappa Alpha's statement read [20],

> The University violated the previous FOA as well as student individual and organizational rights." It did so by initiating a system-wide suspension for reasons that were revealed to be untrue. Then U.Va. used the suspension as leverage to require compliance with a new contract which violated its own FOA policy, Virginia law and students' constitutional rights. Moreover, Kappa Alpha already maintains a high-level of risk management at all its events and expressed concern that "the university's revision to the [new] FOA may create new liability for individual members of our organizations that is more properly a duty to be borne by the university itself.

In a *National Review* article, "The Brute-Force Left. The Left lost the argument, but is determined to win the fight," Kevin D. Williamson wrote [21], "[T]he Left has become much more intensively coercive in recent years....The enthusiasm for coercion and the substitution of enemies for ideas – Christians, white men...take your pick – together form the basis for understanding the Left's current convulsions." The decades-long PC argument is entering its final phase: brute force that is justified by brute reason (law).

The myth is sensational

> [F]rom where I sit in Charlottesville [site of U.Va.], to let fact checking define the narrative would be a huge mistake. –Julia Horowitz, assistant managing editor at U.Va.'s school paper. [22]

Narrative first, facts second.

Nothing grabs attention and short circuits critical thought as surely as a lurid tale that slaps hard at the emotions. Typically, the most revolting aspects of a useful tale are presented upfront and then wrapped in social commentary that is followed by calls for action. The mixture of graphic sex, violence, innocence betrayed and righteousness is galvanizing. It attracts ratings to media, votes to politicians and funding to bureaucrats. If the word "culture" can be attached, then the call will be for systemic change rather than for the arrest of one individual responsible for an isolated act. The call will be for the reconstruction of institutions rather than for redress of a harm.

Sensationalism invites snap judgments before evidence or arguments can be heard. It also demonizes the accused(s) and maintains a fury toward them by rehashing graphic details in a near-pornographic manner. At its worst, the hyperbole creates an unthinking or epidemic mass hysteria that tolerates no skepticism.

The U-Va. story was released in this yellow-journalism style. Extensive, revolting and graphic detail was plentifully provided by *Rolling Stone*. The narrative began with Jackie as she naively followed her date into an upstairs bedroom at the frat house. Then, "Jackie began to scream." The salacious narrative continued in a fashion that people could consume without feeling guilt at their own fascination because the story was being related [23] in a good cause: sexual justice.

> "Shut *up*," she heard a man's voice say as a body barreled into her, tripping her backward and sending them both crashing through a

low glass table. There was a heavy person on top of her, spreading open her thighs, and another person kneeling on her hair, hands pinning down her arms, sharp shards digging into her back, and excited male voices rising all around her. When yet another hand clamped over her mouth, Jackie bit it, and the hand became a fist that punched her in the face. The men surrounding her began to laugh. For a hopeful moment Jackie wondered if this wasn't some collegiate prank. Perhaps at any second someone would flick on the lights and they'd return to the party.

"Grab its motherfucking leg," she heard a voice say. And that's when Jackie knew she was going to be raped.

She remembers every moment of the next three hours of agony, during which, she says, seven men took turns raping her, while two more – her date, Drew, and another man – gave instruction and encouragement. She remembers how the spectators swigged beers, and how they called each other nicknames like Armpit and Blanket. She remembers the men's heft and their sour reek of alcohol mixed with the pungency of marijuana. Most of all, Jackie remembers the pain and the pounding that went on and on.

Unfortunately for *Rolling Stone*, the details were either totally inaccurate or outright lies. Erdely may have believed them or she may have suspended her disbelief because Jackie's story fitted her needs so.well. In an interview presented by the *New Yorker* [24], Erdely was asked why she wrote about Jackie's campus rape as opposed to any other. She admitted to dismissing stories from a number of other universities because the rapes lacked desirable elements that were present in Jackie's. The article hinted that the other stories had *un*desirable elements, such as both parties drinking heavily or some confusion about what happened. In short, the other rapes were too easily interpreted – and, perhaps, correctly so – as acts of willing sex that were mitigated by circumstance. By contrast, Jackie barely touched alcohol before the incident, and the alleged sex was not vaguely consensual. Moreover, Jackie was reportedly rift with "self-blame," which Erdely found compelling. The *New Yorker* concluded, "the other women's stories (which could be found in great numbers) weren't what *Rolling Stone* was looking for."

Jackie's story was cherry-picked for its shock-value and, probably, for how damaging it was to the fraternity system. Its sensationalism was so perfect that fact-checking by Erdely and *Rolling Stone* editors fell by the wayside, as did the skepticism of a broader media.

The myth is backed by junk science

Junk science consists of research, data, or analysis that are spurious and it often attempts to promote a legal or political agenda by surrounding itself with what appears to be evidence. The term *"junk* science" indicates that the results may be deliberately sloppy or fraudulent, and should be discarded along with the agenda.

Today's laws and policies are driven as much by opinions as they are by legal principles; for example, policies on freedom of speech draw on surveys about whether a word is offensive rather than on the First Amendment. Those who want specific results in law and policy, therefore, use studies and surveys to create data that provide them with a desired and useful result whether or not the data are accurate. This is different in kind from a researcher who produces results in a scientifically-sound manner which happen to favor his or her own political viewpoint.

In the hard sciences, such as geology, the subject of study is usually an object or tangible thing that can be measured in precise units, such as weight or duration of time. Junk science is more common in the soft sciences, like psychology, where measurement and verification are problematic because the subjects of study are usually human beings and their reactions. The soft sciences deal with intangibles such as attitudes or social impacts, which are notoriously difficult to measure accurately. For one thing, a double-blind study is often impossible. In order to quantify intangibles, therefore, the soft-science researcher often creates a tailor-made index that relies upon techniques such as ranking answers to directed questions. Rather than introduce objectivity, however, the indexes and questions usually create greater subjectivity. Yet results from the soft sciences are presented in the same manner as those from the hard sciences. They use mathematical formulas, comparative charts, tables, academic jargon, data from other supporting soft studies, statistical analysis and comparison.

Junk science embodies certain characteristics that are distinct from real science. For example, junk scientists tend to be politically oriented and so, either purposefully or from inherent bias, they introduce skewed data that counter disproving evidence or confuses rather than enlightens. An article, "Researchers find researchers overestimate soft-science results– US the worst offender" in *Phys.org*, explained [25],

> In the science community, soft research has come to mean research that is done in areas that are difficult to measure– behavioral science being the most well known. Science conducted on the ways

people...respond in experiments is quite often difficult to reproduce or to describe in measurable terms. For this reason, the authors claim, research based on behavioral methodologies has been...at higher risk of bias, than with other sciences. Such biases, they suggest, tend to lead to inflated claims of success....[R]esearchers have more room to engineer experiments that will confirm what they already believe to be true. Thus, success in such sciences is defined as meeting expectations, rather than reaching a clearly defined goal or even discovering something new.

The battle between hard and junk science is as enduring as that between truth and lies. It is the background music to the lie of the rape culture. (Chapters Four and Five deal extensively with both hard and junk science.)

The myth is attached to a clear agenda

The article [on the U.Va. gang-rape in *Rolling Stone*] is a textbook case of putting the ideological cart before the factual horse. It is a mind-meltingly egregious example of journalistic malfeasance, of activists posing as reporters, facts be damned because by their own admission they didn't even bother to corroborate the facts because they didn't want to further traumatize the reputed victim. –Jim Goad [26]

"A Rape on Campus" was the perfect vehicle for Erdely's agenda to reform the manner in which administrations handled campus rape and to demonize fraternities. In November 2014, Erdely told *PBS Newshour [27]*, "I looked around at a lot of different campuses and I interviewed a lot of different students. I was looking to set this story at a university that had a good reputation, but also felt very representative of what was going on at American colleges across the country with regard to sexual assault....I was also hoping that it would be a college that was under Title IX investigation, and on top of that, a place where people were willing to talk to me about their sexual assault experiences. And I found all that at University of Virginia."

Erdely wanted the rape to have occurred on an elite but representative campus. U-Va. is not Ivy League but the university has a venerable history that dates back to its founding in 1819 by Thomas Jefferson. U-Va. is frequently cited as the highest ranked public university in America. *NBC29*, a news venue in U-Va.'s hometown of Charlottesville, interviewed Erdely [28] about the specific criteria she sought. *NBC29* reported, "She also wanted a school with an open Title IX sexual violence investigation. Title IX is the federal law that prohibits schools from discriminating on the basis of gender. UVA, along with 87 other schools, is under investigation for possible violations of federal law over the handling on sexual violence and harassment complaints." Added to the foregoing advantages was the unusual drama of Jackie's story. It was not merely a rape but a savage gang-rape. The victim was not a drunken party girl but a sober and representative student. The villain was not a single misogynist male student but an entire frat house, which enabled a hue and cry against the system of fraternities itself.

Journalistic advancement may have been part of Erdely's agenda as well; the possible self-interest of rape culture advocates should always be considered. After cherry-picking the U-Va. story, Erdely applied a formula to the story that had served her career well for over two decades. The formula: lurid accounts of abusive sex as told by an anonymous source with a plethora of details that are difficult to verify or disprove. In September 2011, for example, *Rolling Stone* ran another piece by Erdely, "The Catholic Church's Secret Sex-Crime Files," which alleged child abuse by two priests and a school teacher. The men reportedly had "passed" the child back and forth between them for years. As with "A Rape on Campus," Erdely referred to the now-adult accuser by a pseudonym – "Billy Doe."

The veracity of the 2011 article came under heavy and sustained attack. Ralph Cipriano, who writes for the *National Catholic Reporter*, literally campaigned for years to reveal the article as a lie. In a December 2014 article, "Before *Rolling Stone* Ran with Jackie's Story They Fell for Billy's", Cipriano commented [29], "if you think the factual discrepancies in Jackie's story are 'deeply unsettling', wait till you read all the factual discrepancies in Billy's story, documented for the past two years on this blog. Sadly, the stakes here are a lot higher than in Virginia, where none of the alleged attackers have even been outed. In Philly, three priests and a school teacher wound up going to jail over Billy's story, which has since unraveled. One of those priests died in prison last month after he spent his last hours handcuffed to a hospital bed while suffering from untreated coronary disease."

Erdely's extreme bias and sloppy journalism have been questioned repeatedly. At the time she wrote "The Catholic Church's Secret Sex-Crime Files," her husband worked as a criminal prosecutor at the District Attorney's Office in Philadelphia. This was the office prosecuting the Billy Doe case. According to *The Washington Post*, however, *Rolling Stone* did not see a problem with possible bias. The *Post* reported [30], "A *Rolling Stone* spokeswoman, Melissa Bruno, said Peter Erdely's work in the DA's office didn't pose a conflict of interest because he wasn't part of the unit trying the men. In hindsight, the Billy story might have been a warning of sorts." In short, *Rolling Stone* did not consider their contributor to be involved in the prosecution even though there was an intimate and obvious connection. It became more difficult to distance Erdely from the prosecution when the fact that the police had earlier discredited Billy Doe's story came to light. It is unlikely the court case would have occurred without the exposure of Erdely's article and her political crusading.

Erdely's past writings are now under a microscope. [31] A repeating pattern has been revealed. Again, victims are protected by false names while "victimizers" are either named or easily identifiable. A plethora of "facts" are presented but many, if not most, cannot be independently verified. Based upon emotional reactions, a cry for social justice erupts. The mainstream media picks up on the outrage and it is widely circulated. Erdely becomes a journalist-celebrity on talk shows. Legal and political agendas are attached and advanced.

The myth is presented by a credible source

The credible source promoting the rape culture myth can be anyone who speaks with authority. Often he or she also has a vested interest in the story.

The source can be a vote-seeking politician who grabs on to an issue around which the public will flock and applaud. It can be a religious figure who is dedicated to a moral principle that he is willing to impose by law. A trusted news source may want to break a hot story to keep watchers riveted and away from competitors. Government experts, university professors, bureaucrats, consultants, researchers, journalists...an army of professionals draw salaries and prestige from PC ideas, including the rape culture.

In the U-Va. case, the initial authority was a credible news source and a celebrated reporter. Readers found it difficult to believe a prominent magazine like *Rolling Stone*, published since 1967, would have released an in-your-face article without the due diligence of fact-checking. Moreover, Erdely was an award-winning journalist whose work appeared in prominent venues such as *GQ, the New Yorker, Mother Jones,* and, *Men's Health.* Both *Rolling Stone* and Erdely lent a credibility to Jackie's story that continued until the "facts" utterly collapsed. At that point, the more honest rape culture supporters had the same reaction as Anna Merlan, a contributor to the PC feminist site Jezebel. A staunch champion of Jackie, Merlan was forced to admit [32], "This is really, really bad. It means, of course, that when I dismissed Richard Bradley and Robby Soave's doubts about the story and called them 'idiots' for picking apart Jackie's account, I was dead fucking wrong, and for that I sincerely apologize. It means that my conviction that Sabrina Rubin Erdely had fact-checked her story in ways that were not visible to the public was also wrong."

U-Va. faculty added to the credibility of rape culture accusations when dozens of PC administrators and professors rushed to denounce Phi Kappa Psi. Not surprisingly, politicians also called for tougher campus policies and more punitive laws. The tone of discussion had been set months earlier by President Obama who spoke from the bully pulpit of the Oval Office. On January 22, 2014, the White House blog announced "A Renewed Call to Action to End Rape and Sexual Assault" in order to address "alarming rates of sexual assault on college campuses." Repeating the 1-in-5 figure for women who experienced "rape or attempted rape in their lifetime," Obama created a "White House Task Force to Protect Students from Sexual Assault." The Task Force is an extension of Obama's 2010 call to action, in which he urged the federal government to be more active in supporting survivors and discouraging assault. [33]

The U-Va. gang-rape fiction reinforced the scenario of a campus rape epidemic which had been officially validated by the White House. How much more credibility could a myth attain than being stamped with a Presidential seal?

Critics are rendered non-credible

Anyone who questions rape culture ideology is immediately labeled as part of the rape crisis itself. If the skeptic is a man, then he can be dismissed as a participant in and beneficiary of the rape culture. Women skeptics are problematic, but only slightly so. And, in the end, it is dissenting women who receive the most vicious attacks from rape culture warriors.

The conservative-libertarian commentator Cathy Young is a case in point. Known for her even-handed approach and extensive documentation, Young showed restraint in addressing Jackie's role in the U-Va. debacle. Her article, "The UVA Story Unravels: Feminist Agitprop and Rape-Hoax Denialism" in *Real Clear Politics* opened [34], "We will almost certainly never know for sure what actually happened to Jackie, the troubled young woman at the center of the now-discredited *Rolling Stone* tale of rape and impunity at the University of Virginia that riveted the nation for two weeks before it came apart."

Instead of focusing on the "troubled" Jackie, Young documented the shoddy journalism of the original article and the extraordinary backlash that PC feminists directed toward Jackie skeptics. Young noted that the *New York Times* was actually able to find "a couple of journalism professors who were willing to defending *Rolling Stone*'s methods" even after the story collapsed. Meanwhile, "the feminist media set about shooting the messenger." Skeptics became "rape apologists" who would have attacked Erdely's article "no matter how thorough a job she had done."

A prominent rape culture warrior "not-so-subtly insinuated that the 'rape denialist movement' [which includes many women, including Young] is driven by men who are themselves rapists." The preceding insinuation occurred prior to the thorough debunking of Jackie's story by the *Washington Post*. After the debunking? The same prominent advocate tweeted, "Interesting how rape apologists think that if they can 'discredit' one rape story, that means no other rape stories can be true, either." Young responded, "Needless to say, she does not give an example of a single person who believes that rape never happens." Young might have added, "Interesting how a series of rape accusations being revealed as false does not make 'rape culture' adherents question whether other rape stories can be *un*true."

What is a rape denialist? It is a person who denies that rape occurs. In PC usage, however, it becomes anyone who doubts the existence of a rape culture, minimizes its importance, or questions a victim's accusation no matter how improbable it may be. In other words, to question the details of a specific rape or the validity of a political construct is the equivalent of denying that the crime of rape occurs at all. The backlash of slander aimed at skeptics comes fast and furious. When blogger Bradley first expressed skepticism about Jackie's story, Marin Cogan of *New York Magazine* labeled him a "UVA truther." (She has since apologized.) Cogan's term hearkened back to the "truthers" who claim that 9-11 was a government conspiracy.

Young received a full blast of PC rage for coverage of another faux campus rape – her article in *The Daily Beast,* "Columbia Student: I Didn't Rape Her." [35] The "I" was Columbia student Paul Nungesser who was accused of raping fellow student Emma Sulkowicz in August 2012. After a campus investigation dismissed the case, Sulkowicz began to carry a mattress around campus with her, partly as a protest, partly as an art project for her senior thesis. The performance art was entitled "Carry That Weight."

Sulkowicz pursued a judgment against Nungesser in what she called "the court of public opinion." The public prosecution reached a peak when she prominently attended Obama's 2015 State of Union address as Senator

Kirsten Gillibrand's guest. Gillibrand is an outspoken advocate for legislation to combat the rape culture, especially on campus. *New York Magazine* ran an article [36] on Sulkowicz's attendance, which mentioned her disappointment at the President's lack of comment on sexual violence. Sulkowicz subsequently stated, "I can't say I was entirely surprised because since when has violence against women ever been a man's issue?" Sulkowicz was fast replacing Jackie as the official face of raped and abused women. Her poster-victim status may have been diminished, however, by a subsequent hardcore porn video in which she starred and released under the title, "This is not a rape." [37]

Young occasioned fury because she interviewed Nungesser about his alleged rape of Sulkowicz. She did what Erdely neglected to do. Young sought out evidence and verified it, which included exculpatory facts from the accused. Her article highlighted inconsistencies in Sulkowicz's account and raised serious doubts about its legitimacy, to say the least. Young noted, for example, "Sulkowicz has said in interviews that she was too embarrassed and ashamed to talk to anyone about the rape, let alone report....Yet Nungesser says that for weeks after that night, he and Sulkowicz maintained a cordial relationship, and says she seemingly never indicated that anything was amiss." Nungesser produced Facebook messages which were flirtatious rather than accusatory even though they were written immediately after the alleged attack. In one of them, Sulkowicz accepted Nungesser's invitation to a party with the words, "*lol yusss. lso I feel like we need to have some real time where we can talk about life and thing because we still haven't really had a paul-emma chill sesh since summmmmerrrr.*"

Young chronicled the rape accusation in meticulous detail before concluding that Nungesser's "case is far from as clear-cut as much of the media coverage has made it out to be. And if Nungesser is not a sexual predator, he could be seen as a true victim: a man who has been treated as guilty even after he has proved his innocence."

On the same day as Young's article appeared, Julie Zeilinger, founder of the feminist blog *The F Bomb*, published a rebuttal. In "The Treatment of Emma Sulkowicz Proves We Still Have No Idea How to Talk About Rape," [38] Zeilinger quoted Sulkowicz as calling Young "an anti-feminist" who wrote the article "to shame me." Zeilinger further accused Young of perpetuating "the perfect victim narrative through speculation" that worked "to shame and silence victims." Also on the same day, *Salon*'s politics writer Katie McDonough published [39], "The 'perfect victim' myth: How attempts to discredit rape survivors stand in the way of real change," in which she referred to Young's alleged "history of writing to discredit victims."

The "perfect rape victim" meme was off and running. It amounts to the allegation that critics like Young disparage victims like Sulkowicz because the latter does not live up to the ideal of victimhood. (In truth, Young doubted Sulkowicz because her story was implausible.) The meme's campaign was topped off by the Twitter hashtag, #TheresNoPerfectVictim. [40] The "perfect victim defense" seems to preclude the questioning or examination of *any* testimony given by *any* accuser; it is a reiteration of the demand to always believe the accuser. In the future, responsible journalists who examine all of the evidence will be vilified for requiring perfection from alleged victims. Thus, the focus is shifted from the facts to the character of an investigator.

Other responses make the "perfect victim" attack on Young look civil. On the *Feminist Current* site, for example, founder Meghan Murphy called Young a "virulent anti-feminist" who "continues to be published by otherwise seemingly legit publications." Accusing Young of being a "rep" for the men's rights movement, Murphy appealed several times for *The Daily Beast* to reconsider running Young's articles. For example, Murphy used a handful of words to mockingly paraphrase the article in question [41] and told the periodical to run her version instead of paying "someone whose sole purpose...is to discredit female victims and paint the feminist movement as a group intent on targeting males at any cost, carrying around mattresses on our backs and whatnot just for the hell of it."

Murphy's précis:

- *Head: But she was nice to him*
- *Subhead: Here are some private messages that show rape victim knew her rapist.*
- *Body: But she was nice to him.*
- *Also some other people think he is nice.*

The parody in no way reflects the content or attitudes in Young's article.

Urging a boycott of Young's work is a variation on the attacks that are launched against academicians who question the rape culture or any aspect of PC feminism. In academia, outraged rape culture ideologues typically demand that administrations fire, untenure, denounce, or disinvite anyone who asks questions. In many cases, their demands succeed.

> If science could cross breed a jellyfish with a parrot, it could create academic administrators.–Thomas Sowell [42]

In a *Boston Review* article [43], Judith Levine captured the backlash dynamic well. "[I]f men are slapped down when they question these orthodoxies, special punishment attends female critics. One alleged serial offender is *Slate's* Emily Yoffe...a consistently responsible, intelligent commentator on women's issues. Last year, Yoffe wrote a well researched and empathetic piece about the link between binge drinking and campus rape. In it, she gave some common-sense advice: rapists target drunk women. To reduce the risk of assault, don't get plastered to unconsciousness. The response was fierce. *Feministing* pronounced the column a 'rape denialist manifesto.' *Jezebel's* Erin Gloria Ryan accused Yoffe of 'admonishing women for not doing enough to stop their own rapes.'" Many other rape culture warriors piled on. [44]

Terms of denigration hurled at women dissenters include "rape denier," "Auntie Thomasina," "rape trivializer," "victim blamer," "woman hater," "gender traitor," "rape facilitator," "sister punisher," "MRA (men's rights activist) stooge," "self hater," "rape apologist," and "chill girl." (The latter term refers to females who would rather chill – that is, hang-out – with men.) These are some of the more polite terms.

Arguably, gender traitor is the most common accusation and the most interesting one. It reveals the PC belief that there can be no righteous disagreement between women on subjects of incredible complexity, such as rape. A single political or legal position, such as "always believe the woman," must be accepted without hesitation on the grounds of shared womanhood. Gender creates a duty of allegiance to share an ideology, approach and attitude.

Critics who retain any credibility are ignored

Voices that resist being discredited or silenced are ignored. Several common strategies are used, including charging the critic with being ignorant, corrupt or ungrateful. Any of the foregoing sins disqualifies the critic from having an opinion worth heeding. The charge of ingratitude springs from the following argument: "If the founding mothers of feminism had not gone to prison and marched in the streets, you wouldn't have an education or own property or...[fill in the blank.]" The argument is ridiculous because no one is casting doubt on issues such as the propriety of women attending university. Critics question the reality of one thing and one thing only – the rape culture or the validity of a specific account of rape. Asking such questions is not a rejection of feminist victories of the past. The accusation is absurd and, yet, it is commonplace.

The foregoing dynamics typify the manner in which the rape culture myth is maintained by those with a vested interest in its success.

Psychology of Rape Culture Warriors

A special psychology is required to victimize people while claiming *you* are the victim and they are the aggressors. An arrogant brutality is necessary to attack an innocent person simply because he or she does not conform down to the syllable with a PC agenda.

Many people hesitate in responding to attack-dog dynamics. They withdraw or apologize for innocuous or non-existent actions. The apology is understandable. It is confusing to be hit by a sudden barrage of accusations shouted in your face. And, so, the dissenter unwittingly vindicates the PC zealot by feeling or acting guilty even though she or he has done nothing wrong. The people at fault are those who wield so-called justice as an excuse for being vicious. They are the victimizers. It is important to recognize that fact, and to deal with such people as the vicious autocrats they are.

Kafkatrapping

Those who attempt to reason with SJWs will almost certainly encounter a tactic known as kafkatrapping. It occurs when a person is accused of a thought crime, such as racism or sexism, due to a disagreement on theory or fact. For example, a man may dispute the accuracy of the 1-in-5 rape statistic because he is familiar with studies that offer far lower estimates. Instead of addressing his argument, the SJW calls the man a "rape denier" who oppresses women by facilitating sexual violence against them.

The accused usually responds with a protestation of innocence, which is used as confirmation of guilt. The more the accused attempts to prove a negative for which no evidence has been provided, the more guilty he appears. Certainly, the more frustrated he becomes. The accused is now trapped in a circular and unfalsifiable argument because he has been kafkatrapped.

The term derives from Franz Kafka's novel *The Trial* in which a nondescript bank clerk named Josef K. is arrested; no charges are revealed to him or to the reader. Josef is prosecuted by a bizarre and tyrannical court of unknown authority, and he is doomed by impenetrable red tape. In the end, two strange men inexplicably abduct Josef and execute him. *The Trial* is Kafka's comment on totalitarian governments, like the Soviet Union, through which justice is twisted into a bitter, horrifying parody of itself that serves those in charge and never makes sense. Whoever is accused of a vague crime is automatically guilty with no prospect of an effective defense. Kafkatrapping turns reason and truth inside out to become self-mockeries. The process serves SJWs who wish to avoid evidence and reasoned arguments which are not friendly to their positions.

The term appears to have originated in a 2010 article by Eric S. Raymond. [45] Raymond's piece opened by acknowledging the worth of showing respect for those with whom you interact. But, he noted, "good causes [such as showing respect] sometimes have bad consequences," especially when dealing with a SJW. One consequence: the civil arguer is open to tactics that veer "into the creepy and pathological, borrowing the least sane features of religious evangelism." The civil person is vulnerable to kafkatrapping. His arguments are ignored in favor of an attack his character and motives.

Raymond's article offered models of how kafkatrapping operates, of which the most common ones are A and C.

Model A: The SJW states, "Your refusal to acknowledge that you are guilty of racism, sexism, homophobia, and the oppression of minorities confirms that you are guilty of racism, sexism, homophobia and the oppression of minorities." Harking back to *The Trial*, Raymond explained how its plot parallels the structure and purpose of the SJW's nonargument. Josef was never accused of a specific act, which made the indictment unfalsifiable because there was nothing specific to refute. The vague charge centered on a thought crime, which also made it unfalsifiable. Why? Because, ultimately, a person cannot prove that what he says is what he actually thinks. He could be lying. How can a man prove that he is not secretly a woman-hater? All he can say is that there is absolutely no evidence to support that accusation.

At this point, the SJW pipes up, "Ah, but there *is* evidence. You question the latest data on the prevalence of campus rape, which is a blatant display of hatred for women and contempt for their safety. And, then, you respond to the charge with a vehemence that shows I've hit a nerve." Some SJWs will offer the man a way out. Namely, he may be unaware of how sexist and hate-filled his comments are because they so often pass for normal in a rape culture.

As in *The Trial*, the process is designed to throw an accused off-balance, to create guilt and to destroy resistance so that he becomes malleable. Indeed, Raymond concluded, "the only way out...is...to acquiesce in his own destruction." Even if the person is innocent, the only path to redemption is to plead guilty and embrace the self-blame that leads to exoneration. Of course, this includes accepting the rape culture against which he had been arguing. Ideally, for the accuser, the person may even come to believe in his own guilt.

Model C is a common variant on the same theme. The SJW does not directly accuse the rape culture skeptic of doing, feeling or thinking anything hateful. Nevertheless, the person is guilty of oppressing women because, as a male, he benefits from a position of privilege that was created by others who act, feel or think in a hateful manner. In other words, being white, male and heterosexual makes him part of the patriarchy.

The accusation makes the skeptic responsible for the actions of strangers whose behavior he cannot control and of which he may not approve. Indeed, the person is held responsible for actions of white males who lived centuries before his birth. Raymond wrote, "The aim ... is to produce a kind of free-floating guilt ... a conviction of sinfulness that can be manipulated by the operator [the accuser] to make the subject say and do things that are convenient to the operator's personal, political, or religious goals." To be reborn, the skeptic must cease to disagree with the rape culture and condemn his entire identity group. The process becomes an effective but perverse type of white-, male-, and het-shaming because it is done by a white, male heterosexual.

What happens when an accuser confronts someone in the same identity group to which she belongs? What happens when a PC feminist interacts with a skeptic who is also female? A different dynamic emerges. Obviously, the dissenter will not be encouraged to condemn herself for being a woman. A common reaction is to define her out of the group.

In logic classes, the redefinition process has been called the "No True Scotsman" fallacy. The British philosopher Antony Flew described the error, which he also named. It occurs when someone confronts an example that disproves a universal claim of which he is fond. The fallacy goes like this: One day Hamish McDonald reads an article in the *Glasgow Morning Herald* which reports on an attack by a sex maniac in England. Hamish declares aloud, "No Scotsman would do such a thing!" The next day, the *Glasgow Morning Herald* reports on an even worse attack in Scotland. Rather than reject his original statement, Hamish exclaims, "No *true* Scotsman would do such a thing."

Thus, conservative women like Sarah Palin and aberrant feminists like Christina Hoff Sommers are not *true* women because they do not accept the rape culture ideology. Sommers is a self-described equity feminist, for example, who rejects entitlements for women and promotes real equality under the law for both sexes. For this sin, she is defined out of the identity group of "woman." A similar tactic is used against blacks who question the validity of white privilege; they cease to be *truly* black and can be dismissed as dupes of white power. Jewish people who reject Israeli policy are sometimes called "self-hating Jews," and so on and so on.

The sort of act, feeling or thought that can result in being booted out of an identity group includes:

- Requesting a statement of exactly what an accusation is based upon. For example, if the accusation is homophobia, then the accused asks for the precise behavior of his that prompted it.

- Pointing to an injustice committed by the SJW's identity group. Perhaps he raises a case in which there was a false rape report.

- Applying a single standard to all individuals. For example, he refuses to accept that blacks cannot be racist and, instead, considers racism to be a behavior or attitude that any group or individual can manifest.

- Expressing skepticism about any aspect of victimhood ideology, including the plausibility of anecdotal evidence or the methodology of a study.

- Being uninterested in the PC topic under discussion. If transgender politics bores him to the point of yawning, then he hates the transgendered.

- Stating the wrong sort of approval. For example, saying "some of my best friends are X" will be seen as patronizing.

Cost to social justice warriors

Kafkatrapping would seem to be a win-win situation for an accuser. In the short term, this may be true but the long-term impact can be devastating.

A movement becomes popular because its message contains basic truth and its demand for justice has validity. For example, homosexuals were hideously abused through much of history. In the '60s and '70s, when they demanded the right to live openly and in peace, the movement blossomed. It could not have done so without broad support outside the gay and lesbian community, however. The average person will not tolerate a massive injustice that is occurring in his or her own backyard – that is, once it becomes apparent to them.

But a movement dies when it discards the truth and the demand for justice that made it flourish. When a cause favors ideology and insults over facts and reason, it is on the decline. Raymond observed, "[m]anipulative ways of controlling people tend to hollow out the causes for which they are employed, smothering whatever worthy goals they may have begun with and reducing them to vehicles for the attainment of power and privilege over others." This is what is currently happening to PC feminism and rape culture ideology.

The SJW is more likely to seek power for women and to impose social control over everyone else. "Everyone else" will resent the imposition of double-standards. They will resist regulation by an elite class who wants to dictate what they allowed to say and think. SJWs are creating a society in which there can be no compromise, no meeting of minds...only conflict and "winner take all." The system of privilege and dominance envisioned by SJWs can only deepen gender conflict and obstruct good will efforts to resolve social problems.

The true believer does great damage to herself as well, especially if she believes her own kafkatrapping. A PC feminist may honestly view all white men as oppressors and all objections to data as expressions of hatred. If so, she is unlikely to cooperate with white males or female skeptics, who are class enemies, in order to solve social problems. By politically shunning half of society, she greatly reduces the chance of effectively addressing issues like sexual violence.

She also becomes increasingly isolated from the majority of people who are viewed as opponents or as unenlightened because they have little interest in the rape culture world view. She becomes increasingly unable to communicate with or have empathy for a broad spectrum of people. Thus, the kafkatrapper may win a particular argument but such victories come at the cost of abandoning a shared humanity. (Chapter Six, Harms of the Rape Culture explores in detail the damage inflicted on SJWs by their own beliefs.)

Cost to recipients of Kafkatrapping

Anyone conversing with a kafkatrapper can expect to encounter several of the following tactics. They are unpleasant and often offensive.

Devaluing Individuals. Individuals are not judged on their merit, character or on the content of their actions. They are judged as members of a category who are held responsible for the presumed agenda and actions of that group.

Declaring War Between Categories of People. Men versus women, whites versus blacks, heterosexuals versus homosexuals, dissenting women versus enlightened ones. There is no sense of shared humanity which is essential to the natural compassion people feel toward each other. Instead, there is class warfare, and no act of integrity or expression of benevolence can exonerate an individual who belongs to the wrong class.

Refusing to acknowledge counter-evidence. The SJW will sometimes ignore contradicting data or arguments as though the words had not been spoken. The unacknowledged does not exist because reality is subjective and constructed. At other times, the words will used against the speaker in order to springboard into a personal attack. In either case, facts have no place in the exchange.

Constructing straw men. A straw man is an informal fallacy by which the SJW misrepresents an argument and proceeds to refute the misrepresentation. An example is the claim that a skeptic denies the existence of rape because she questions a specific report. If deftly done, the debunking of a misrepresentation gives the appearance of an effective counter-argument; in reality, it shifts the ground of discussion away from addressing the issue.

Evincing indignation. This is the "how dare you!" tactic. In a flash, the focus moves to a full-bore attack on the skeptic's character. The rage with which the assault is launched can pass as a sort of persuasion because bystanders assume the recipient must have done something wrong to deserve it. The tactic frequently involves accusing the critic of hidden motives or an unholy agenda.

Attacking an opponent to make him lose composure. Jeering and humiliation are common SJW tactics. I attended a sex workers' rights conference at which I critiqued the methodology of key studies of PC researchers; I argued that sex workers' safety requires a accurate view of their reality, not a political one. Another panelist disdainfully accused me of killing women on the streets because the studies in question were keeping them alive. She achieved her goal: I lost my composure, and I did not respond well.

Refusing to acknowledge unfair treatment of white men or dissenting women. By definition, white males are privileged and cannot be oppressed; the possible exception is white males who are not heterosexual. Dissenting women are gender heretics, and heretics are always hated more than infidels; they cannot be oppressed because they are part of the patriarchy despite their genitalia.

Pathologizing disagreements. Content is ignored in order to dissect the alleged pathology underlying a position. For example, a man argues against affirmative action and for a meritocracy because the latter is more conducive to civil society. Instantly, he is called a "racist" whose white elitism once created slavery. In short, the kafkatrapper rephrases an opponent's argument in a manner that pathologizes it and eliminates the need to deal with any evidence presented.

Playing the Victimhood Card. This nuclear option is played not merely to silence but to devastate. Someone who persists in questioning an account of assault is accused of *making* the victim relive her rape, of raping her all over again. Even silence can be interpreted as a "re-rape" because it is a refusal to acknowledge the pain of an attacked woman, which also makes her relive the assault.

Demanding Infinite Respect While Giving None. PC feminists make amazingly cruel, vicious comments about men under the guise of humor. These are comments they would not tolerate about women, blacks or other marginalized group. Sometimes it is not clear if they actually view white males as real human beings. In *The Merchant of Venice,* Shylock cried out against those who hated him for being a Jew, "If you cut me, do I not bleed?" Apparently, white males cannot bleed.

Zero Tolerance. Total war has been declared on "incorrect" thoughts and words with every PC advocate acting as a holy crusader who takes no prisoners and brooks not a syllable of disagreement. Civilized concepts like negotiation, polite discussion, forgiveness, compassion and empathy are discarded. Just as using force (law) has become the first option rather than a last resort so, too, has viciousness become the default.

Using Anecdotes as Data. PC activists tell graphic stories of rape, beatings and humiliation in order to stir a useful fury in listeners – useful to the activists, that is. The stories are terrible to hear. But they do not indicate how pervasive a problem is and they cannot substitute for solid data. Yet the anecdotes are presented as evidence of a systemic problem. The emotions stirred are used to eliminate the need for real proof. Indeed, people who ask for facts in the wake of a horror story are likely to be shouted down.

A question remains. How should people react when such tactics arise in conversation? My advice: Make a statement that's been planned in advance and calmly walk away. In my experience, nothing productive will come from playing a rigged game with someone who cares nothing for fairness. If there are third parties who are listening and with whom you wish to continue, then do it later and as a separate conversation.

Conclusion

Political correctness demands respect for historically oppressed categories of people. This is laudable. But respect flows both ways. I will not offer appreciation to any individual who responds to me with abuse, especially when the abuse does not come from my actions or character but is based upon class hatred. Extending a hand of friendship should not occasion a slap in the face. When it does, the gesture and feeling of good will should be withdrawn.

If SJWs wish to create a society of respect, then they are going about it in a manner that will establish the opposite. If their goal is social control in order to impose a specific vision, then they are proceeding in a straight line toward that clear objective.

For the sake of argument, let me accept at face value the demand to respect the disadvantaged. The approach has a deep and resonating appeal but I would use words such as "empathy" or "decency" instead of respect. The reason: I believe respect needs to be earned but common decency is a moral debt that each human being owes to every other person.

In reality, what is demanded is a faux respect. That is, law and policy force individuals to treat specific people with *deference*, not *respect*. One difference between the two attitudes is that deference frequently demeans the person extending it, especially when the response is coerced. SJWs seem to seek the debasement of so-called privileged classes as much or more than the elevation of disadvantaged ones.

The air of crusading righteousness is maintained by claiming respect is a civil right. It is not. Respect is an attitude of approval and appreciation which one person feels toward another. No one can properly assert a right to the emotional reactions or intellectual judgment of another. To do so is slavery of the most intimate sort – enslavement of another's soul. The most a person can properly claim is respect of his or her body and property in the legal sense; this claim is commonly known as individual rights.

Notes

[1] Sabrina Rubin Erdely, "A Rape on Campus: A Brutal Assault and Struggle for Justice at U.Va.," *Rolling Stone*, Nov. 19, 2014. http://www.rollingstone.com/culture/features/a-rape-on-campus-20141119 *Rolling Stone* has retracted the story and the preceding URL now leads to "Rolling Stone and UVA: The Columbia University Graduate School of Journalism Report" on what went wrong. Retrieved Sept. 23, 2015.

[2] "Important Message from President Sullivan Addressing Sexual Misconduct," *UVA Today*, Nov. 19, 2014. http://news.virginia.edu/content/important-message-president-sullivan-addressing-sexual-misconduct Retrieved Sept. 23, 2015.

[3] Sara Rourke and Victoria Moran, "Community confronts sexual assault on Grounds," *The Cavalier Daily*, Nov. 21, 2014. http://www.cavalierdaily.com/article/2014/11/community-confronts-sexual-assault Retrieved Sept. 23, 2015.

[4] Petition, "End the Culture of Rape at U.Va.," Nov. 21, 2014. https://www.change.org/p/the-president-and-board-of-visitors-of-the-university-of-virginia-end-the-culture-of-rape-at-U.Va. Petition no longer active at this site. Text of the petition: https://www.change.org/p/the-president-and-board-of-visitors-of-the-university-of-virginia-end-the-culture-of-rape-at-uva Retrieved Sept. 23, 2015.

[5] "Rape at U.Va.: Readers Say Jackie Wasn't Alone," *Rolling Stone*, Nov. 21, 2014. http://www.rollingstone.com/culture/news/rape-at-uva-readers-say-jackie-wasnt-alone-20141121 Retrieved Sept. 23, 2015.

[6] "A Message from President Sullivan Regarding Sexual Violence," *UVA Today*, Nov. 22, 2014. https://news.virginia.edu/content/message-president-sullivan-regarding-sexual-violence Retrieved Sept.23, 2015.

[7] As quoted by Jennifer Steinhauer and Richard Perez-Pena, "University of Virginia Officials Vow to Combat Campus Rape Problem," *New York Times*, Nov. 25, 2014. http://www.nytimes.com/2014/11/26/us/university-of-virginia-officials-vow-to-combat-campus-rape-problem.html Retrieved Sept. 23, 2015.

[8] T. Rees Shapiro, "McAuliffe urges investigation at U-Va. after Rolling Stone depiction of sexual assault," *The Washington Post*, Nov. 20, 2014. http://www.washingtonpost.com/local/education/mcauliffe-urges-investigation-at-u-va-after-rolling-stone-depiction-of-sexual-

assault/2014/11/20/21f45eac-70ec-11e4-8808-afaa1e3a33ef_story.html Retrieved Sept. 23, 2015.

[9] Richard Bradley, "Is the Rolling Stone Story True?" *Shots in the Dark*, Nov. 24, 2014. http://www.richardbradley.net/shotsinthedark/2014/11/24/is-the-rolling-stone-story-true/ URL returns an error message. Much of the article reprinted here: http://www.unz.com/isteve/richard-bradley-is-the-rolling-stone-story-true/ Retrieved Sept. 23, 2015.

[10] Cathy Young, "Columbia Student: I Didn't Rape Her," *The Daily Beast*, Feb. 3, 2015. http://www.thedailybeast.com/articles/2015/02/03/columbia-student-i-didn-t-rape-her.html Retrieved Sept. 23, 2015.

[11] "A Rape on Campus," op. cit.

[12] Colin Downes, "Greek Gangs. States should treat rogue fraternities as criminal organizations and seize their assets," *Slate*, Dec. 5, 2014. http://www.slate.com/articles/news_and_politics/jurisprudence/2014/12/fraternity_sexual_assault_and_criminal_activities_states_should_use_gang.html Retrieved Sept. 23, 2015.

[13] As quoted by Michael McDonald and Allyson Versprille, "UVA Faculty Propose Extending Frat Ban Through School Year," *Bloomberg*, Dec. 3, 2014. http://www.bloomberg.com/news/2014-12-03/uva-faculty-propose-longer-frat-ban-as-alleged-rape-investigated.html Retrieved Sept. 23, 2015.

[14] "Dean Wormer's Favorite Editorial," *Bloomberg*, Jan. 7, 2014. http://www.bloombergview.com/articles/2014-01-07/dean-wormer-s-favorite-editorial Retrieved Sept. 23, 2015.

[15] Zerlina Maxwell, "No matter what Jackie said, we should generally believe rape claims," *The Washington Post*, Dec. 6, 2014. http://www.washingtonpost.com/posteverything/wp/2014/12/06/no-matter-what-jackie-said-we-should-automatically-believe-rape-claims/ Retrieved Sept. 23, 2015.

[16] Wendy McElroy, "Accused Denied Due Process in Duke Lacrosse Case?" *FOX News*, Sept. 19, 2006. http://www.foxnews.com/story/2006/09/19/accused-denied-due-process-in-duke-lacrosse-case/ Retrieved Sept. 23, 2015.

[17] Sean Collins, "UVA scandal: fight for the right to fraternise," *Spiked*, Dec. 15, 2014. http://www.spiked-online.com/newsite/article/uva-scandal-

fight-for-the-right-to-fraternise/16350#.VPN7bYam1Ss Retrieved Sept. 23, 2015.

[18] "U.Va. Adopts New Fraternal Organization Agreement Aimed to Enhance Safety," *UVA Today*, Jan. 6, 2015. http://vpsa.virginia.edu/fraternal-organization-agreement URL changed from original. Retrieved Sept. 23, 2015.

[19] "Could You Plan a Fraternity Party Under U.Va.'s New Rules?" *The Chronicle of Higher Education,* Jan. 8, 2015. http://chronicle.com/article/Could-You-Plan-a-Fraternity/151073/ Retrieved Sept. 23, 2015.

[20] Kappa Alpha Order's Statement Regarding Revised Fraternity Operating Agreement, ND. http://s3.amazonaws.com/content.washingtonexaminer.biz/web-producers/011315-fraternity-statement-2.pdf Retrieved Sept. 23, 2015.

[21] Kevin D. Williamson, "The Brute-Force Left. The Left lost the argument, but is determined to win the fight," *National Review,* Feb. 8, 2015. http://www.nationalreview.com/article/398133/brute-force-left-kevin-d-williamson Retrieved Sept. 23, 2015.

[22] Julia Horowitz, "Why We Believed Jackie's Story," *Politico*, Dec. 6, 2014. http://www.politico.com/magazine/story/2014/12/why-we-believed-jackies-story-113365.html#.VJB86dLF864 Retrieved Sept. 23, 2015.

[23] "A Rape on Campus," op. cit.

[24] Amy Davidson, "What Rolling Stone Did to 'Cindy'," *The New Yorker*, Dec. 11, 2014. http://www.newyorker.com/news/amy-davidson/rolling-stone-cindy-uva-rape-story Retrieved Sept. 23, 2015.

[25] Bob Yirka, "Researchers find researchers overestimate soft-science results– US the worst offender," *Phys.org*, Aug. 27, 2013. http://phys.org/news/2013-08-overestimate-soft-science-resultsus-worst.html Retrieved Sept. 23, 2015.

[26] Jim Goad, "A Rolling Stone Gathers No Rape," *Taki Magazine*, Dec. 8, 2014. http://takimag.com/article/a_rolling_stone_gathers_no_rape_jim_goad/print Retrieved Sept. 23, 2015.

[27] As quoted in "Article on brutal sexual assault provokes investigation at the University of Virginia," *PBS Newshour,* Nov. 21, 2014.

http://www.pbs.org/newshour/bb/article-brutal-sexual-assault-provokes-investigation-university-virginia/ Retrieved Sept. 23, 2015.

[28] "NBC29 Speaks with Rolling Stone Article Author," *NBC29,* Nov. 20, 2014. http://www.nbc29.com/story/27442741/nbc29-speaks-with-rolling-stone-article-author Retrieved Sept. 23, 2015.

[29] Ralph Cipriano, "Before Rolling Stone Ran with Jackie's Story They Fell for Billy's," *Big Trial,* Dec. 6, 2014. http://www.bigtrial.net/2014/12/before-rolling-stone-was-conned-by.html Retrieved Sept. 23, 2015.

[30] Paul Farhi, "Rolling Stone magazine has often thrived on controversy. Is this time different?" *The Washington Post*, Dec. 12, 2014. http://www.washingtonpost.com/lifestyle/style/rolling-stone-magazine-has-often-thrived-on-controversy-is-this-time-different/2014/12/12/b92c5974-8171-11e4-8882-03cf08410beb_story.html Retrieved Sept. 23, 2015.

[31] Mollie Hemingway, "Sabrina Rubin Erdely's Old Stories Read Like Bad Lifetime Movies," *The Federalist*, Dec. 8, 2014. http://thefederalist.com/2014/12/08/sabrina-rubin-erdelys-old-stories-sure-read-like-bad-lifetime-movies/ Retrieved Sept. 23, 2015.

[32] Anna Merlan, "Rolling Stone Partially Retracts UVA Story over 'Discrepancies'," *Jezebel,* Dec. 5, 2014. http://jezebel.com/rolling-stone-partially-retracts-uva-story-over-discrep-1667329573 Retrieved Sept. 23, 2015.

[33] "A Renewed Call to Action to End Rape and Sexual Assault," The White House Blog, Jan. 22, 2014. http://www.whitehouse.gov/blog/2014/01/22/renewed-call-action-end-rape-and-sexual-assault Retrieved Sept. 23, 2015.

[34] Cathy Young, "The UVA Story Unravels: Feminist Agitprop and Rape-Hoax Denialism," *Real Clear Politics*, Dec. 8, 2014. http://www.realclearpolitics.com/articles/2014/12/08/the_uva_story_unravels_feminist_agitprop_and_rape-hoax_denialism_124891.html Retrieved Sept. 23, 2015.

[35] "Columbia Student: I Didn't Rape Her," op. cit.

[36] As quoted by Katie Van Syckle, "Emma Sulkowicz Was 'Let Down' by Obama SOTU Speech," *New York Magazine,* Jan. 21, 2015. http://nymag.com/daily/intelligencer/2015/01/sulkowicz-was-let-down-by-state-of-the-union.html Retrieved Sept. 23, 2015.

[37] Milo Yiannopoulos, "This is not a rape," *Breitbart*, June 5, 2015. http://www.breitbart.com/big-hollywood/2015/06/05/mattress-girl-emma-sulkowicz-just-released-a-sex-tape-heres-my-review/ Retrieved Sept. 23, 2015.

[38] Julie Zeilinger, "The Treatment of Emma Sulkowicz Proves We Still Have No Idea How to Talk About Rape," *Mic*, Feb. 3, 2015. http://mic.com/articles/109446/the-treatment-of-emma-sulkowicz-proves-we-still-have-no-idea-how-to-talk-about-rape Retrieved Sept. 23, 2015.

[39] Katie McDonough, "The 'perfect victim' myth: How attempts to discredit rape survivors stand in the way of real change," *Salon*, Feb. 3, 2015. http://www.salon.com/2015/02/03/the_perfect_victim_myth_how_attempts_to_discredit_individual_survivors_stand_in_the_way_of_real_change/ Retrieved Sept. 23, 2015.

[40] https://twitter.com/hashtag/theresnoperfectvictim Retrieved Sept. 23, 2015.

[41] Meghan Murphy, "Cathy Young doesn't understand even the most basic truths about rape," *Feminist Current*, Feb. 3, 2015. http://feministcurrent.com/10583/cathy-young-doesnt-understand-even-the-most-basic-truths-about-rape/ Retrieved Sept. 23, 2015.

[42] Thomas Sowell, "Random Thoughts," *Townhall,* Dec. 30, 2014. http://townhall.com/columnists/thomassowell/2014/12/30/random-thoughts-n1936707/page/full Retrieved Sept. 23, 2015.

[43] Judith Levine, "Feminism Can Handle the Truth," *Boston Review*, Dec. 6, 2014. http://bostonreview.net/blog/judith-levine-uva-rape-denialism-rolling-stone-hoax-feminism Retrieved Sept. 23, 2015.

[44] Erin Gloria Ryan, "How To Write About Rape Prevention Without Sounding Like An Asshole," Jezebel, Oct. 16, 2013. http://jezebel.com/how-to-write-about-rape-prevention-without-sounding-lik-1446529386 Retrieved Sept. 23, 2015. Readers should judge Yoffe's writing for themselves. See Emily Yoffe, "The College Rape Overcorrection," *Slate*, Dec. 7, 2014. http://www.slate.com/articles/double_x/doublex/2014/12/college_rape_campus_sexual_assault_is_a_serious_problem_but_the_efforts.html?wpsrc=sh_all_dt_tw_bot Retrieved Sept. 23, 2015.

[45] Eric Raymond, "Kafkatrapping," *Armed and Dangerous*, July 18, 2010. *http://esr.ibiblio.org/?p=2122* Retrieved Sept. 23, 2015.

Chapter Four: Data, Valid and False

Zombie statistics
PC Feminist research
- Feminism is a perspective
- Feminists use many research methods
- Feminist research involves ongoing criticism of nonfeminist scholarship
- Feminist research is guided by feminist theory
- Feminist research may be trans-disciplinary
- Feminist research aims to create social change
- Feminist research strives to represent human diversity
- Feminist research frequently involves the researcher as a person
- Feminist research frequently attempts to develop special relations with the people studied (in interactive research)
- Feminist research frequently defines a special relationship with the reader

How to Interrogate Rape Culture Studies and Statistics
- Does the researcher have a clear bias?
- What is the source of the findings I'm hearing?
- Does the research include an explicit public policy recommendation?
- Is the sample biased – that is selective – or too small?
- Does the research proceed from a false assumption that is stated as established fact?
- Is a margin of error not present or misreported?
- Does the researcher assume a correlation means causation?
- Is the sample further biased by adding incentives?
- Do the questions skew participants toward the desired answer?
- Does it draw upon prestigious but dubious authority?
- Does the study ignore contradicting evidence?
- Do the results make sense or do they contradict your own experience?

Applying the Preceding Questions to Specific Research
The Saga of Missing Data
Stats That Are Impossible to Accurately Calculate
- The sticky question of false accusations

The Touchstone Moment of Feminist Research on Rape

Conclusion
Notes

Zombie Statistics

> Zombie stats are numerical factoids that just won't quit, however dead they get. They lurch up from their graves in every subject, drawn to the juicy warm flesh of public consciousness by some unkillable primal instinct, spreading their intelligence-murdering contagion wherever they shamble. –Sarah Ditum [1]

Zombie statistics are spurious "facts" that assume a life of their own. The faux facts circulate because they are sensational and useful to those with political agendas who wish to establish a specific narrative. Sometimes, the statistic is framed by meaningless but emotional rhetoric, such as "record numbers of women could be in danger of being raped this year," or "abortion rights have never been so besieged." Sometimes they are specific, such as "1-in-5 women will be raped." Zombie stats permeate discussions of the rape culture and are instrumental in creating the hysteria surrounding it.

There are several reasons for the hysteria. One of them: Discussion of the rape culture is drenched in ideology by adherents who seem more interested in imposing a PC agenda than in open debate or hard evidence. The only statistics they embrace are sensational ones that support their positions and create a sense of crisis in listeners.

Rape culture discussions also brim over with gut-wrenching accounts of victimization. Anyone who brings sexual violence out of the shadows should be roundly applauded. But that humanitarian act is damaged when it is politicized. The emotionally-charged atmosphere produced by graphic accounts of attack causes an automatic acceptance of rape culture claims and makes listeners less willing to entertain contradicting stories or data. Those who continue to question receive a backlash of anger because they are seen as denying the importance of rape or its existence. And, so, emotionalism drives out reasoned argument and leaves a void into which zombie stats shamble.

Other aspects of rape data also produce a confusion that favors zombie statistics even when they are not creations of rape culture ideology.

"Rape" is an elastic term, and it is not always clear which behavior it describes. (See Chapter Five for specifics on how varying definitions are commonly used.) Legally speaking, the definition varies from state to state and even from one police department to another. Many academics and researchers seem to define the term in whatever manner facilitates the results they wish to reach. In a single discussion, the definition can shift ground repeatedly, which prevents productive dialogue. Sometimes, rape refers only to forced intercourse or penetration. At other times, it incorporates attempted rape or unwanted sexual touching. Increasingly, rape has come to include sex in the presence of alcohol or other impairments by which the woman is deemed to be unable to consent. With odd logic, an equally impaired male partner is almost never viewed as a co-victim but almost always as a perpetrator who is fully responsible for his actions. The word "rape" has even been stretched to include verbal harassment in situations where no physical contact has occurred.

Yet the public has a sense that the word "rape" means a violent sexual assault and so reacts with healthy outrage. Researchers who misuse the anger-evoking word can draw upon the natural response of horror to advance acceptance of the agendas attached to their findings.

The methods by which data are collected and processed also deviate, which can produce dramatically different results. The National Research Council (NRC) pointed to huge discrepancies in the number of sexual assaults reported for 2010 by the Federal Bureau of Investigation (85,593), the National Crime Victimization Survey (188,380), and the Centers for Disease Control (1.3 million). The *Huffington Post* news editor Emily Thomas commented [2], "Either someone's not counting properly, or there's a problem with the methods of collecting and analyzing data about rapes." Her article was prompted by the release of a study by the NRC, "Panel on Measuring Rape and Sexual Assault in Bureau of Justice Statistics Household Surveys." [3] The panel had been requested by the Bureau of Justice Statistics (BJS) in order to evaluate whether the rate of sexual assault was being miscalculated by some agencies. If so, then the BJS wanted to know *why*.

Another obstacle to clarity: Many rape statistics are "dark numbers," which means they either are not or cannot be identified with confidence. The darkness of the data makes it difficult or impossible to assess its accuracy.

Rape stats are dark for several reasons. A large number of alleged sexual assaults suffer from the "he said/she said" problem. Even in the absence of dishonesty, disparate accounts often surround reported rapes, especially ones that involve alcohol or drugs. Assessing the reality of what happened may come down to nothing more than a judgment call not only on the part of third parties but also for the people who engaged in sex. Even if circumstantial evidence is present, it may say little about whether the act was consensual. Other crimes, like murder, do not suffer from similar confusion. The dead body with a protruding knife is a clear indication that a crime of a specific nature *has* occurred. There is an indisputable victim and a perpetrator, known or not.

Another darkness problem is exemplified by the question, "how many rapes go unreported every year?" Criminologists use the phrase "the dark figure of crime" to indicate the amount or rate of a crime that is unreported or undiscovered. Rape may be one of the most unreported crimes in society because many victims feel deeply shamed and are understandably reluctant to relive the experience at a police station or in a court docket. Statistical estimates of how many dark rapes occur are all over the map. The resource website, Sexual Assault in Canada, claims [4], "Of every 100 incidents of sexual assault, only 6 are reported to the police." That's an amazing 94 percent rate of non-reporting. By contrast, the American Rape, Abuse & Incest National Network (RAINN) places the rate at 68 percent. [5]

One of the most important questions about rape is, "how can anyone know the rate of non-reporting with confidence?" By definition, the person attempting to answer is measuring something for which there is no hard evidence. A common method of measurement is to survey a slice of the population and ask the participants if they have been raped. If so, did they report it?

This method raises severe problems, however. Such surveys are often nothing more than SLOPs (Self-Selected Listener Opinion Polls) or the equivalent. In a SLOP, the population surveyed is typically not random but selected by researchers, albeit in an indirect manner. For example, a set of questions may be posted on a PC feminist website that is frequented almost exclusively by women who accept the rape culture and see it everywhere. Such a website self-selects against the participation of devout Christian, conservative or skeptical women. The site's results will differ dramatically from the data returned by religious ones.

The possible bias involved in SLOPs was vividly illustrated by a 2013 incident at Occidental College where an online form allowed students to anonymously report sexual assault with the stated purpose of gathering data. It failed miserably. The *Business Insider* explained [6], "overzealous 'men's rights' activists flooded the form with false reports of sexual assault, rendering it useless to those gathering data. If you look through the thread, a few people point out that the effort is in vain, but they are silenced by the wave of Redditors giddily sharing descriptions of their false reports." There is no reason to believe the information provided by rape culture zealots is any more accurate or less biased.

The foregoing are merely a handful of reasons that statisticians give SLOPs little weight. In fact, the *mis*information provided by SLOPs is worse than having no data whatsoever because bad research can result in bad policy or law. Moreover, flawed statistics tend to drive out good ones.

Nevertheless, online surveys and other SLOPs are popular because they offer distinct advantages. Some advantages are reasonable and neutral in nature. For example, online SLOPs are far easier and cheaper to administer than traditional studies which require built-in safeguards and hands-on participation by researchers.

Other advantages are less honest. Respondents can be guided toward the desired answers in various ways. As mentioned earlier, a common method is to post the survey to a site visited by a specific population that is likely to validate the positions favored by researchers. Or the Framing Effect may be present. The term describes a situation in which the same person will give contradictory answers to equivalent questions, depending upon how the question is phrased. The phrasing determines the answer.

A wide array of fallacies haunt SLOP data. Two of the most common ones are:

- The Ecological Fallacy by which inferences about an individual are based upon statistics for the population group to which the individual belongs. An example is to infer an individual is above average in intelligence because a study of his or her ethnic group demonstrates that result. This is a version of the Fallacy of Division, which assumes something true about the whole must be true about its parts.

- The Exception Fallacy reverses the Ecological Fallacy. A researcher reaches conclusions about a population based upon a few outlying individuals. An example is concluding that all men are rapists because some men rape. This is an expression of the Fallacy of Composition, which assumes something true about a part must be true about the whole.

The two proceeding errors are frequently employed by researchers who wish to manufacture a factual basis for a position or argument. Unfortunately, zombie stats can become deeply entrenched, partly because the production of hysteria is valuable not only to ideologues but also to bureaucrats and PC politicians. In a *USA Today* article, "The great campus rape hoax," law professor Glenn Harlan Reynolds astutely observed [7], "This kind of hysteria may be ugly, but for campus activists and bureaucrats it's a source of power: If there's a 'campus rape crisis', that means that we need new rules, bigger budgets, and expanded power and self-importance for all involved, with the added advantage of letting you call your political opponents (or anyone who threatens funding) 'pro rape'. If we focus on the truth, however – rapidly declining rape rates already, without any particular 'crisis' programs in place – then voters, taxpayers, and university trustees will probably decide to invest resources elsewhere. So for politicians and activists, a phony crisis beats no crisis."

How do you kill a zombie statistic? The same way you kill a zombie in movies. You aim for the head and not for the heart. Rape culture adherents want to claim both the factual (head) and the moral (heart) high ground. But the morality of their position rests on its factual support; the facts must be the target of attack. If critics respond in kind to the emotional soundtrack of rape culture adherents, then they play into the strength of dissembling opponents. But if critics deal in evidence and reason, then they stand on solid ground where the advantage is theirs.

PC Feminist Research

> What began as a useful sensitization of police officers, prosecutors and judges to the claims of authentic rape victims turned into a hallucinatory overextension of the definition of rape to cover every unpleasant or embarrassing sexual encounter. Rape became the crime of crimes, overshadowing all wars, massacres and disasters of world history. The feminist obsession with rape as a symbol of male-female relations is irrational and delusional. From the perspective of the future, this period in America will look like a reign of mass psychosis, like that of the Salem witch trials....The fantastic fetishism of rape by mainstream ... feminists has in the end trivialized rape, impugned women's credibility, and reduced the sympathy we should feel for legitimate victims of violent sexual assault. –Camille Paglia [8]

Before analyzing specific instances of PC feminist research, defining such research is useful. PC research differs dramatically from the traditional version which is based on scientific method, controls, replicable results, etc. The traditional methodology allows people to compare or merge studies with some degree of confidence because the research follows the same basic rules. If they do not, then comparing them only blurs understanding.

Over the past several decades the new methodology of "feminist research" has evolved. It flies in the face of the scientific method, which most people assume is still conducted at universities. In fact, feminist research is the mirror image of scientific or unbiased methodology. When a PC feminist speaks of a "study," the word means something very different than when a traditional researcher uses the same word.

What is feminist research, and what gave rise to it? In her path-breaking book *The Science Question in Feminism* (1986), the feminist philosopher Sandra Harding questioned whether it was possible to use traditional science, which was "steeped in Western, masculine, bourgeois endeavors," as a vehicle to emancipate women and other marginalized groups. Harding stated [9], "When we began theorizing our experiences during the second women's movement a mere decade and a half ago, we knew our task would be a difficult though exciting one. But I doubt that in our wildest dreams we ever imagined we would have to reinvent both science and theorizing itself to make sense of women's experience."

The publisher of Harding's book, Cornell University Press, called it [10], "the first comprehensive and critical survey of the feminist science critiques," which "examines inquiries into the androcentricism that has endured since the birth of modern science. Harding critiques three epistemological approaches: feminist empiricism, which identifies only bad science as the problem; the feminist standpoint, which holds that women's social experience provides a unique starting point for discovering masculine bias in science; and feminist postmodernism, which disputes the most basic scientific assumptions."

Traditional science and associated concepts, such as objectivity, were male constructs and part of the problem, not the solution. The entire approach and framework of traditional research needed to be deconstructed and reconstructed in order to express a feminist perspective or, at least, a female one that was aligned with PC ideology.

> Objectivity is a word men use to describe their own subjectivity. – Adrienne Rich

What does the reconstruction look like? There is controversy as to *exactly* what constitutes feminist research or whether there is one approach that is feminist. A touchstone book by sociologist Shulamit Reinharz, *Feminist Methods in Social Research* (1992), provided guidelines rather than hard-and-fast rules for the conduct of feminist research. [11] The book offers an excellent summary. Reinharz loosely defined feminist research as anything produced by an author who identified herself "as a feminist doing research." Within that loose framework, Reinharz makes ten vague claims about the typical characteristics of feminist research. [12] (Note: Text in boldface reflects Reinharz's own words.)

1. Feminism is a perspective

Even hard sciences that are traditionally considered bastions of objectivity, such as physics or geology, are seen as subjective because they are socially constructed by men. They must be reinterpreted through an explicitly feminist lens.

Another word for "feminist perspective" is ideology because feminism in its varied forms is a set of ideas and principles. All self-identified "feminist research" unabashedly begins with ideology. It is not value-neutral, nor is it meant to be.

> The argument that there is a specifically feminist methodology implies not just that feminists select research topics on a different basis to non-feminists, but that when a feminist investigates a particular topic, the whole process of research will reflect her commitment to feminism. –Martyn Hammersley [13]

2. Feminists use many research methods

The methodology is intentionally flexible and can include *both* quantitative and qualitative approaches. Quantitative research asks structured questions in order to produce hard facts that are as unbiased as possible. The group Feminist Perspectives on Media and Technology, based at York University, described qualitative methods as [14],

> '[R]esearch procedures which produce descriptive data: people's own written or spoken words and observable behavior'....In the past several years the feminist community has increasingly debated the merits of traditional research, specifically the quantitative methodologies used in that research.... '[M]any feminists...argue that traditional research in the social sciences is used as a tool for promoting sexist ideology and ignores issues of concern to women and feminists'....Feminists indicate that until recently, social scientific knowledge was based on men's experiences of the world and women's experiences were particularly missing. Males are establishing the norms; more specifically they are playing the dominant roles. As a result of this, some feminists have suggested the increased use of qualitative research.

Qualitative methods include subjective approaches. They produce subjective data that cannot be verified, generalized or replicated by scientific methods. Qualitative methods include stream-of-consciousness, SLOPs, auto-biographies, group diaries, unstructured interviews, and consciousness-raising. They step in the opposite direction from traditional research. And, yet, they are often quoted to contradict and dismiss more careful research. In reality, the two types of research cannot be meaningfully compared to each other, as PC feminists sometimes concede.

> Feminist claims are 'unthinkable' within the domain assumptions of established social science not only because they forthrightly assert that the discourses of science are man made, but also because they ascribe to the far more radical claims that the epistemologies and the theories of knowledge that produced these discourses are systematically skewed by both Eurocentric and masculinist interpretative and textual practices. –S.C. Jansen [15]

3. Feminist research involves ongoing criticism of nonfeminist scholarship

The approach includes a persistent attack on all scholarship, investigation and commentary that contradicts feminist ideology or conclusions. The constant onslaught is conscious and occurs solely because the research produces results that are non- or anti-feminist. The contrary evidence is not weighed or considered except in order to discredit it. By contrast, traditionally-conducted studies often cite research that differs from their own results and then they attempt to account for the difference; for example, a contradicting study might have surveyed a more restricted population.

The process of accounting for differences is *not* what is meant by "ongoing criticism of nonfeminist scholarship." The feminist researcher's ongoing criticism aims at diminishing the reputations and character of those who disagree, especially dissenting women researchers.

4. Feminist research is guided by feminist theory

Investigation is not neutral but driven by ideology. The bias is reflected in the phrasing of questions, the populations selected for survey, the methodology, the weighing of data, the manner in which data are released, and virtually every other aspect of the process.

> Feminist research is guided by feminist theory and most often is conducted about women and the various dilemmas that concern them including children, family, education, and health. Such research values women and sees their lives as important. It acknowledges that much of the regarded truths in the world have been forged from within patriarchic viewpoints that have

dominated the production of knowledge for centuries. –Audrey M. Dentith. [16]

5. Feminist research may be transdisciplinary

In her work *Essentials of Transdisciplinary Research: Using Problem-Centered Methodologies,* Patricia Leavy defined the title's key term. [17] "Transdisciplinarity is an approach to conducting social research that involves synergistic collaboration between two or more disciplines with high levels of integration....Transdisciplinary research follows responsive or iterative methodologies and requires innovation, creativity, flexibility and often employs research design strategies."

Transdisciplinary research addresses social questions from a range of perspectives without being restricted by the traditional boundaries of disciplines or methodology. It creates new conceptual frameworks by introducing PC analysis into fields of study that have been viewed as politically neutral. Everything becomes a feminist issue. An example would be the text *Feminist Geography in Practice: Research and Methods*. [18]

6. Feminist research aims to create social change

The primary purpose of feminist research is *not* to obtain the truth by following evidence and reason wherever they may lead. The purpose is to advance a predetermined social or political agenda that the research is meant to support. Point 4, "Feminist research is guided by feminist theory," leads naturally into an agenda of social change. Thus, a characteristic that typifies feminist research is the explicit presence of policy and/or legal recommendations, which are routinely included in concluding remarks. Often, they are also stated in the summary or opening comments and scattered throughout the report. In their essay in *Handbook of Feminist Research: Theory and Praxis,* Sarah Madison and Frances Shaw explained [19], "Feminist research methodologies are often 'impelled by a concern for social justice' and therefore 'are designed to reveal the gender problematic'."

> In one respect, almost every feminist research is inevitably futuristic. As feminism is a program for social change, feminists are concerned with offering alternative visions of the future. Change is also incorporated into the feminist understanding of social reality. Seeing, for example, norms of the objectivity, customs, law, religion, science, and other areas as historically and socially constructed, gives greater opportunity for redefinition, for reconstruction, for questioning

givens, for more radical transformation, for change. *What is seen as man made could be woman remade*. Therefore, feminist research does not only include extrapolation, forecasting, and analysis of current trends but alternative visions, as well, even if these are seen by many as unfeasible utopias. [Emphasis in the original] –Ivana Milojević [20]

7. Feminist research strives to represent human diversity

In the preface to the anthology *Handbook of Diversity in Feminist Psychology*, the editors commented [21], "Each author brings her own cultural perspective, values, and concerns to her chapter.... 'Women of color [and other marginalized groups] complain...about the cultural bias of reviewers and editors who transform what they never understood into something the author never wrote, thereby excluding the diversity we ostensibly seek to achieve'." As diverse as this may sound, such anthologies will almost assuredly *not* welcome authors who question concepts such as "social construction" or authors who fall into "undesirable" categories such as conservative women.

By *diversity,* PC feminists do not mean the delightful range of differences between human beings. Their diversity rarely embraces a representative sampling of people. For one thing, half the human race (males) are ignored or crudely stereotyped. For another, feminist researchers are overwhelmingly white affluent academics who demand conformity from others. The feminist definition of diversity is extremely exclusionary.

8. Feminist research frequently involves the researcher as a person

In her book *Emotionally Involved: The Impact of Researching Rape* [22], Rebecca Campbell explained how erasure of the emotional line between researcher and subject was inevitable and valuable. "We were studying something from which we have no immunity. There is no line that separates us, the researchers, from them, the survivors. We knew we could be or could have been on the other side of the interview– telling a story of surviving rape, not listening to one. It became more and more difficult to 'think' about rape when the very things we were hearing and learning in our research project reminded us of our own vulnerabilities."

Traditionally, the ideal researcher attempts to be a neutral presence. The reason: Personal involvement is likely to bias the results. For example, it is common for subjects to provide the responses they believe a researcher wants. PC feminism reverses this ideal of a neutral researcher.

> It is we [the feminist researchers] who have the time, resources and skills to conduct methodical work, to make sense of experience and locate individuals in historic and social contexts....[I]t is an illusion to think that, in anything short of a participatory research project, participants can have anything approaching 'equal' knowledge to the researcher. –L. Kelly and S. Burton [23]

9. Feminist research frequently attempts to develop special relations with the people studied (in interactive research)

Interactive research is a collaborative venture. In their introduction to a special issue of *International Journal of Action Research* [24], editors Lennart Svensson, Per-Erik Ellstrom and Goran Brulin defined the term.

> Interactive research is characterised by a continuous joint learning process between the researcher and the participants. The main focus is on the outcome of the research in terms of new theories and concepts. We will argue that the inclusion of the participants in the whole research process is a way to increase the validity of the research. The change process should be owned by the participants, but these changes will be more sustainable.

An example of interactive research is called "active listening" by which the voices of women are heard through semi-structured or unstructured interviews. The literal responses are heard but the tone, body language and other indications are interpreted as well. The interpretation is used as evidence of the subject's reaction and is sometimes given priority over the verbal response.

Again, this reverses the traditional researcher's role of neutrality.

10. Feminist research frequently defines a special relationship with the reader

The researcher engages the reader in various ways, including personally addressing her or him in the text of the study by asking questions. Sharlene Nagy Hesse-Biber in, *Feminist research practice: a primer,* offered an example. [25] She wrote within a study, "This brief remembrance of the first day of my class came to mind as I began to think of a way to provide you, the reader, with a re-invitation to feminist research. While each student's experience is real, it also arises out of very different life circumstances. While most women in my class start out with the common goals of equality and of social justice for all women, they do not share the same lived reality; these differences cause these women to provide different answers to the question of whether or not feminism is still needed and relevant today." The researcher acts as an advocate and a guide rather than a reporter of data.

Feminist research is the reverse of the scientific method that attempts to establish a neutral environment. Nevertheless, feminist research draws authority from its conventional counterpart by presenting findings in a manner that mimics scientific research. The mimicry makes their data appear *hard* and so it receives more widespread acceptance than if people viewed it as a subjective interpretation of biased evidence.

The readers' confusion is understandable, for several reasons. The research is published in peer-reviewed journals, albeit PC ones, with the peer review performed by academics who share the researchers' politics, methodology and purpose. The presence of graphs and mathematics seems to indicate an exact measurement of objective facts rather than the subjective measurement of an interpretation. Because many studies are conducted at universities by researchers with Ph.D.s, an academic atmosphere also lends credibility to the results. The same is true of the academic grants that fund the research, and the dense academic jargon in which it is expressed. As a result, a highly ideological report reaps the benefit of appearing objective while being sensational at the same time.

Feminist research must be denied the appearance of objective fact. In order to do so, it is important to know how to interrogate feminist studies and surveys.

How to Interrogate Rape Culture Studies and Stats

> Politicians use statistics in the same way that a drunk uses lampposts– for support rather than illumination. –Andrew Lang

First, an acknowledgement. Not all bad data come from dishonest or biased research. The ensuing are honest reasons why data may prove unreliable or *bad.*

- There is inadequate definition of the subject matter under study

- The study is based on assumptions that are not justified or proven

- There are ethical or financial constraints

- It is a meta-analysis, combining several earlier studies that use different definitions or have other significant incompatibilities

- The researcher does not credit alternate explanations for data

- The researcher is an expert in the field of study but not a competent statistician

- The researcher is competent with statistics but not an expert in the field of study and so misinterprets results

There are specific rules by which studies and statistics must abide if they are to have a place in principled, informed discussion. The rules aim at producing valid results rather than ideology and advocacy. People should ask the following question of any finding before they accept it as fact. (Note: The next section of this chapter applies the questions to a specific study in order to illustrate the process.)

Does the researcher have a clear bias?

If so, the bias does not invalidate the data but it does indicate a need to scrutinize a study more closely. This is particularly true if the researcher doesn't have a solid background in statistical method, if she states the results in a sensational manner or expresses them as conclusions rather than indications.

What is the source of the findings I'm hearing?

Never accept findings on the basis of a media report or a brief synopsis from the researchers because such accounts are often incorrect or misleading. Seek out an neutral source or the complete report along with the raw data, if possible. If the report is not available, then bump up your level of skepticism. Unpublished research is a red flag because sloppy or dishonest researchers prefer to block scrutiny. Moreover, non-transparency prevents the research from being duplicated, which is a standard form of verification.

Does the research include an explicit public policy recommendation?

Feminist research has the explicit and inherent goal of achieving political change. In traditional research, a study provides an indication of what might be true of a situation and points to further research that could be be useful. In an ideological approach, the findings are offered as *the* truth and accompanied by recommendations of how law or policy should respond.

The suggested response may or may not have merit but the ideological nature of the data should bring greater scrutiny to any claims.

Is the sample biased – that is selective – or too small?

A sample bias means that a researcher selectively includes some members of a target population and excludes others. The stated target could be female students and, yet, all participants may be drawn from the Gender Studies program. The study might accurately reflect students in that program but its results cannot be generalized to say anything about the entire or average female population on campus.

Other forms of sample bias include selecting participants from one location and generalizing results to all locations. For example, the target population may be "male students." But a survey of male students at a Baptist college in the Midwest may differ significantly from the same survey conducted at a Miami party-college. Data from the former cannot be generalized as representing male students nationwide. [26] Equally, small samples say little about the target population as a whole.

Does the research proceed from a false assumption that is stated as established fact?

This practice is commonplace in rape culture research. For example, it is taken for granted that 1-in-5 female students will be sexually assaulted while on campus even though the figure is widely disputed. After stating the assumption as a fact, the researcher then proceeds to ask, "why?" or "under what circumstances?" The bias introduced is so obvious as to need no explanation. [27]

Always question the assumptions from which a study proceeds. They may be sound or they may express the ideology of the researcher or flawed findings from past studies. Researchers are human beings and we all make assumptions. But an honest researcher will attempt to be as fact-based as possible, and some make a point of stating their own bias. A quick but not sure test of the honesty and competence of the researcher is to look for a stated margin of error.

Is a margin of error not present or misreported?

A margin of error indicates the "confidence interval," which is an estimate of the expected range of variability that will occur when applying the results from sample to sample or to the general public. It tries to establish boundaries for the reproducibility of the statistic. The margin is obtained through a set of formulas and it is usually expressed as a percentage. For example, if an ice cream survey finds that 50 percent of respondents prefer chocolate over vanilla and the margin of error is 10 percent, then the 50 percent should be interpreted as indicating that a range of 40-60 percent of the general population is likely to be chocolate-lovers.

A study's margin of error is important for a number of reasons. If no margin is included, then people may consider the reliability to be 100 percent even if it is closer to 50 percent. Of course, the reaction to 100 percent reliability will be different than to 50 percent. This includes the reaction of media and funders, both of whom the researcher may be courting. The practice of doing so is sometimes called "P-value fishing" or "data dredging," and a margin of error can interfere with it.

Does the researcher assume a correlation means causation?

A correlation is a mutual relationship between two or more things. For example, a mutual relationship may exist between a society's prosperity and the sale of cars; as one goes up, so does the other. When X and Y are correlated, however, it is not clear that there is a cause and effect relationship. The classic example of a correlation **not** implying causation is the sale of ice cream and the murder rate, both of which rise in tandem. A *Slate* article, "When Ice Cream Sales Rise, So Do Homicides. Coincidence, or Will Your Next Cone Murder You?," explained [28], "The idea that frozen treats cause crime is obviously ridiculous....But it does stand to reason that ice cream sells better in warm weather, and there is in fact plenty of evidence to suggest that murder rates rise when temperatures rise." This is an example of a correlation occurring because of a separate variable – the heat.

When X and Y correlate, several explanations are possible. Y could cause X or they could be causing each other. X and Y may both be caused by a third factor. Or it could be a statistical fluke.

Is the sample further biased by adding incentives?

It is common to induce members of a target population to participate in research by offering incentives. The practice seems especially popular at universities where students are readily available as subjects. The incentives vary from gift cards to cash to academic credit.

But offering enticements is controversial. Some believe incentives skew the study by affecting how respondents answer questions. For example, if a professor offers extra credit for participating, then students are more likely to give the answers they think the professor wants to hear. Those attracted by an incentive could also constitute a biased sample. Extra credit will appeal most to those who need it to pass a class or to the lazy. Equally, a gift card will appeal most to students who are struggling rather than to those who come from wealthy families.

Always check whether the results were purchased and ask what the currency was.

Do the questions skew participants toward the desired answer?

Again, this is the Framing Effect. There are several ways to skew a question. The wording may predispose participants to answer in a specific manner. "Do you believe female students deserve the best protection possible against being raped while on campus?" is likely to receive a high "yes" rate. "Does protecting female students from rape require stripping due process from accused males?" is likely to receive a high "no" rate. The phrasing is all.

Another skewing tactic is to provide biased background information before asking a question. The researcher may explain that she cares deeply about the rape epidemic on campus and thank the participant for being part of the solution by participating. Or she may ask him to read a sheet of statistics, including the common misstatement, "1-in-5 female students will be raped." Only then are the questions posed.

Does it draw upon prestigious but dubious authority?

One method of validating dubious research is to publish it in peer-reviewed journals. A peer review is an evaluation of scholarly work by academics or experts who work in the same field. It is meant to be a guarantee of quality but it has come to mean little. The popular *JoNova* site – subtitled "Skeptical Science for dissident thinkers" – recently reported on a peer-reviewed study that found the age of respondents had no correlation with any of "the indicator variables." In an article entitled "Lewandowsky peer reviewed study includes someone 32,757 years old," Joanne Nova wrote [29], "The data sample is not large, but despite that, it includes...[a] Neanderthal, as well as a precocious five year old and some underage teenagers too." Some responses were pranks. Remove them and, suddenly, age correlates well with the indicator variables, which is the opposite of what the study concludes. Even worse, the prestigious publishers of the paper in question neglected to correct the error after it was brought to their attention. Perhaps their lack of action was because the publishers favored the study's conclusions on climate change.

And, then, there was the research paper discussed in the *Slate* article, "This Is What Happens When No One Proofreads an Academic Paper." [30] "Variation in Melanism and Female Preference in Proximate but Ecologically Distinct Environments" appeared in the peer-reviewed journal *Ethology*. It accidentally included a question intended only for co-authors; the researcher asked, "Should we cite the crappy Gabor paper here?"

A peer review is no guarantee of quality or accuracy. As research is increasingly driven by politics or a desire for funding, the academic filtering becomes less and less effective.

Does the study ignore contradicting evidence?

Industries often sponsor multiple studies and release only the ones with favorable results. The tobacco industry is notorious for doing so.

Researchers who want a particular result also discard contradicting evidence within their own studies. This is called cherry picking or the fallacy of selective attention. [31] It is extremely difficult to judge whether information has been discarded without checking the raw data or going outside of the study to check if it is widely contradicted by other research. Fortunately, a great deal of research is currently available online for free.

Do the results make sense or do they contradict your own experience?

Your own experience of a situation may not reflect the truth of the larger picture. But be wary of conclusions that seem counterintuitive, of results that run counter to common sense.

The foregoing questions are far from definitive but they are good place to start in honing your skills as a skeptic. [32]

Applying the Preceding Questions to Specific Research

And if all others accepted the lie which the Party imposed – if all records told the same tale – then the lie passed into history and became truth. 'Who controls the past', ran the Party slogan, 'controls the future: who controls the present controls the past'. And yet the past, though of its nature alterable, never had been altered. Whatever was true now was true from everlasting to everlasting. It was quite simple. All that was needed was an unending series of victories over your own memory. 'Reality control,' they called it: in Newspeak, 'doublethink'. –George Orwell, *1984* [33]

Early in 2015, the results of a study, which was actually a survey, exploded across the media due to its sensational message. "Denying Rape but Endorsing Forceful Intercourse: Exploring Differences Among Responders" [34] was conducted at the University of North Dakota, Grand Forks, a national public research university. The results were released in the journal *Violence and Gender*. They claimed that approximately 1-in-3 male students would rape their female counterparts, "if nobody would ever know and there wouldn't be any consequences." Virtually every major media venue parroted the claim with an appropriately mixed tone of outrage and titillation.

"Denying Rape" descends to the level of "Potemkin data." The phrase refers to Russian lore in which Gregory Potemkin erected fake settlements along the Dnieper River in order to deceptively impress his paramour Catherine II as she toured the newly acquired Crimea (1787). The faux villages were akin to movie props with no substance behind their fronts. Potemkin wished to trick Catherine into believing a situation was far better than it really was. The North Dakota study wants people to believe a situation is far *worse* than it really is but the technique is much the same. And it has the same purpose – to secure an advantage.

What happens when we apply the questions sketched in the preceding section to "Denying Rape?"

(Note: I use the originally-issued study even though the publisher recently issued a correction [35] that read,

> Understanding how people define rape is an important topic in research, intervention and prevention of sexual assault, intimate partner violence and domestic violence, among other issues. "Denying Rape but Endorsing Forceful Intercourse: Exploring Differences Among Responders" by Sarah R. Edwards, Kathryn A. Bradshaw and Verlin B. Hinsz, *Violence and Gender* December 2014, 1(4) 188-193 explored this topic. However, after publication of the article, Dr. Edwards contacted the editorial office to explain that the data presented inadvertently duplicated a dataset that was

previously published in *Problems of Psychology in the 21ˢᵗ Century.* Two similar datasets (the other focusing on rape perceptions and how they differ in individual vs. group judgments) were collected at the same time, but from different individuals. The error does not affect the results or conclusions of either paper, but the method section as it was published does not fully reflect the lineage of the data.

"Denying Rape" analyzed the wrong dataset, which should instantly invalidate its results. Nevertheless, the publisher defended the findings. The original "1-in-3" conclusion remains the one with which people are familiar because the media blared it without so much as mentioning the subsequent massive error. The original conclusions are what stand in the public mind and record.)

Does the researcher have a clear bias?

The research team was led by psychology professor Sarah R. Edwards, who does feminist counselling and has a track record of conducting similar research with similar results. The study displays a clear bias. It states of rapacious males, "We believe that men exhibiting higher levels of hostility toward women will exhibit awareness that their behaviors constitute rape, and still endorse use of force given that the motivation of the encounter is to punish women." In other words, the researchers base the study on their own gender beliefs and enter with strong assumptions about the participants.

What is the source of the findings I'm hearing?

The ultimate source is the academic journal *Violence and Gender,* which issued the bizarre non-retraction retraction. The popularizing source was the mainstream media who noted the study's original conclusions without examining its methodology or noting the rather amazing correction. It is difficult to take either source seriously.

Does the survey or study include an agenda such as a public policy recommendation?

"Denying Rape" has at least two stated agendas. *Campus Reform* reported [36],

> According to Edwards, such behavior [rape] is closely associated with hypermasculinity – the noticeable accentuation of masculine

traits such as strength, aggression, and an enhanced sexual appetite. Edwards and her colleagues suggested that male students receive educational programming focused on "clarifying different behaviors that all constitute sexual assault, but do not follow the stereotypically imagined scenarios related to rape."

In short, the policy recommendation is for mandatory training to change the attitudes of male students through "cultural messages that do not condone the use of force."

This recommendation emerged from the public commentary that surrounded the survey more than from the report. The report itself concluded, "Our results suggest that there is no one-size-fits-all approach to sexual assault prevention." Instead, it called for more research which presumably means more tax funding for the researchers.

The second agenda item embodied one of the feminist research characteristics stated by Reinharz: "3. Feminist research involves ongoing criticism of nonfeminist scholarship." The introduction to "Denying Rape" stated, "some mainstream media and social network users" have "suggested that rape only occurs if a woman labels it as such." A study arguing with Facebook and Twitter commentators is odd enough but, then, it continued, "Such sentiments contribute to a culture that...normalizes sexual aggression as part of the male gender role." In other words, rape culture skeptics are part of what causes rape.

Is the sample biased – that is selective – or too small?

Of the approximately 15,000 students at the University of North Dakota, only 86 male students were surveyed with no sense of how they were chosen or how many were rejected. The "Materials and Method" section presents itself scientifically through the use of mathematics and formulas. For example, it states of the 86 respondents, "All participants were over 18 (M=21, SD=3.6) and most were juniors in college. The overwhelming majority of participants (> 90 percent) identified as Caucasian, consistent with the general student make up at this university, and all identified as heterosexual, with prior sexual experiences."

The math does not place the study on sounder scientific grounds, however; it merely highlights limitations over and above the very small number of participants. Namely, the respondents were drawn from the same basic ethnic group and shared the identical sexual orientation.

Moreover, only 73 surveys were used for analysis, which means a significant number were discarded: 13 out of 86. The high discard rate is particularly puzzling as the report stated, "A male research assistant collected informed consent and administered the survey in a private location." The fact that the survey was supervised and the respondents "informed" should have greatly reduced errors. Confusingly, elsewhere the report seemed to indicate that the surveys were self-reported. (The confusion may result from the report referencing the wrong dataset, as later admitted.)

"Denying Rape" only touched upon the reasons for its significant discard rate. "There was one participant who indicated that he would rape a woman, but denied any likelihood to use force to obtain intercourse. Because we did not know how to make sense of this answer and could not exclude a random error (e.g., careless marking), this case was dropped from the analysis." The specifics of why the 12 other surveys were dismissed is not explained.

The resulting data: Of 73 surveys, 23 respondents were deemed to have "intentions to force a woman to sexual intercourse." As the wording of questions and answers do not appear to be available, it is impossible to verify the conclusion or assess the process by which answers were "deemed" to express one intention rather than another. But the word "deemed" indicates subjectivity on the part of researchers.

Can such a miniscule and biased sample be generalized? No. In fairness, according to the *Campus Reform* article [37], "Edwards warned against interpreting the study as a representation of the entire collegiate male population." Instead she called the study an "initial investigation."

And, yet, the study is not shy about applying broad hypothetical statements to a group of males. The researchers stated, "Therefore, we hypothesize that men [who] do not endorse any intentions for sexual aggression will differ from the other two groups of men primarily on a dimension characterized by hostility toward women as the strongest loading factor. Men who openly endorse intentions to rape women versus those who only endorse intentions to use force but deny rape are hypothesized to differ along a second dimension on which callous sexual attitudes play a more important role. In other words, we expect a pattern of results showing two significant functions along which we can differentiate the three groups of men." Predictably, the survey validated the presumed hypothesis. Expectations are conclusions in progress.

Does the research proceed from a false premise or assumption that is stated as an "established" or presumed fact?

The opening sentence of "Denying Rape" states, "Federal data estimate that about one in five women becomes the victim of sexual assault while in college, most of which is committed by assailants known to the victim." The 1-in-5 figure has been exhaustively debunked. [38] The zombie stat should have been buried by the Bureau of Justice Statistics (BJS) report (Dec. 2014) that found the actual rate of rape to be 0.61 percent per year – or 6.1 per 1,000 students. (More on the BJS report in Chapter Five.)

Is a margin of error presented or misreported?

"Denying Rape" commented on the reliability of two surveys taken by respondents as a prelude to their filling out the one around which the study is centered. It explained,

> The hostility toward women scale: "Judgments were made on a 0 (strongly agree) to 6 (strongly disagree) response scale, with higher scores indicating more hostility. The scale demonstrated good reliability ($\alpha = .87$) in the current study."

> The Hypermasculinity scale: "The subscale consisted of 10 forced choice items. The scale demonstrated good reliability in this study ($\alpha = .86$)."

Forced choice questions eliminate neutral options and demand that the subject choose between defined answers. Sometimes the questions are multiple choice, which may present false options; the question might be, "Do you prefer A or B," when the respondent dislikes both. There is great debate on whether forced choice questions provide any valuable data.

The mathematical formulas give the appearance of science while offering little information. For one thing, the noted reliability of the two surveys is a misleading measure. [39] Moreover, the third and presumably most important pre-survey was not included in the statement of reliability. That pre-survey was the "attraction to sexual aggression scale." So, no; there was no margin of error presented.

Does the researcher assume a correlation means causation?

The researchers assumed a cause-and-effect relationship between a respondent's reported hostility to women and his intentions to rape.

Again, the report mimicked objectivity. It stated, "Understanding the motives and meaning associated with such rapes is beyond this scope of the present research." Nevertheless, it included statements such as, "Given that hostility toward women involves resentment, bitterness, rejection sensitivity, and paranoia about women's motives, we consider the inverse of hostility toward women in men that intend to use force to be indicative of an affable, trusting, and nonreactive affect toward women. When combined with callous sexual attitudes, we interpret this function as representing personality characteristics that might lend themselves to allowing men to not perceive his actions as rape and may even view the forced intercourse as an achievement." Clearly, assumptions on the "motives and meaning" associated with rape were **not** beyond the scope of the study.

Is the sample further biased by adding incentives?

The respondents, who apparently were volunteers, received academic credit. It is not clear whether the wrongfully-used dataset also received a credit incentive.

The respondent surveys seem to have been submitted anonymously. The report stated, "After finishing the survey, participants dropped the survey into a mailbox." If anonymity was observed, then the participants would have received credit no matter how dishonestly they answered. In short, there was no reason beyond inherent honesty for the them to provide real data, especially if they resented the "men are rapists" attitude of the questions. In a *Washington Examiner* article [40], "No, we did not just learn 1 in 3 college men would rape if they could get away with it," Ashe Schow commented, "Even in a world where college men take everything seriously, nine guys does not equal a mass epidemic of would-be rapists. A more sound reading is that nine college boys didn't take the survey too seriously."

The researchers did not consider alternate explanations for the answers.

Does the researcher ask questions that skew participants toward the desired answer?

The specific wording of questions does not seem to be available. But in at least one important regard, the questions seem deeply skewed. The researchers painted a specific scenario to respondents. A rape they committed would never be discovered and would never have consequences. This means the rape took place in a universe other than the one we inhabit because the real world never offers a guarantee of non-discovery and no consequences. When you take the real-world context and consequences away from behavior, then a great many people might contemplate actions they would never take otherwise. For example, many people might admit to considering the murder of an ex-spouse, a swindling partner, a romantic rival, a hated relative. But they would consider it *only* because the crime was guaranteed to remain unknown and be consequence-free. That doesn't mean they would murder in real life. Many people who would never steal might be tempted by a hypothetical scenario in which they could loot a bank with impunity. By removing reality, the validity of the responses is removed as well.

Does the survey draw upon prestigious but dubious authority?

The 6-page study cites almost 30 studies for authority; indeed, the last of the 6 pages is a list of references. The list is impressive in length but many of the supporting studies have themselves been debunked. [41]

"Denying Rape" wraps itself in authoritative jargon and dense mathematical formulas.

> In discriminant function analysis, each function consists of a unique linear combination of the predictor variables used (here: hostility toward women and callous sexual attitudes). Function 1 significantly discriminated among groups: $\lambda=0.65$, $\chi^2(4)=32.76$, $p<0.001$. Observing the standardized canonical function coefficients and structure matrix suggests that the first function is very strongly related to hostility toward women ($r_s=0.87$), and moderately strongly related to callous sexual attitudes ($r_s=0.75$).
>
> Function 2 was also significant: $\lambda=0.91$, χ^2 (1)=7.20, $p<0.01$. Function 2 appears to represent moderately strong callous sexual attitudes ($r_s=0.66$), and a moderate inverse of hostility ($r_s=-0.50$).

The foregoing is immensely complicated for a self-reporting survey that includes "yes" and "no" answers as well as imprecise responses rated on a scale from 1-to-6. Frankly, the formulation seems deliberately arcane and confusing in order to borrow scientific authority to bolster a brief, simplistic survey.

A mathematician friend who reviewed the formulas commented to me, "No clue as to what the impressive statistics being cited here might mean, with the exception of '$p<0.001$'. But, then, that is your point. No one except a specialist will know what it means, and the average reader will only see (and, perhaps, be impressed by) the dense jargon and arcane symbols."

Do the results make sense or do they contradict your own experience?

Every reader must answer this question for him- or herself based on personal experience.

Electrifying headlines followed the release of "Denying Rape." Fortunately, the calls for sanity were also immediate. Katherine Timpf commented [42] in a *National Review* article, "'1 in 3 College Men Would Rape a Woman' Stat is Based on a Survey of 73 Dudes." She noted how hyped the headlines seemed given the extraordinarily small sample. "These [sensational] headlines seem like a pretty big jump: 'Study: 1 in 3 Men Would Rape if They Wouldn't Get Caught or Face Consequences' (*Cosmopolitan*), 'Study Finds That a Third of College Men Would Rape if They Could Get Away With It' (*Feministing*), '1 in 3 Male University Students Would Sexually Assault a Woman If They Could Get Away With It' (*Crave Online*), and '1 in 3 College Men Admit They Would Rape If We Don't Call it Rape' (*Jezebel*)."

The sensational rape stat and headlines do not mirror my real-life experience or that of women I know.

The Saga of Missing Data

> Yesterday, upon the stair,
> I met a man who wasn't there.
> He wasn't there again today,
> I wish, I wish he'd go away... –Hughes Mearns

The findings of "Denying Rape" are strikingly reminiscent of an earlier statistic in the book *Body Wars: Making Peace with Women's Bodies* by the clinical psychologist Margo Maine. [43] A lurid stat from the book has been frequently quoted. "Eight percent of college men have either attempted or successfully raped. Thirty percent say they would rape if they could get away with it. When the wording was changed to 'force a woman to have sex,' the number jumped to 58 percent. Worse still, 83.5 percent argue that 'some women look like they are just asking to be raped'." [44]

I stumbled over the 83.5 percent figure. It seemed improbably high because it contradicted my own experience. It also seemed improbable that a scientifically-conducted study would ask the question, "if you could get away with it," which almost mandated a speculative response.

I was not the only skeptic. In the article "Is there an epidemic of 'rape culture' at Canadian universities?," the *National Post* reported on an attempt to track down the statistic's source. "Reached in Connecticut this week, Ms. Maine acknowledged she does not know the original source of her numbers. She said she pulled some of the figures from another author's book, published in 1988." Maine ultimately said she did not have time to find the source of her data.

The *National Post* continued to probe and found [45] "the scholar responsible for some of the data...mentioned" thought "the *Body Wars* passage misrepresents his work." The scholar is Neil Malamuth who researches topics relating to men and violence against women at the University of California, Los Angeles. Malamuth could not recall any study that indicated 83.5 percent of men from any population believed that "some women look like they are just asking to be raped."

The same article highlighted exactly how a tangled mess of research could become worse. In *Body Wars*, Maine had also claimed, "In one study over half of high school boys and nearly half of the girls stated that rape was acceptable if the man was sexually aroused." So far, no one – including Maine – has produced the referenced study. The *National Post* concluded, "The 'one study' to which she refers in her book, and which is promulgated by so many others, simply does not exist."

Missing stats are prevalent and powerful forces in the construction of the rape culture. A considerable number of the stats cited and repeated as absolutes are without supporting data. Those who try to track them down discover that there is no *there*.

Stats That Are Impossible to Accurately Calculate

An uncomfortable circumstance surrounds research on rape. Many aspects are extremely difficult or impossible to accurately quantify because they are "dark numbers," which were previously discussed. Consider a highly contested rape statistic – the rate at which false accusations occur. Various statistics that claim to accurately measure the rate are wildly contradictory, with claims that range from 1.5 to 90 percent.

A 2006 paper by Philip N.S. Rumney in the *Cambridge Law Journal* reviewed studies of the false reporting of rape in the US, New Zealand and the UK. [46]

	Number	False reporting rate (percent)
Theilade and Thomsen (1986)	1 out of 56 4 out of 39	1.5 percent (minimum) 10 percent (maximum)
New York Rape Squad (1974)	n/a	2 percent
Hursch and Selkin (1974)	10 out of 545	2 percent
Kelly et al. (2005)	67 out of 2,643	3 percent ("possible" and "probable" false allegations) 22 percent (recorded by police as "no-crime")
Geis (1978)	n/a	3–31 percent (estimates given by police surgeons)
Smith (1989)	17 out of 447	3.8 percent
U.S. Department of Justice (1997)	n/a	8 percent
Clark and Lewis (1977)	12 out of 116	10.3 percent
Harris and Grace (1999)	53 out of 483 123 out of 483	10.9 percent ("false/malicious" claims) 25 percent (recorded by police as "no-crime")
Lea et al. (2003)	42 out of 379	11 percent
HMCPSI/HMIC (2002)	164 out of 1,379	11.8 percent
McCahill et al. (1979)	218 out of 1,198	18.2 percent
Philadelphia police study (1968)	74 out of 370	20 percent
Chambers and Millar (1983)	44 out of 196	22.4 percent
Grace et al. (1992)	80 out of 335	24 percent
Jordan (2004)	68 out of 164 62 out of 164	41 percent ("false" claims) 38 percent (viewed by police as "possibly true/possibly false")
Kanin (1994)	45 out of 109	41 percent

	Number	False reporting rate (percent)
Gregory and Lees (1996)	49 out of 109	45 percent
Maclean (1979)	16 out of 34	47 percent
Stewart (1981)	16 out of 18	90 percent

Discerning the actual rate of false accusations is further complicated by how passionately some factions defend *their* statistic as though the figure were dogma rather than fact.

It is time to get back to basics. A false accusation of rape is a deliberate report of sexual assault when none has occurred; an unfounded accusation is one that cannot be supported with enough evidence to make an arrest. No one accurately knows the rate at which false allegations occur; no one knows the rate at which unfounded but true accusations occur. The rarest type of false report, according to police, is one in which the accuser willingly admits to having lied. Thus many false accusations may be classified as unfounded.

Other circumstances confuse the rate of false allegations. As mentioned, false reports are often conflated with *unfounded* ones. How to assess if an accusation is false also varies. Some data sources tally the number of rape reports and compare that total to the number of successful prosecutions. But it is invalid to claim that if only 8 percent of rape accusations result in a "not guilty" verdict, then 92 percent of reports are true. The high conviction rate may mean that standards of guilt and evidence have been lowered; for example, campus sexual misconduct hearings use the civil court standard of "a preponderance of the evidence" rather than the criminal standard of "beyond a reasonable doubt." It is equally invalid to assume that an 8 percent "guilty" verdict means that 92 percent of accusations are false. The low conviction rate may reflect another flaw in the legal system.

Other factors mask the rate of false accusations. Real victims sometimes drop accusations. Or a victim might legitimately believe she was raped even though circumstances are unclear, perhaps due to alcohol. There are cases of mistaken identity in which innocent men have spent years in jail before being exonerated. There are also cases in which an accuser truly believes she was raped although an examination reveals there was no sexual encounter. Rumney reported [47] on a 2005 study, "Recent research by Kelly et al. has found another category of technically false, but non-malicious allegations of rape. They found a group of no-crimed cases that arose from complainants who thought they might have been sexually assaulted while asleep or intoxicated, but subsequent forensic examination indicated that no sexual contact had taken place."

A world of complexity hides behind the words "false," "unfounded," and "proven," with many accusations falling into a grey area. Third parties rarely know with certainty if an allegation is true or false. This argues for never prejudging the validity of an accusation. It argues for evaluating the unique circumstances and evidence that surround each case.

The rate of rape is important to estimate, nevertheless, even if it cannot be clearly ascertained. For one thing, the rate has practical value. Rape prevention draws upon a knowledge of why, when, and how the crime happens. If there are patterns surrounding rape within a jurisdiction, then identifying them may protect potential victims. The data also provide feedback on whether specific preventative measures are successful, and they can reveal the presence of a serial rapist.

For better or worse, estimates of the rate of rape also have political importance. For example, the claim that 1-in-5 women will be raped in their lifetime creates an atmosphere of hysteria which enables the passage of draconian laws and policies. It directs funding toward specific programs and individuals, creating a profitable "sexual assault industry." By contrast, a low rate of rape and a high rate of false accusations defuses political hysteria and creates public skepticism toward sentiments such as "always believe the woman."

The sticky question of false accusations

No one knows the rate at which false accusations of sexual assault occur.

A commonly cited source for rates on the high end is a 1994 peer-reviewed study by Eugene J. Kanin of Purdue University. Kanin reviewed all rapes reported to the police department in a small urban community over a 10 year period. "False Rape Allegations" is a touchstone study for several reasons. Kanin did not seem to have a foregone conclusion or an ideological bias. His methodology was spelled out and scientific. Kanin targeted a small community because, unlike inner cities, the police force there was well-funded and it pursued every single reported rape regardless of its surface merit. Moreover, each investigation was well documented and included an attempt to have the accuser take a polygraph or otherwise to test the accusation. Kanin stated [48],

> Additionally, [in the examined cases] for a declaration of false charge to be made, the complainant must admit that no rape had

occurred. She is the sole agent who can say that the rape charge is false. The police department will not declare a rape charge as false when the complainant, for whatever reason, fails to pursue the charge or cooperate on the case, regardless how much doubt the police may have regarding the validity of the charge. In short, these cases are declared false only because the complainant admitted they are false.

The total number of rape allegations during the period was 109. The number classified as false allegations was 45, or 41 percent of the total, with Kanin's follow-up research indicating that the rate might be as high as 50 percent.

Generalizing the study immediately encounters problems, however. For one thing, the results from one small community cannot be generalized to say anything definite about broader societies. They could be atypical or due to factors that are specific to the area, such as demographics. A further barrier is that police departments, then and now, differ in their definition and processing of rape, which makes comparisons difficult. At most, Kanin's study is an intriguing indication of what *may* be true of the broader population; it is a reason to scrutinize research that claims a far, far lower rate of false accusations.

Another criticism: A 1994 study based on a review of data from 1978 to 1987 is antiquated. What was true of rape and rape allegations then is not necessarily true now, especially since the approach to rape has changed both legally and culturally. Nevertheless, more recent studies confirm Kanin's findings. In an article, "Memo to VP Biden: Male Rapists Are Not Lurking on Every Campus Corner," rape-culture skeptic Suzanne Venker explained [49], "three peer-reviewed studies [Kanin's plus two] have found the rate of false accusations of rape to range from 41 percent to 60 percent." Moreover, a mass of anecdotal evidence points to a substantial rate of false accusations. [50]

The low end of the false accusations rate is the 2 percent figure favored by rape culture adherents. The original source of the statistic is Susan Brownmiller's *Against Our Will: Men, Women and Rape*. She stated [51], "When New York City created a special Rape Analysis Squad commanded by police-women, the female police officers found that only 2 percent of all rape complaints were false– about the same false-report rate that is usual for other kinds of felonies." The 2 percent figure was ostensibly lifted from a talk delivered by Judge Lawrence H. Cooke before the Association of the Bar of the City of New York.

In his 2006 essay "False Allegations of Rape," the British researcher Philip N.S. Rumney commented [52] on an earlier 2000 article by Edward Greer which had been published in the *Loyola of Los Angeles Law Review*. Rumney wrote, "In a recently published article, Greer recounts his attempts at tracking down the origins of this statistic [Brownmiller's 2 percent] and concludes that there is no evidence that it was the product of any systematic research. Yet within the scholarly literature and elsewhere, repeated reference is made to 'research' or 'studies' in the context of the New York figure even though the original source for this figure cannot be identified." Greer listed various scholarly articles that referenced each other as a way to put authority behind the 2 percent figure but all seemed to ultimately rely upon the report from *Against Our Will*.

Rumney continued, "In developing legal policy, one might question the wisdom of relying upon a statistic that has never been published or subject to peer review, that is several decades old, and in the context of its use in this country [England], is derived from a foreign jurisdiction. Of course, there are a small number of studies that lend support to the 2 percent claim, though they are rarely cited."

A popular method by which rape culture proponents validate the 2 percent figure is by claiming the rate of false accusations for rape is the same as it is for other felonies. The FBI places that general rate at about 2 percent.

Rumney commented [53], "An integral part of the 2 percent figure is the claim that the false reporting rate for rape is no higher than for other offences. Yet rarely do scholars actually cite studies of false complaints for offences other than rape....In a direct comparison with rape complaints and those involving non-sexual assaults, Theilade and Thomsen found that the highest rate of false complaints was for non-sexual assault. By contrast, Gregory and Lees cite a no-crime rate for non-sexual assaults of 3 percent, while the no-criming [sic] rate for rape in their study was 45 percent. Chambers and Millar cite research suggesting a no-crime rate for general crime reports of between 1.6 percent and 6 percent."

The claim that the false reporting on rape is no higher than for other offences seems flawed. The oft-quoted FBI report, *Crime in the United States, 1996*, stated that 8 percent of rape accusations were unfounded or false, which is four times the rate for most other crimes. [54] Consider just three possible reasons for the higher rate of false or unfounded reports of rape.

First, property theft is rarely motivated by anger, revenge or other intimate emotions. They are for-profit crimes in the literal sense. But the crime of rape, like domestic violence, is intensely personal. Unlike reporting the theft of a car, an accusation of rape is extremely emotional and often involves someone the accuser knows. Even if the accused is a stranger, however, the rape remains painfully personal, and involves deep-seated attitudes toward the opposite sex, sexuality and self. Reports of rape are more likely to be confused or misused than reports of theft.

Second, rape accusations often require less tangible proof than property theft, which makes them easier to lodge.

A third reason? Few false accusers experience legal consequences. By contrast, an accuser who falsely files a murder report, perjuring himself to police and in court, is treated harshly by the law.

An article in *The Guardian,* "Rape investigations 'undermined by belief that false accusations are rife'," explained [55] that a "study released...by the Crown Prosecution Service (CPS) reveals that during the 17-month test period...there were 5,651 prosecutions for rape and 111,891 for domestic violence in England and Wales. By comparison, over the same timespan, there were only 35 prosecutions for making false allegations of rape, six for false allegations of domestic violence and three that involved false allegations of both rape and domestic violence."

A later *Guardian* article [56] indicated that the extremely low prosecution rate in the UK was actually higher than prosecutions in "the United States, Canada and Australia." The article observed, "Prof Lisa Avalos, of the University of Arkansas, said false allegations in the US were dealt with as a misdemeanour offence, not a felony – and most women were not jailed if found guilty....Prof Claire Ferguson, a forensic criminologist from the University of New England in New South Wales, Australia, said it was not the norm to prosecute women for false allegations and that only those in the most egregious cases were charged, often where the accused man had spent time in custody." A lack of legal consequences encourages false accusations.

But the key question remains. What is the most likely rate at which false accusations occur?

If pressed to estimate, I would place the lower boundary of false rape reports made to the police at about 8 to 10 percent, which is where some of the more careful studies with large samples converge. That makes the frequency of false reports 4 or 5 times what is claimed by rape culture adherents.

The rate is heavily influenced by institutional circumstances, however, and false accusations are much more likely at universities than in the criminal system. Universities apply extraordinarily broad definitions of rape as well as low standards by which to credit and adjudicate reports. They also have a political and financial bias toward believing the accuser. In *American Thinker*, Ben Cohen observed [57], "By demanding that colleges lower the standard of proof to 50.1 percent, they roll out the red carpet for false accusers. If an insurance company declared that they would no longer conduct arson investigations, they would go out of business within weeks."

By contrast, police departments have a stricter definition of rape, higher standards of evidence along with more neutral and professional investigations.

The Touchstone Moment of PC Feminist Research on Rape

No discussion of rape statistics is complete without an analysis, however brief, of the touchstone moment of PC feminist research into sexual assault: the Koss study, which was released in 1988 through the book *I Never Called It Rape: The Ms. Report on Recognizing, Fighting, and Surviving Date and Acquaintance Rape.* [58] Arguably, the study established the model for future feminist research as well as the quintessential zombie rape stat: 1-in-4 women will be raped.

(Note: The specific 1-in-5 stat for rape and sexual assault does not arise from the Koss study but from a 2007 online survey at two universities. The Campus Sexual Assault Study [59] returned high positives because of factors such as equating drunken sex with rape. Christopher Krebs, the lead researcher, cautioned against expanding the results beyond the two universities because "sexual assault is a phenomenon that is potentially unique at each university." Of course, the results were not only generalized across universities but also applied to the public at large. [60] Indeed, the White House used the figure in its recent declaration of war on sexual assault. [61]

Some rape culture warriors clearly realize the statistic is shaky. In a *Washington Examiner* article, Ashe Schow explained [62], "Sen. Kirsten Gillibrand, D-N.Y., one of the most prominent lawmakers working to curb campus sexual assault, has removed from her website the debunked claim that one in five women will be sexually assaulted while in college, according to *Politico*. Using the tracking website ChangeDetection.com, *Politico*'s Caitlin Emma found that a sentence claiming that incredibly high rate of sexual assault had been deleted from Gillibrand's website page about her bill, the Campus Accountability and Safety Act. The change was first detected by *Inside Higher Ed* reporter Michael Stratford.")

The history behind the statistic-establishing Koss study is fascinating and revealing. Barbara Kaye relayed some of it in a *National Post* article, "'Rape culture' fanatics don't know what a culture is'." [63] "In 1982, Mary Koss, then a professor of psychology at Kent State University in Ohio, published an article on rape in which she expressed the orthodox gender feminist view that 'rape represents an extreme behavior but *one that is on a continuum with normal male behavior within the culture'*." [Emphasis in the original.]

In her book *Who Stole Feminism?: How Women Have Betrayed Women* [64], the iconoclastic feminist Christina Hoff Sommers sketched the origins of the study. "Some well-placed feminist activists were impressed by her. As Koss tells it, she received a phone call out of the blue inviting her to lunch with Gloria Steinem. For Koss, the lunch was a turning point. *Ms.* magazine had decided to do a national rape survey on college campuses, and Koss was chosen to direct it. Koss's findings would become the most frequently cited research on women's victimization, not so much by established scholars in the field of rape research as by journalists, politicians, and activists."

The survey sampled thousands of female college students who were randomly selected from over thirty campuses nationwide. It consisted of ten basic questions with follow-ups to elicit details. The key questions were as follows:

> 4. Have you had a man attempt sexual intercourse (get on top of you, attempt to insert his penis) when you didn't want to by threatening or using some degree of force (twisting your arm, holding you down, etc.) but intercourse *did not* occur?

> 5. Have you had a man attempt sexual intercourse (get on top of you, attempt to insert his penis) when you didn't want to by giving you alcohol or drugs, but intercourse *did not* occur?

> 8. Have you had sexual intercourse when you didn't want to because a man gave you alcohol or drugs?

> 9. Have you had sexual intercourse when you didn't want to because a man threatened or used some degree of physical force (twisting your arm, holding you down, etc.) to make you?

> 10. Have you had sexual acts (anal or oral intercourse or penetration by objects other than the penis) when you didn't want

to because a man threatened or used some degree of physical force (twisting your arm, holding you down, etc.) to make you?

The definition of rape employed by Koss included penetration by penis, finger, or other objects while in the presence of physical force, alcohol, threats or other coercive forces. Affirmative responses to questions 4 and 5 were counted as attempted rape. Affirmative responses to any of the last three questions were counted as completed rape. The survey found that 15.4 percent of the women had been raped; 12.1 percent had experienced attempted rape. In other words, 27.5 percent were victims of rape or attempted rape. Thus, 1-in-4 women were deemed to be rape victims.

The Koss study has been so thoroughly discredited that a rebuttal would merely repeat the meticulous work of others. [65] Instead, consider just a few flaws that, in and of themselves, should cause Koss's findings to be dismissed.

The definition of rape used by Koss and her colleagues differed from the definition accepted by the study respondents themselves. The variance was so significant that 73 percent of the women whom Koss classified as rape victims did not agree with her description. That is, they did not believe they had been raped, with many of them blaming the experience on "miscommunication." 42 percent of alleged rape victims went on to have sex again with the man in question; 35 percent of attempted rape victims did so as well.

In this, the Koss survey expressed one of Reinharz's guidelines for feminist research. "9. *Feminist research frequently attempts to develop special relations with the people studied (in interactive research)."* This is the use of interviews in which the subject's response is not merely recorded but also analyzed and interpreted. Koss and her colleagues simply reinterpreted many of the women's statements to reach a conclusion of rape or attempted rape.

Another problem was the vagueness of key questions. For example, "Have you had sexual intercourse when you didn't want to because a man gave you alcohol or drugs?" Several critics asked, "What does it mean to have sex *because* a man gave you alcohol or drugs?" Was there coercion involved? Or did active consent occur due to lowered inhibitions? In response to such criticism, Koss subsequently added the following words to the question: "to *make* you cooperate." But this only highlights the problem with the original question and invalidates the original answers, which invalidates the famous stat. Moreover, the rewording seems to say that the alleged rape victim *did* cooperate rather than being forced. After all, if coercion or threats were present, then there was no cooperation, only compliance. The clarification clarifies nothing.

The Koss survey is so rife with methodological problems and bias that no one concerned with truth can credit it.

Conclusion

In *Against Our Will*, Brownmiller asked, "...does one need scientific methodology in order to conclude that the anti-female propaganda that permeates our nation's cultural output promotes a climate in which acts of sexual hostility directed against women are not only tolerated but ideologically encouraged?" [66]

The answer is a resounding *yes!* Scientific methodology is required to test any empirical claim that wants to assume the status of truth. Without such methodology, research becomes mere opinion. Or worse. It becomes a barrier to genuine studies conducted by those who wish to reach conclusions based on evidence.

Notes

[1] Sarah Ditum, "Feminism's zombie stats: 63 percent of young women would rather be glamour models," *Paperhouse*, April 23, 2012. http://sarahditum.com/2012/04/23/feminisms-zombie-stats-63-of-young-women-would-rather-be-glamour-models/ Retrieved Sept. 27, 2015.

[2] Emily Thomas, "Rape Is Grossly Underreported In The U.S., Study Finds," *Huffington Post*, Nov. 21, 2013. http://www.huffingtonpost.com/2013/11/21/rape-study-report-america-us_n_4310765.html Retrieved Sept. 27, 2015.

[3] The National Research Council report, "Panel on Measuring Rape and Sexual Assault in Bureau of Justice Statistics Household Surveys" was published in 2014. http://www.nap.edu/openbook.php?record_id=18605 Retrieved Sept. 27, 2015. An online synopsis is available http://www.ncbi.nlm.nih.gov/books/NBK202268/?report=classic#sec_00101 Retrieved Sept. 27, 2015.

[4] Sexual Assault Statistics in Canada. http://www.sexassault.ca/statistics.htm Retrieved Sept. 27, 2015.

[5] American Rape, Abuse & Incest National Network, "Reporting Rates." Note: the rate of unreported male rape is rarely if ever discussed.

https://rainn.org/get-information/statistics/reporting-rates Retrieved Sept. 27, 2015.

[6] Dylan Love, "'Men's Rights' Activists Spam A College's Rape Reporting System With False Accusations," *Business Insider*, Dec. 18, 2013. http://www.businessinsider.com/mens-rights-activists-make-false-rape-reports-at-occidental-2013-12 Retrieved Sept. 27, 2015.

[7] Glenn Harlan Reynolds, "The great campus rape hoax," *USA Today*, Dec. 15, 2014. http://www.usatoday.com/story/opinion/2014/12/14/campus-rape-uva-crisis-rolling-stone-politics-column/20397277/ Retrieved Sept. 27, 2015.

[8] Camille Paglia, *Vamps & Tramps: New Essays*, (New York: Vintage, 1994), p.24. http://www.amazon.ca/Vamps-Tramps-Essays-Camille-Paglia/dp/0679751203 Retrieved Sept. 27, 2015.

[9] Sandra Harding, *The Science Question in Feminism,* (Ithaca, N.Y.: Cornell University Press; Reprint edition, 1986), p.250. http://www.cornellpress.cornell.edu/book/?GCOI=80140100841900 Retrieved Sept. 27, 2015.

[10] Ibid.

[11] Shulamit Reinharz, *Feminist Methods in Social Research,* (Oxford University Press, 1992). http://www.amazon.ca/Feminist-Methods-Research-Shulamit-Reinharz/dp/019507386X Retrieved Sept. 27, 2015.

[12] University of Strathclyde, "Defining feminist research: Reinharz," http://www.strath.ac.uk/aer/materials/6furtherqualitativeresearchdesigna ndanalysis/unit4/definingfeministresearchreinharz/ Unable to retrieve website Sept. 27, 2015. For a counter perspective, Susan Haack's *Manifesto of a Passionate Moderate: Unfashionable Essay*, provides a highly critical view of whether there is a specifically female perspective on logic and scientific truth. She argues that many such feminist critiques are overly concerned with political correctness. http://press.uchicago.edu/ucp/books/book/chicago/M/bo3614193.html Retrieved Sept. 27, 2015.

[13] Martyn Hammersley, (1992) 'On Feminist Methodology', *Sociology*, vol. 26, no. 2, pp. 187 – 206, as quoted in D. Millen (1997) "Some Methodological and Epistemological Issues Raised by Doing Feminist Research on Non-Feminist Women," *Sociological Research Online*, vol. 2, no. 3. http://www.socresonline.org.uk/2/3/3.html Retrieved Sept. 27, 2015.

[14] "Feminist Research Methods," Feminist Perspectives on Media and Technology, University of York. http://www.yorku.ca/mlc/sosc3990A/projects/femresearch/femresearch.ht ml Retrieved Sept. 27, 2015.

[15] Sue Curry Jansen, *Critical Communication Theory: Power, Media, Gender, and Technology*, (Washington, D.C.: Rowman & Littlefield, 2002) p.30.

[16] Audrey M. Dentith "Feminist Research," *Encyclopedia of Activism and Social Justice,* Gary L. Anderson and Kathryn G. Herr, eds, (SAGE, 2007) p.561.

[17] Patricia Leavy, *Essentials of Transdisciplinary Research: Using Problem-Centered Methodologies*, (Left Coast Press, 2011), p.9. http://www.amazon.ca/gp/search? index=books&linkCode=qs&keywords=9781598745931 Retrieved Sept. 27, 2015.

[18] Pamela Moss (Editor), *Feminist Geography in Practice: Research and Methods,* (Hoboken, N.J.: Wiley-Blackwell, 2002). http://ca.wiley.com/WileyCDA/WileyTitle/productCd-0631220194.html Retrieved Sept. 27, 2015.

[19] Sarah Madison & Frances Shaw, *Handbook of Feminist Research: Theory and Praxis*, Sharlene Nagy Hesse-Biber, ed, "Feminist Perspectives on Social Movement Research," (SAGE, 2012), p.416. http://www.amazon.ca/Handbook-Feminist-Research-Theory-Praxis/dp/1412980593 Retrieved Sept. 27, 2015.

[20] Ivana Milojević, "Feminism, Futures Studies And The Futures of Feminist Research," Metafuture. http://www.metafuture.org/articlesbycolleagues/IvanaMilojevic/FeministF utures.htm Retrieved Sept. 27, 2015.

[21] Nancy Felipe Russo PhD, Hope Landrine PhD (eds) *Handbook of Diversity in Feminist Psychology*, (New York: Springer, 2009), p.xxi. https://books.google.ca/books? id=9lLcCxRe4WQC&dq=Feminist+research+diversity.&source=gbs_navli nks_s Retrieved Sept. 27, 2015.

[22] Rebecca Campbell, *Emotionally Involved: The Impact of Researching Rape,* (London: Routledge, 2001), p.39. http://www.amazon.ca/Emotionally-Involved-Impact-Researching-Rape/dp/0415925940 Retrieved Sept. 27, 2015.

[23] L. Kelly and S. Burton, "Researching Women's Lives or Studying Women's Oppression? Reflections on what Constitutes Feminist Research," *Researching Women's Lives from a Feminist Perspective,* Mary Mayard and June Purvis, eds. (Taylor & Francis, 1994), p.37.

[24] Lennart Svensson, Per-Erik Ellstrom, and Goran Brulin (eds), *International Journal of Action Research* (2007, volume 3, issue 3), p.233. http://www.hampp-verlag.de/hampp_e-journals_IJAR.htm#307 Retrieved Sept. 27, 2015.

[25] Sharlene Nagy Hesse-Biber, ed. *Feminist research practice: a primer.* (Thousand Oaks, California: Sage, second edition, 2014) pp.21-22. There is confusion as to the publication date. 2014 refers to the copyright date on the edition. Checked Sept. 27, 2015.

[26] Always review the size and location of the sample, as well as the method by which participants were selected. Darrell Huff, author of *How to Lie with Statistics* reported an experiment in which a coin was tossed into the air ten times. Eight times it landed heads up; two times it landed heads down. From this he concluded that a tossed coin landed heads up 80 percent of the time. The issue Huff was highlighting is that the results of limited research can indicate little more than the laws of probability. This is true even if the researcher does not bias the results in any manner. A good study on attitudes or behavior that wishes to generalize should include random participants from a reasonably sized sample of the target population. https://archive.org/details/HowToLieWithStatistics Retrieved Sept. 27, 2015.

[27] Christopher Krebs and Christine Lindquist, "Setting the Record Straight on '1 in 5'," *Time,* Dec. 15, 2014. The article offers a prime example of research, the Campus Sexual Assault Study, that proceeds directly from a false assumption. http://time.com/3633903/campus-rape-1-in-5-sexual-assault-setting-record-straight/ Retrieved Sept. 27, 2015.

[28] Justin Peters, "When Ice Cream Sales Rise, So Do Homicides. Coincidence, or Will Your Next Cone Murder You?" *Slate,* July 9, 2013. http://www.slate.com/blogs/crime/2013/07/09/warm_weather_homicide _rates_when_ice_cream_sales_rise_homicides_rise_coincidence.html Retrieved Sept. 27, 2015.

[29] Joanne Nova, "Lewandowsky peer reviewed study includes someone 32,757 years old," JoNova, Jan. 11, 2015. http://joannenova.com.au/2015/01/lewandowsky-peer-reviewed-study-includes-someone-32757-years-old/#more-40327 Retrieved Sept. 27, 2015.

[30] Will Oremus, "This Is What Happens When No One Proofreads an Academic Paper," *Slate*, Nov. 11, 2014.
http://www.slate.com/blogs/future_tense/2014/11/11/_crappy_gabor_pa
per_overly_honest_citation_slips_into_peer_reviewed_journal.html
Retrieved Sept. 27, 2015.

[31] Another method of cherry picking is to select participants who are likely to provide the desired results while ignoring those who are unlikely. The researcher chooses participants from a group exhibiting the behaviors or attitudes that are consistent with the conclusions she wishes to reach. An example is to survey only religious people on abortion in order to demonstrate how women's reproductive rights are in dire jeopardy.

[32] Helen M. Walker's *Elementary Statistical Methods,* (H. Holt, 1943) is also excellent. http://www.amazon.com/Elementary-Statistical-Methods-Helen-Walker/dp/B001M29N3U Retrieved Sept. 27, 2015.

[33] George Orwell, *Nineteen Eighty-four.*
https://ebooks.adelaide.edu.au/o/orwell/george/o79n/chapter1.3.html
Retrieved Sept. 27, 2015.

[34] Sarah R. Edwards, Kathryn A. Bradshaw, and Verlin B.Hinsz, *Violence and Gender.* "Denying Rape but Endorsing Forceful Intercourse: Exploring Differences Among Responders," December 2014, 1(4): 188-193.
http://online.liebertpub.com/doi/abs/10.1089/vio.2014.0022?
journalCode=vio Retrieved Sept. 27, 2015.

[35] Unfortunately, the study is not reliably accessible. As of September 24, 2015, it cost $51 for 24 hour access. As of September 27, the report had reappeared online for free. Correction to original study appears here:
http://online.liebertpub.com/doi/abs/10.1089/vio.2014.0022.cxn
Retrieved Sept. 27, 2015.

[36] Gabriella Morrongiello, "Study: Some men have a distorted understanding of rape," *Campus Reform*, Jan. 13, 2015.
http://www.campusreform.org/?ID=6196 Retrieved Sept. 27, 2015.

[37] Mark J. Perry, "No polling organization would ever be taken seriously if its sample size was 73, and neither should this 'study' on college rape," American Enterprise Institute, Jan. 14, 2015.
https://www.aei.org/publication/polling-organization-ever-taken-seriously-sample-size-73-neither-study-college-rape/print/ Retrieved Sept. 27, 2015.

[38] Ashe Schow, "No, 1 in 5 women have not been raped on college campuses," *Washington Examiner*, Aug. 13, 2014.

http://www.washingtonexaminer.com/no-1-in-5-women-have-not-been-raped-on-college-campuses/article/2551980 Retrieved Sept. 27, 2015.

[39] Op.cit., "Denying Rape." It seems likely that this α refers to Cronbach's alpha, which is an "estimate of the reliability of a psychometric test." https://en.wikipedia.org/wiki/Cronbach%27s_alpha This is not "reliability" in the common sense. It says nothing about whether the test, or its results, are accurate, valid, dependable, or meaningful. Rather, it is a measure of the internal consistency of the test questions. https://en.wikipedia.org/wiki/Reliability_(psychometrics) Both retrieved Sept. 29, 2015.

[40] Ashe Schow, "No, we did not just learn 1 in 3 college men would rape if they could get away with it," *Washington Examiner*, Jan. 13, 2015. http://www.washingtonexaminer.com/no-we-did-not-just-learn-1-in-3-college-men-would-rape-if-they-could-get-away-with-it/article/2558579 Retrieved Sept. 27, 2015.

[41] Christina Hoff Sommers, "Researching the 'Rape Culture' of America. An Investigation of Feminist Claims about Rape," *The Real Issue Reprint*, 1995. *http://www.d.umn.edu/cla/faculty/jhamlin/3925/Readings/RapeCultureSummers.pdf* Retrieved Sept. 27, 2015.

[42] Katherine Timpf, "'1 in 3 College Men Would Rape a Woman' Stat is Based on a Survey of 73 Dudes," *National Review*, Jan. 12, 2015. http://www.nationalreview.com/article/396233/1-3-college-men-would-rape-woman-stat-based-survey-73-dudes-katherine-timpf Retrieved Sept. 27, 2015.

[43] Margo Maine, *Body Wars: Making Peace With Women's Bodies*, (Gürze, 2000). http://www.amazon.com/Body-Wars-Margo-Maine-Ph-D/dp/0936077344 Retrieved Sept. 27, 2015.

[44] As quoted by Brian Hutchinson, "Is there an epidemic of 'rape culture' at Canadian universities?" *National Post*, March 7, 2014. http://news.nationalpost.com/news/is-there-an-epidemic-of-rape-culture-at-canadian-universities Retrieved Sept. 27, 2015.

[45] Ibid.

[46] Philip N.S. Rumney, *Cambridge Law Journal* 65 (1): 128–158, "False Allegations of Rape," (2006). http://journals.cambridge.org/production/action/cjoGetFulltext? fulltextid=430300 Rerieved Sept. 27, 2015.

[47] Ibid, p.130. The referenced study is L. Kelly et al., "A gap or a chasm? Attrition in Reported Rape Cases," Home Office Research Study 293 (London 2005), 46–47. http://webarchive.nationalarchives.gov.uk/20110218135832/rds.homeoffi ce.gov.uk/rds/pdfs05/hors293.pdf Retrieved Sept. 27, 2015.

[48] Eugene J. Kanin, "False Rape Allegations," 1994, False Rape Archives. http://falserapearchives.blogspot.ca/2009/06/archives-of-sexual-behavior-feb-1994.html Retrieved Sept. 27, 2015.

[49] Suzanne Venker, "Memo to VP Biden: Male Rapists Are Not Lurking on Every Campus Corner," *Women for Men*, Jan. 27, 2014. http://womenformen.org/2014/01/27/an-open-letter-to-joe-biden/ Retrieved Sept. 27, 2015.

[50] Avid news readers encounter accounts of false accusations on a daily basis. This is a typical example: "Police: False Criminal Reports Must Stop," *WESH*, Jun 22, 2010. http://www.wesh.com/Police-False-Criminal-Reports-Must-Stop/13150934?_escaped_fragment_=bazOQ0#!bazOQ0 Retrieved Sept. 27, 2015.

[51] Cited by Brownmiller, "Remarks of Lawrence H. Cooke, Appellate Division Justice, Before the Association of the Bar of the City of New York," 16 January 1974 (mimeo) p. 6, *Against Our Will: Men, Women and Rape* (Harmondsworth 1975). For background, please see Edward Greer, *The Truth behind Legal Dominance Feminism's Two Percent False Rape Claim Figure,* (2000) 33 Loyola of Los Angeles Law Review 947, 949, 954–8. http://digitalcommons.lmu.edu/cgi/viewcontent.cgi? article=2216&context=llr Retrieved Sept. 27, 2015.

[52] Op.cit., Rumney, p.143.

[53] Op.cit., Rumney, p.143, p.146.

[54] *Crime in the United States 1996: Uniform Crime Statistics. Section II: Crime Index Offenses Reported,* FBI, 1997. http://www.fbi.gov/about-us/cjis/ucr/crime-in-the-u.s/1996/96sec2.pdf Retrieved Sept. 27, 2015.

[55] Owen Bowcott, "Rape investigations 'undermined by belief that false accusations are rife'," *The Guardian*, March 13, 2013. http://www.theguardian.com/society/2013/mar/13/rape-investigations-belief-false-accusations Retrieved Sept. 27, 2015.

[56] Sandra Laville, "109 women prosecuted for false rape claims in five years, say campaigners," *The Guardian,* Dec. 1, 2014.

http://www.theguardian.com/law/2014/dec/01/109-women-prosecuted-false-rape-allegations Retrieved Sept. 27, 2015.

[57] Ben Cohen, "Amanda Marcotte: The face of rape hysteria," *American Thinker,* Dec. 21, 2014.
http://www.americanthinker.com/blog/2014/12/amanda_marcotte_the_fa ce_of_rape_hysteria.html Retrieved Sept. 27, 2015.

[58] Robin Warshaw, *I Never Called It Rape: The Ms. Report on Recognizing, Fighting, and Surviving Date and Acquaintance Rape,* (New York: Harper & Row, 1988). https://en.wikipedia.org/wiki/I_Never_Called_It_Rape Retrieved Sept. 27, 2015.

[59] Christopher Krebs, Christine H. Lindquist, Tara D. Warner, Bonnie S. Fisher, and Sandra L. Martin, National Criminal Justice Reference Service, *The Campus Sexual Assault Study*, 2007.
https://www.ncjrs.gov/pdffiles1/nij/grants/221153.pdf Retrieved Sept. 27, 2015.

[60] Libby Nelson, "'1 in 5': how a study of 2 colleges became the most cited campus sexual assault statistic," *Vox,* April 27, 2015.
http://www.vox.com/2014/12/11/7377055/campus-sexual-assault-statistics Retrieved Sept. 27, 2015.

[61] Charlotte Hays, "More on the White House's Bogus Rape Statistic," The Independent Women's Forum, May 1, 2014.
http://www.iwf.org/blog/2793850/More-on-the-White-House percent27s-Bogus-Rape-Statistic Retrieved Sept. 27, 2015.

[62] Ashe Schow, "Sen. Kirsten Gillibrand removes debunked sexual assault statistic from website," *Washington Examiner*, Dec. 22, 2014.
http://www.washingtonexaminer.com/sen.-kirsten-gillibrand-removes-debunked-sexual-assault-statistic-from-website/article/2557717 Retrieved Sept. 27, 2015.

[63] Barbara Kaye, "'Rape culture' fanatics don't know what a culture is'," *National Post,* March 8, 2014.
http://www.nationalpost.com/m/wp/blog.html?
b=news.nationalpost.com/2014/03/08/barbara-kay-rape-culture-fanatics-dont-know-what-a-culture-is Retrieved Sept. 27, 2015.

[64] Christina Hoff Sommers, *Who Stole Feminism? How Women Have Betrayed Women* (New York: Simon & Schuster, 1994).
http://www.amazon.ca/Who-Stole-Feminism-Women-Betrayed/dp/0684801566 Retrieved Sept. 27, 2015.

[65] Op.cit., Sommers, (Chapter 10) as cited by False Rape Net, Researching the "Rape Culture" of America."
http://www.falserape.net/rape_culture.html Retrieved Sept. 27, 2015.

[66] Brownmiller, op.cit, p.395.

Chapter Five: Comparison of the Key Surveys Regarding Rape

One thing that can help [the problem with misleading results] – though it's by no means a catch-all solution – is to let people who don't know the answer say so. A surprising amount of surveys...force people to choose between 'agree' or 'disagree'. And that means that people who genuinely don't know (or don't care) have to misrepresent their opinions. Then again, 'Majority of Americans noncommittal about DNA' doesn't make such a catchy headline, does it? –anonymous [1]

(Note: Much of this chapter is dry exposition and analysis of surveys with scant attempt to editorialize. Indeed, so much editorializing has occurred in other venues that a straight-forward presentation of their contents seems most appropriate. The word "study" and "survey" are used interchangeably.

I am deeply indebted to a statistician colleague who co-authored this chapter but wishes to remain anonymous due to the controversial nature of the book.)

Why Do Rape Statistics Vary So Widely?
Introduction

The National Crime Victimization Survey (NCVS), which the Department of Justice (DOJ) conducts by telephone, has been called the gold standard of statistics on rape. Released in October 2012, the NCVS found that there had been 243,800 rapes or sexual assaults in the preceding year (2011). This was a decline. In Table 1 of "Criminal Victimization, 2011," the DOJ reported on former NCVS data. [2] The survey cited the number of rapes or sexual assaults in 2002 as 349,810 and in 2010 as 258,570. (p.2). The rate declined by 30 percent between 2002-2011, and declined by 9 percent between 2010-2011. This would seem to be good news but the survey came under heavy criticism. Why?

Also focusing on the 2011 rate of rape, the Centers for Disease Control (CDC) issued a report that suggested "the NCVS is failing to capture a large portion of victims– as much as 88 percent." The CDC concluded "almost one in five women (and 1.7 percent of men) have been raped in their lifetimes." [3]

The *New Republic* offered plausible reasons [4] for the jarring discrepancy in statistics. For example, the questions differed. "The NCVS's questions required the victims to identify the crime as a rape or sexual assault, asking questions like 'How were you attacked?' and providing answers like 'raped', 'tried to rape' and 'sexual assault other than rape and attempted rape'." By contrast, the CDC avoided legal terms and asked "questions like, 'How many people have ever used physical force or threats to physically harm you to make you have vaginal sex?'" Victims who did not believe a sexual encounter was rape may have been willing to describe it in terms of "physical force."

A second reason was a difference in the definitions of sexual assault. Significantly, the CDC considered females who had sex while under the influence to be victims of sexual assault because they were considered incapable of rendering consent. The NCVS made no such assumption.

The foregoing merely foreshadows the discrepancies between two key surveys from which rape stats are drawn. The rape data offered by standard reports have come to resemble chaos. Some confusion comes from honest incompatibilities between studies, such as a difference in the reporting period or in the age range of participants. Other problems are less pardonable. For example, the methodology of many surveys is so poor that their results should be discarded. (Chapter Four dwells upon the research habits and tactics that produce useless data...or worse.)

Yet other factors hinder the search for credible numbers. For example, political advocates and the media routinely misstate the basic findings of straight-forward reports. The previously mentioned *New Republic* article stated the NCVS findings for 2011 as **243,800** rapes or sexual assaults. An article in *Time*, which linked to the *New Republic* piece, declared, "While the CDC estimates that nearly 2 million adult American women were raped in 2011 and nearly 6.7 million suffered some other form of sexual violence, the NCVS estimate for that year was **238,000** rapes and sexual assaults." [5] The difference is not great but it is disconcerting to see *any* variation in the reporting of fundamental findings from a single source.

This chapter explores the four most cited surveys in close detail. The chapter does not endorse any one report as *the* truth about the rate of rape or sexual assault. The four sources are:

- **NCVS:** The National Crime Victimization Survey, published by the Bureau of Justice Statistics in December 2014. [6]

- **NISVS:** The National Intimate Partner and Sexual Violence Survey, published by the Centers for Disease Control in 2011. [7]

- **CSAS:** The Campus Sexual Assault Study, published by the National Institute of Justice in December 2007. [8]

- **UCR:** The FBI Uniform Crime Reporting Program, 2013 data. [9] The UCR is not a survey, but rather an administrative compilation of crime reports.

The statistics are all over the map but the four preceding sources are the most significant ones and the most frequently consulted. Nevertheless, this chapter compares three additional surveys in a passing manner:

- **SVCW:** "Sexual Victimization of College Women," a research report published by the National Institute of Justice in December 2000. [10]

- **NVAWS:** "Prevalence, Incidence, and Consequences of Violence Against Women: Findings of the National Violence Against Women Survey," published by the National Institute of Justice in November 1998. [11]

- **DOE:** Jeanne Clery Disclosure of Campus Security Policy and Campus Crime Statistics Act and the Higher Education Opportunity Act, 2013 data. [12]

Unfortunately, much of the data cannot be directly compared. For example, some studies report *incidence* (how many assaults occurred); others report *prevalence* (how many women were assaulted). [13] Some render a one-year account while others gather lifetime totals or examine varied periods. There are surveys that include women of all ages, while others address only women of college age or they focus exclusively upon students. Some require an assault to be reported to an authority before counting it while others use self-reporting surveys. Many researchers randomize their sample population but some use self-selected samples. To add more confusion, completed and attempted assaults are often grouped into one statistic. And, as mentioned earlier, definitions differ widely.

But, with wide room for approximation, data comparison can be attempted. **Table 1** is a summary chart of the rates of rape and sexual assault, both attempted and completed, of women on college campuses. These numbers are rates per thousand women per year. Numbers are prevalence (number of women affected), except for the DOE (Clery Act) ones which are incidence (number of reports). Boxes shaded in gray indicate data that is not available.

The table demonstrates how various studies classify and lump together different types of sexual violence. For example, the NCVS separates forcible rapes from sexual assault other than rape, but it does not include incapacitated rape (sex while unable to consent due to alcohol or drugs). The DOE provides a combined total for forcible rapes, sexual assault and incapacitated rapes.

Table 1. Rate of Campus Rape and Sexual Assault

per thousand women, per year

Study	attempted sexual assault	attempted rape	forcible rape	incapacitated rape	sexual assault other than rape	sexual coercion [1]
DOE, 2013			0.52 [2]			
NCVS, 2014		1.5	2.0		2.6 [3]	?[3]
UCR, 2013		12 est. [4]				
NISVS, 2011		18 est. [5]		30 est. [5]	105 est. [6]	60 est. [6]
CSAS, 2007 [7]	31		8.5	21	10	
SVCW, 2000	49.9 [8]	11.0	16.6		37.1 [9]	16.6
NVAWS, 1998		9 est. [10]				

Table 1 Notes:

1. Sexual coercion is generally defined as non-physical punishment, promise of reward or verbal pressure.

2. Based on 6,069 incidents in the year 2013, over a female student population of 11,612,000.

3. NCVS counts "coerced" sex as rape but does not define coercion. This chart includes "threat of rape or sexual assault" with sexual assault.

4. Estimate is based on 0.8 per thousand reported for all ages, and assumes (per NCVS) that only 20% of rapes/attempted rapes of college students are reported to police. It also assumes the rate for the "college" age group is roughly 3x that for all ages. (See Note 11 below)

5. Estimate is based on reported 16 per thousand of all rapes/attempted rapes, of which 10 per thousand are alcohol- or

drug-facilitated. It assumes the rate for the "college" age group is roughly 3x that for all ages. (See Note 11 below).

6. Estimate is based on reported 55 per thousand of all assaults, of which 20 per thousand are sexual coercion. It assumes the rate for the "college" age group is roughly 3x that for all ages. (See Note 11 below)

7. CSAS four-year figures, divided by four. Categories overlap so the totals cannot be calculated by summing the columns. One-year rate for all sexual assault is 49 per thousand.

8. Sum of prevalence figures for "attempted sexual contact" with force and without force; this almost certainly overstates the total prevalence due to victims responding in both categories. It does not include "attempted sexual coercion" at 13.5 per thousand.

9. Sum of prevalence figures for "completed sexual contact" with force and without force; this almost certainly overstates the total prevalence due to multiple responses.

10. Estimate is based on reported 3 per thousand rapes/attempted rapes the previous year, all ages. It assumes the rate for the "college" age group is roughly 3x that for all ages. (See Note 11 below).

11. The NISVS reports 38.3% of rapes are *first* experienced at ages 18-24; for ease of calculation, this can be rounded upward to 40%. As a reasonable approximation, multiple rapes are ignored and it is assumed that 40% of rapes happen to women at ages 18-24. Per the 2010 Census, the college-age population is 10% of the total. If 40% of rapes happen to 10% of women, then the per-capita rate of rape for those women is 4 times the per-capita rate for all ages.

The NVAWS reports that 29.4% of rapes are first experienced at ages 18-24. If we round this up to 30 percent, the per-capita rate for college-age women can be calculated at 3 times the per-capita rate for all women.

The NCVS reports, "In 2013, college-age females had a similar rate of rape and sexual assault regardless of enrollment status (about 4.3 victimizations per 1,000), while the victimization rate for not college-age (ages 12 to 17 and 25 or older) females was 1.4 victimizations per 1,000." The per-capita rate for college-age women can be calculated at 2.5 times the per-capita rate for all women. [14]

The discrepancy could be due to multiple rapes (e.g. women raped at 18-24 also being raped after age 24), or due to methodological differences in the surveys. As a reasonable "middle ground," the chapter assumes the reported data indicates that the college-age rate is three times the all-age rate.

What lessons can be drawn from the preceding data?

One lesson: The truth is in there. But where? In 2011, the National Research Council asked much the same question when it convened a panel of experts to review the methodology of the NCVS survey. In their report, the panel compared the NCVS to older surveys [15], (pp.3-4),

> The panel found that a comparison across these sources of estimates of rape was particularly problematic because of the differences in the populations targeted, the definitions used, the data collection methodology, and the survey timing. The panel determined that it could not scientifically conclude which source was overall better, and it does not recommend any source as the best or as a standard. However, in reviewing all of this material, the panel judges that it is likely that the NCVS is under-counting rape and sexual assault victimization...

> It is important to note that the panel did not perform the same in-depth examination of the error structure of the other surveys for measuring rape and sexual assault because of limitations of time and resources. Presenting findings focused on the NCVS does not imply that the panel believes that the other surveys have fewer errors: the panel did not examine them carefully and so cannot draw overall conclusions about their error structures.

There is no statistically meaningful way to average such disparate reports. Only inferences can be drawn. Assuming from the CSAS that there are 2.5 incapacitated rapes for every 1 forcible rape on campus, then the NCVS would seem to overlook 5 incapacitated rapes per thousand women per year. The discrepancy is massive.

Perhaps the most informative approach to the differing surveys is to view them as a way to set an upper and lower bound on the real numbers. If so, it is safe to conclude that the rate of forcible rape on campus is more than 2.0 per thousand women per year (NCVS), and less than 16.6 per thousand per year (SVCW). But the surveys offer more information than merely setting a range.

To decide how much weight to give the data from each survey, however, it is necessary to compare their methodology and definitions. Start with the most basic question: How are rape and sexual assault defined?

How are Rape and Sexual Assault Defined?

Compilations of data use different definitions for rape and sexual assault. As mentioned earlier, the NCVS does not consider sex while incapacitated by alcohol or drugs to be rape. The FBI's UCR has only counted such sexual acts as rape since 2013 when its definition was updated.

Table 2 below presents a summary of acts that may or may not be considered rape or sexual assault. It indicates how they are classified by the NCVS, NISVS, CSAS, UCR, SVCW and NVAWS – or, at least, they are categorized based upon a reasonable reading of the varying definitions. The authors, researchers, survey subjects and law enforcement officers may classify borderline cases differently. For example, no survey defines "regret the next morning" as rape. But if it were reported as non-consensual, then it could be counted as rape. These studies are unable to provide such distinctions.

A more subtle difference was noted by the National Research Council [16]:

> There are two quite different perspectives for the measurement of rape and sexual assault– the criminal justice perspective and the public health perspective. These different perspectives have led to methodological differences in designing and implementing surveys, which, in turn, have resulted in different estimates of the incidence rates. The NCVS reflects the criminal justice perspective, and its purpose is to measure criminal victimizations: "point-in-time" events that are judged to be criminal. In contrast, surveys that reflect the public health perspective look at victimization as a condition that endures over a period of time, and may not necessarily be criminal.

To distinguish between rape and sexual assault, Table 2 follows the updated FBI definition, which may be the simplest and least ambiguous of the various definitions of rape: "penetration, no matter how slight, of the vagina or anus with any body part or object, or oral penetration by a sex organ of another person, without the consent of the victim." All other unwanted sexual contact is classified here as "sexual assault."

Table 2. Definitions of Rape and Sexual Assault

	NCVS	NISVS	CSAS	UCR	SVCW	NVAWS
RAPE (penetration by penis, other body part, or object)						
1. Threat of death or injury (lethal threat)	X	X	X	X	X	X
2. Threat to another (e.g. child)	?		X	X	X	X
3. Physically overpowered (e.g. pinned down)	X	X	X	X	X	X
4. Unconscious or incapacitated		X	X	Note 1		
5. Involuntarily drugged (e.g. with "date rape" drugs)		X	X	Note 1		
6. Inebriated (voluntarily drunk, conscious)		X	X			
7. Threat to reputation (e.g. blackmail)	X	X	?	?	Note 5	
8. Threat of demotion (e.g. workplace harassment)		X			Note 5	
9. Emotionally/socially pressured into having sex	?	X			Note 5	
10. Telling lies or false promises ("rape by deception")		X				
Failure to stop when requested during sex						
Failure to use a condom when requested						
Regret the next morning						
Regret six months later						
Re-evaluation after counseling						
ATTEMPTED RAPE						
As 1-9 above, but uncompleted (no penetration)	Note 2	Note 3		X	Note 3	Note 3

	NCVS	NISVS	CSAS	UCR	SVCW	NVAWS
SEXUAL ASSAULT incl. "unwanted sexual contact"						
Groping of breasts or genitals (without penetration)	X	X	X		X	
Forced removal of clothing	?	X	X		?	
Forced kissing	?	X	X		X	
Grabbing, fondling, "rubbing up against you in a sexual way"	X	X	Note 4		X	
Incidental contact with breasts or genitals						
"Flashed"		X				
Forced to view sexually explicit media		X				
Sexually suggestive remarks		X				
Insulting remarks about appearance						
Telling sexual stories/jokes						
Leering or ogling						

Table 2 Notes:

A question mark "?" indicates that it is not clear whether the act is deemed to be rape or sexual assault.

1. Included in FBI statistics since their 2013 redefinition of rape.

2. Attempted rape includes verbal threats of rape.

3. Attempted rape is counted only for force or threats of harm (rows 1-3 above).

4. Yes, if by physical force or when incapacitated or drunk.

5. Counted as sexual coercion by the SVCW.

The NCVS has the narrowest definition of rape, followed by the UCR, and then the CSAS. The NISVS has the most expansive definition of rape by far; for example, it is the only survey that counts "rape by deception," which means you have sex with someone because he or she lies to you. It is no surprise that, in Table 1, the NCVS reports the lowest rate of rape, followed by the UCR and CSAS; the NISVS reports the highest.

The NISVS also has the broadest definition of sexual assault, which includes sexually suggestive remarks and being forced to view sexually explicit media. (Note: The UCR does not count sexual assaults, only rapes.) Again, these definitions are subject to interpretation by the victim. For example, one victim may regard a dirty joke as a "sexually suggestive remark" but another may not.

The following sections offer an in-depth look at these four touchstone sources of rape statistics.

National Crime Victimization Survey, Bureau of Justice Statistics (NCVS, December 2014)

In December 2014, the BJS issued a Special Report based on NCVS data, which was entitled "Rape and Sexual Assault Victimization Among College-Age Females, 1995–2013 " [17]. (Unless otherwise noted, the page numbers below refer to this report.) The BJS findings caused a sensation because its reported rate of rape and sexual assault among college students was 6.1 per thousand per year, a factor of ten lower than some headlines.

Methodology

According to the report:

> The National Crime Victimization Survey (NCVS) is an annual data collection conducted by the U.S. Census Bureau for the Bureau of Justice Statistics (BJS). The NCVS is a self-report survey in which interviewed persons are asked about the number and characteristics of victimizations experienced during the prior 6 months. The NCVS collects information on nonfatal personal crimes (rape or sexual assault, robbery, aggravated and simple assault, and personal larceny) and household property crimes (burglary, motor vehicle theft, and other theft) both reported and not reported to police... (p.11)

> All first interviews are conducted in person with subsequent interviews conducted either in person or by phone. New households rotate into the sample on an ongoing basis to replace outgoing households that have been in the sample for the 3-year period... (p.11)

> In 2013, 90,630 households and 160,040 persons age 12 or older were interviewed for the NCVS. Each household was interviewed twice during the year. The response rate was 84% for households and 88% for eligible persons. (p.12)

Because the NCVS is a household survey and not based on police reports, it offers a glimpse into "dark" numbers such as how many sexual assaults are *not* reported to police. Because it is conducted annually with a consistent methodology, it also captures trends. Another advantage of the NCVS: As a randomized survey, it is less prone to selection bias. But because it surveys *all* crimes, and not just sexual assaults, the amount of detail on sexual crimes is limited.

Definitions

The NCVS collects information for two sexual crimes – "rape" and "sexual assault." These are defined as follows:

> Rape is the unlawful penetration of a person against her or his will by the use or threat of force, as well as the attempt to commit such an act. Rape includes psychological coercion and physical force. Forced sexual intercourse means vaginal, anal, or oral penetration by the offender. Rape also includes incidents where penetration involves a foreign object such as a bottle. Attempted rape includes verbal threats of rape.

> Sexual assault is defined to include a wide range of acts that are separate from rape or attempted rape. They include attacks or attempted attacks, which usually involving unwanted sexual contact between a victim and an aggressor. They may or may not involve force but they include grabbing or fondling. (p.11)

Actual NCVS questions include:

> –(Other than any incidents already mentioned), has anyone attacked or threatened you in any of these ways:... (e) any rape, attempted rape, or other type of sexual attack; ...

> –Incidents involving forced or unwanted sexual acts are often difficult to talk about. (Other than any incidents already mentioned), have you been forced or coerced to engage in unwanted sexual activity by (a) someone you didn't know before, (b) a casual acquaintance? OR (c) someone you know well? (p.15) [Note: Unfortunately, the question does not specify what constitutes "coerced," so this is left up to the interpretation of the survey respondent.]

Also, "the survey does not specifically ask about incidents in which the victim was unable to provide consent because of drug or alcohol consumption." (p.14) As Libby Nelson observed [18] at *Vox*:

One thing the survey doesn't ask about specifically is incapacitated rape – sex when one person was too drunk or drugged to legally consent. Studies of campus sexual assault have consistently found that this kind of rape is more common than rape under a threat of force. That's one big difference between the National Crime Victimization Survey and other studies about campus sexual assault that have found campus rape to be much more prevalent.

Results

The most frequently cited NCVS result is "6.1 per 1,000" per year for the prevalence of rape and sexual assault (combined) of female college students. This is subdivided (p.4) into: 2.0 per 1,000 completed rape; 1.5 per 1,000 attempted rape; 1.9 per 1,000 sexual assault; and 0.7 per 1,000 threat of rape or sexual assault. (In Table 1 above, threats are counted in with sexual assaults.)

Several other NCVS results are interesting:

The rate is decreasing. The 6.1 per 1000 figure is the average for the years 1995-2013. Figure 2 on page 3 of the¹report shows the trend is decreasing. In 2013, for example, the rate for students was 4.4 per 1,000. (p.17)

Non-students are more likely to be victims. Contrary to the popular belief that college is especially dangerous for women, the NCVS statistics reveal that college-age (18 to 24) women who are non-students have a higher rate of sexual victimization. For the 1995-2013 period, the rate is 7.6 per thousand for non-students, versus 6.1 per thousand for students. (p.1)

Students are less likely to report to the police. "Among student victims, 20% of rape and sexual assault victimizations were reported to police, compared to 32% reported among nonstudent victims ages 18 to 24." (p.1) The most common reasons given for not reporting, by both students and non-students, are "fear of reprisal," "personal matter," and "other reason." (p.9)

College-age is the most vulnerable age group. In 2013, college-age females (students and non-students) were about three times more likely to be victimized than other age brackets: 4.3 per 1,000 for ages 18 to 24, v. 1.4 per thousand combined for ages 12 to 17 and 25 or older. (p.3) (This report does not break out the statistics for 17 and under v. 25 and older.)

Men are victimized but less often. The rate of rape and sexual assault for male students is roughly 1/5 the rate for female students. For the period 1995-2013, 1.4 per 1,000 male students were victimized, compared to 6.1 per 1,000 female students. Male non-students of college age report a rate of 0.3 per 1,000. (p.5)

Gang rape is rare. 95 percent of student rapes and sexual assaults involved only a single offender (v. "two or more" or "unknown number"). (p.8)

Limitations

As noted earlier, the NCVS does not count incidents of sex while incapacitated due to alcohol or drugs or unconsciousness.

Questions were not as specific and guided as NISVS and CSAS. For example, it is not clear if forced kissing, fondling, etc. qualifies as "unwanted sexual acts."

The NCVS takes the "criminal justice perspective" rather than the "public health perspective" in the design of its survey:

> In comparison, the NISVS focused on sexual violence, stalking, and intimate partner violence and was presented as a survey collecting data on a range of behaviors that impact public health. This public health perspective may encourage respondents to recall and report on experiences that they may not typically think of as criminal victimization. It also may result in the collection of incidents that may not be considered criminal behavior. Similarly, the CSA study focused specifically on rape and sexual assault, also from a public health and safety perspective. (p.14)

The NCVS report acknowledges that this may lead to under-reporting:

> The NCVS is an omnibus survey designed to collect information on experiences with a broad range of crimes. It is likewise presented to respondents as a survey about criminal victimization. Because victims of rape or sexual assault may not consider their victimization a crime, this context could discourage or suppress recall and reporting of those incidents. Additionally, because the NCVS covers a wide range of criminal victimization, the number of screening questions related to rape and sexual assault are limited. (p.14)

Also, because of the limited number of screening questions, respondents receive less guidance. The NISVS and CSAS specifically ask about forced kissing and fondling; the NCVS has no such explicit question. It is up to the respondent to decide if a forced kiss is an "unwanted sexual act."

Comparison to Other Studies

Because this Special Report was issued after the NISVS and the CSAS (called CSA in the Special Report), it was able to include comparisons to those prior studies:

The NCVS, NISVS, and CSA target different types of events. The NCVS definition is shaped from a criminal justice perspective and includes threatened, attempted, and completed rape and sexual assault against males and females (see Methodology). The NISVS uses a broader definition of sexual violence....The CSA definition of rape and sexual assault includes unwanted sexual contact due to force and due to incapacitation, but excludes unwanted sexual contact due to verbal or emotional coercion. (p.2)

Returning to the issue of specific questions and focus:

Unlike the NCVS, which uses terms like rape and unwanted sexual activity to identify victims of rape and sexual assault, the NISVS and CSA use behaviorally specific questions to ascertain whether the respondent experienced rape or sexual assault. These surveys ask about an exhaustive list of explicit types of unwanted sexual contact a victim may have experienced, such as being made to perform or receive anal or oral sex. (p.2)

A strength of the NCVS is its high response rate compared to other studies:

Surveys with low response rates have an increased potential for nonresponse bias compared to surveys with higher response rates. Nonresponse bias means that those who participated in the survey may differ in important ways from those who did not participate, which could in turn impact the survey findings. In 2013, the NCVS had an 88% response rate for eligible persons and a combined persons and household response rate of 74%, while the 2011 NISVS had an overall response rate of 33.1%, and the CSA response rate was between 33% and 43% for males and females at the two schools. (p.16)

A second significant and frequently quoted source of data is the NISVS.

2. NISVS: National Intimate Partner and Sexual Violence Survey, Centers for Disease Control (2011)

The NISVS was conducted in the year 2011 by the CDC. In September 2014, the CDC published a Surveillance Summary, "Prevalence and characteristics of sexual violence, stalking, and intimate partner violence victimization – National Intimate Partner and Sexual Violence Survey, United States, 2011" [19]. (Unless otherwise noted, page numbers below refer to this report.)

Methodology

The NISVS survey is a random-sample telephone interview:

> NISVS is a national random-digit-dial telephone survey of the
> noninstitutionalized English- and Spanish-speaking U.S. population
> aged ≥18 years. NISVS gathers data on experiences of sexual
> violence, stalking, and intimate partner violence among adult
> women and men in the United States by using a dual-frame
> sampling strategy that includes both landline and cellular
> telephones. The survey was conducted in 50 states and the District
> of Columbia; in 2011, the second year of NISVS data collection,
> 12,727 interviews were completed, and 1,428 interviews were
> partially completed. (p.1)

> A total of 6,879 women and 5,848 men completed the survey. The
> estimates presented in this report are based on completed
> interviews. An interview is defined as having been completed if the
> respondent completed the demographic and general health
> questions as well as all of the violence victimization questions. (p.3)

Definitions

The survey collected information about many types of "sexual violence":

> The specific types of sexual violence assessed included rape
> (completed or attempted forced penetration or alcohol- or drug-
> facilitated penetration) and sexual violence other than rape,
> including being made to penetrate a perpetrator, sexual coercion
> (nonphysically pressured unwanted penetration), unwanted sexual
> contact (e.g., kissing or fondling), and noncontact unwanted sexual
> experiences (e.g., being flashed or forced to view sexually explicit
> media). (p.3)

The survey's definition of the activities that might constitute "forced sex" –
vaginal sex, anal sex, oral-genital contact, oral-anal contact, inserting
fingers or an object into vagina or anus – is fairly close to the 2013-revised
definition now used by the FBI for the Uniform Crime Reporting program.

The questions about these activities are [20]:

> When you were drunk, high, drugged, or passed out and unable to
> consent, how many people have ever ...

> How many people have ever used physical force or threats to
> physically harm you to make you...

For the question about physical force or threats there is a further option, "sex did not happen", for vaginal/oral/anal sex. This appears to be counted as "attempted forced penetration" in the report's Table 1. (p.5)

There is also a "nonphysical pressure" question [21]:

> How many people have you had vaginal, oral, or anal sex with after they pressured you by...
>
> - doing things like telling you lies, making promises about the future they knew were untrue, threatening to end your relationship, or threatening to spread rumors about you?
>
> - wearing you down by repeatedly asking for sex, or showing they were unhappy?
>
> - using their influence or authority over you, for example, your boss or your teacher?

This appears to be counted as "sexual coercion" in Table 1.

Results

The most frequently cited results from the NISVS are "16 per 1,000" (per year), for the prevalence of rape, and "55 per 1,000" for sexual assault, for all women. From the report's abstract (p.1):

> In the United States, an estimated 19.3% of women and 1.7% of men have been raped during their lifetimes; an estimated 1.6% of women reported that they were raped in the 12 months preceding the survey. The case count for men reporting rape in the preceding 12 months was too small to produce a statistically reliable prevalence estimate. An estimated 43.9% of women and 23.4% of men experienced other forms of sexual violence during their lifetimes, including being made to penetrate, sexual coercion, unwanted sexual contact, and noncontact unwanted sexual experiences. The percentages of women and men who experienced these other forms of sexual violence victimization in the 12 months preceding the survey were an estimated 5.5% and 5.1%, respectively...
>
> With respect to sexual violence and stalking, female victims reported predominantly male perpetrators, whereas for male victims, the sex of the perpetrator varied by the specific form of violence examined. Male rape victims predominantly had male perpetrators, but other forms of sexual violence experienced by men were either perpetrated predominantly by women (i.e., being

made to penetrate and sexual coercion) or split more evenly among male and female perpetrators (i.e., unwanted sexual contact and noncontact unwanted sexual experiences)...

The lifetime and 12-month prevalences of rape by an intimate partner for women were an estimated 8.8% and 0.8%, respectively;
...

The NISVS also reported statistics for stalking but, as none of the other key surveys include stalking, those figures are omitted here.

Also from the abstract (p.1):

Results suggest that these forms of violence frequently are experienced at an early age because a majority of victims experienced their first victimization before age 25 years, with a substantial proportion experiencing victimization in childhood or adolescence.

This suggests that rapes/assaults may be skewed towards younger (college-age) women, which is a finding consistent with the NCVS.

The survey asked respondents to report on acts of sexual violence during a "respondent's lifetime and during the 12 months before interview" (p.3). The latter were used to estimate 12-month prevalences. In some categories, there were too few cases to establish a statistically significant result. Table 1 reports the following 12-month prevalences (p.5):

Rape: 1.6%

- Completed forced penetration – no result

- Attempted forced penetration – no result

- Completed alcohol or drug-facilitated penetration – 1.0%

Other sexual violence: 5.5%

- Made to penetrate – no result

- Sexual coercion – 2.0%

- Unwanted sexual contact – 2.2%

- Noncontact unwanted sexual experiences – 3.4%

Note: There is overlap in the four subcategories of "other sexual violence," which means these numbers cannot be simply added together to compute total risk. Judging from the lifetime prevalence figures, there is likewise an overlap in the three subcategories of rape.

Limitations

This study has, by far, the most expansive definition of sexual violence. Any of the following might be considered sexual assault: Being kissed against your will, being "touched...in a way that made you feel unsafe," being verbally harassed in a public place in a way that made you feel unsafe, or being made to look at sexual photos. Sexual coercion might include a boyfriend saying that if you didn't want to have sex with him, he would end the relationship; "wearing you down by repeatedly asking for sex"; "showing [he is] unhappy"; and "telling lies." All are reported as sexual violence. This may be because reporting a 6 percent chance (per Table 1 above) that a male will lie to a female student in order to have sex is less alarming than a 6 percent chance she will be sexually coerced.

Perhaps due to the low case counts for the 12-month period, the report focuses more heavily on lifetime prevalence rather than the risk per year.

There is no breakdown by age groups. The closest it is possible to come to estimating college-age risk is to look at "age at the time of first victimization" for completed rape. According to the report (pp.11-12):

> Among female victims of completed rape (completed forced penetration and completed alcohol- or drug-facilitated penetration), this form of sexual violence was first experienced by an estimated 78.7% before age 25 years, by an estimated 40.4% before age 18 years (28.3% at ages 11–17 years and 12.1% at age ≤10 years), and by an estimated 38.3% at age 18–24 years (Figure 3). In addition, among female victims of completed rape, an estimated 15.2% first experienced this at age 25–34 years, an estimated 4.6% at age 35–44 years, and an estimated 1.5% at age ≥45 years.

As an approximation, then, assume that 38.3% of the rapes occurring in any given year (estimated in Table 1 as 1,929,000 women) are occurring in the group aged 18-24. Table 1 in the report (p.5) suggests a total female population of 121,000,000. Per the 2010 Census [22], about 10% of the population is age 18-24. So, 738,800 rapes in a population of 12,100,000 is a rate of 6.1%, or 61 per thousand (per year), for college-age victims.

While mentioning the limitations of the report (p.17), the authors speculate (without offering evidence) that the NISVS might be *under-counting* the prevalence of sexual violence:

> The findings of this report are subject to at least five limitations. First, the overall response rate for the 2011 NISVS survey was

relatively low (33.1%). However, the cooperation rate was high (83.5%), and multiple efforts were made to reduce the likelihood of nonresponse and noncoverage bias. These included a nonresponse follow-up in which randomly selected nonresponders were contacted again and offered an increased incentive for participation as well as the inclusion of a cellular telephone sample. Second, although NISVS captures a broad range of self-reported victimization experiences, it is likely that the estimates presented underestimate the prevalence of sexual violence, stalking, and intimate partner violence. Victims who are involved in violent relationships or who have recently experienced severe forms of violence might be less likely to participate in surveys or might not be willing to disclose their experiences because of unresolved emotional trauma or concern for their safety, among other reasons. Third, a telephone survey might be less likely to capture some populations that could be at higher risk for victimization (e.g., persons living in nursing homes, military bases, prisons, or shelters, or those who are homeless). Fourth, self-reported data are vulnerable to recall bias because respondents might believe that events occurred closer in time than they did in actuality (i.e., telescoping) [23], and this type of bias might particularly affect 12-month prevalence estimates. Finally, follow-up questions were designed to reflect the victim's experience with each perpetrator across the victim's lifetime and there were limitations associated with how these questions were asked. Respondents were asked about the impact from any of the violence inflicted by each perpetrator. Therefore, the impact of specific intimate partner violence behaviors cannot be assessed. Also, because victims' reports of the age and relationship at the time any violence began with each perpetrator were used, it was not always possible to assess the age or relationship at the time specific types of intimate partner violence occurred.

It is equally plausible to suggest that victims who have experienced sexual violence could be *more* motivated to participate in the survey, rather than less. This remains unknown.

A third significant and frequently quoted source is the Campus Sexual Assault Study.

3. CSAS: Campus Sexual Assault Study (December 2007), National Institute of Justice

CSAS – also widely known as CSA – surveyed undergraduate women and men on their experiences of sexual assault both before and after entering university. Conducted during the winter of 2005-2006, 5,466 undergraduate women and 1,375 undergraduate men participated.

Methodology

The web-based survey was conducted by RTI International (RTI) at two "large, public universities" under a grant from the National Institute of Justice (NIJ). The NIJ is the research, development and evaluation agency of the Department of Justice. "The Campus Sexual Assault (CSA) Study Final Report" [24] was published in December 2007. (Unless otherwise noted, page numbers below refer to this report.)

CSAS drew from random samples of full-time students aged 18-25. Volunteers were offered a $10 Amazon gift certificate and an iTunes song download as compensation. Nevertheless, the response rate was "relatively low" (p.3-7), 42.2 and 42.8 percent at the two universities. (p.x). The study stated, "about 84% of students who completed the CSA survey followed through to obtain their incentives." (p.3-6) It is not known if the 16% who did not follow through were the result of multiple completions of the study; nor is it known whether only questionnaires with completion codes were counted.

CSAS explained its methodology (p.x):

> We drew random samples of students aged 18-25 and enrolled at least three-quarters' time at each university to participate in the CSA Study. Sampled students were sent an initial recruitment e-mail that described the study, provided a unique CSA Study ID#, and included a hyperlink to the CSA Study Web site...
>
> The survey was administered anonymously. (students did not enter their CSA Study ID # to take the survey)

A follow-up survey of 2,000 non-respondents elicited 296 replies (p.3-9):

> Fourteen sample members stated that they never received the original recruitment e-mails, and 126 students (45%) were not sure whether they had received these e-mails.....Among the sample members who either did receive the e-mails and chose to not participate or said that they would not have participated if they had received the e-mails, the most commonly reported reasons for

nonparticipation were that they did not have time (reported by about two-thirds of the sample members) or that they never participate in Web-based surveys (reported by just over 20% of the sample members). An extremely small number of the respondents to the nonrespondent survey indicated that they did not participate because they had never experienced sexual assault (n=9, 15.0%), or because they did not want to discuss their experiences with sexual assault victimization (n=4, 6.7%).

The foregoing raises a question. Did the non-responsive students simply have nothing to report or no interest? Or had they experienced sexual violence about which they did not wish to speak? Either could bias the results.

Definitions

According to the report (p.xi, emphasis in original):

Sexual assault included forced touching of a sexual nature, oral sex, sexual intercourse, anal sex, and/or sexual penetration with a finger or object [sic]. For both physically forced and incapacitated sexual assault, information was collected on *completed* and *attempted* assaults experienced *before entering college* and *since entering college*. For completed sexual assaults, a series of follow-up questions enabled us to define the assault as sexual battery (i.e., sexual assault that entailed sexual touching only) and/or rape (i.e., sexual assault that entailed oral, vaginal, or anal penetration).

Appendix A of the report (p.A-1) provided the survey questions:

This section of the interview asks about nonconsensual or unwanted sexual contact you may have experienced. When you are asked about whether something happened since you began college, please think about what has happened since you entered any college or university. The person with whom you had the unwanted sexual contact could have been a stranger or someone you know, such as a family member or someone you were dating or going out with.

The questions ask about five types of unwanted sexual contact:

- forced touching of a sexual nature (forced kissing, touching of private parts, grabbing, fondling, rubbing up against you in a sexual way, even if it is over your clothes)

- oral sex (someone's mouth or tongue making contact with your genitals or your mouth or tongue making contact with someone else's genitals)

- sexual intercourse (someone's penis being put in your vagina)

- anal sex (someone's penis being put in your anus)

- sexual penetration with a finger or object (someone putting their finger or an object like a bottle or a candle in your vagina or anus).

In a subsequent article in *Time* magazine, two of CSAS's authors clarified what constituted "rape" and "sexual assault" in evaluating responses [25]:

> Among other items, the students, after being told they were going to be asked about their experiences with unwanted sexual contact, were asked these two key questions:
>
> > *Since you began college, has anyone had sexual contact with you by using physical force or threatening to physically harm you?*
>
> and
>
> > *Since you began college, has someone had sexual contact with you when you were unable to provide consent or stop what was happening because you were passed out, drugged, drunk, incapacitated, or asleep? This question asks about incidents that you are certain happened.*

To be counted as a victim of sexual assault or rape and included in the 1-in-5 statistic (19.8%), a woman would have to be a senior and answer "Yes" to one or both of those questions.

In our reports, sexual-assault victims who selected only "Forced touching of a sexual nature" in a follow-up question asking about the type of contact that happened were classified as victims of sexual battery only, whereas victims who selected any of the other response options (oral sex, sexual intercourse, anal sex, or sexual penetration with a finger or object) were classified as victims of rape.

"Forced" and "incapacitated" were spelled out in the survey questions (pp.A-1, A-2, emphasis in original):

Force could include someone holding you down with his or her body weight, pinning your arms, hitting or kicking you, or using or threatening to use a weapon against you.

> Has anyone had sexual contact with you by using physical force or threatening to physically harm you?

> Has anyone <u>attempted but not succeeded</u> in having sexual contact with you by using or threatening to use physical force against you?

The next set of questions ask about your experiences with unwanted sexual contact while you were unable to provide consent or stop what was happening because you were passed out, drugged, drunk, incapacitated, or asleep. These situations might include times that you voluntarily consumed alcohol or drugs and times that you were given drugs without your knowledge or consent.

> Has someone had sexual contact with you when you were unable to provide consent or stop what was happening because you were passed out, drugged, drunk, incapacitated, or asleep? This question asks about incidents that you are <u>certain</u> happened.

> Have you <u>suspected</u> that someone has had sexual contact with you when you were unable to provide consent or stop what was happening because you were passed out, drugged, drunk, incapacitated, or asleep? This question asks about events that you think (but are not certain) happened.

Results

What does CSAS actually say?

An interesting result is the number of women who experienced sexual assault before college (pp.xii-xiii, emphasis in original):

> Nearly 16% of the 5,446 women experienced attempted or completed sexual assault *before entering college*....Nineteen percent of the women reported experiencing completed or attempted sexual assault *since entering college*....

This is the source of the frequently-heard claim that 1-in-5 women will be sexually assaulted in college. To be precise, 1-in-5 will experience a sexual assault *or an attempt* during a four-year stay on campus. In CSAS, 1,073 women out of the 5,446 (19.7%) reported experiencing an attempted or completed sexual assault since entering college. In Figure 1 (p.xiii) and Exhibit 5-1 (p.5-2) these reports are categorized for assaults since entering college:

I.   Attempted or completed sexual assault since entering college, n=1073, 19%

    A: Attempted, n=682, 12.6%

    B: Completed, n=782, 13.7%

    1.   Physically forced, n=256, 4.7%

        a: Sexual battery only, n=75, 1.4%

        b: Rape, n=181, 3.4%

    2.   Incapacitated, n=651, 11.1%

        a: Sexual battery only, n=144, 2.6%

        b: Rape, n=507, 8.5%

        i. Alcohol and/or other drug (AOD)-enabled SA, n=466, 7.8%

        ii. Certain drug-facilitated SA, n=31, 0.6%

        iii. Suspected drug-facilitated SA, n=103, 1.7%

        iv. Other incapacitated SA (e.g. asleep), n=48, 1.0%

It is not clear from the report how subcategories I.B.2.a/b and I.B.2.i/ii/iii/iv overlap; that is, it is not clear how many rapes had drug involvement.

Subcategories I.B.1 and I.B.2 do overlap. 782 women reported completed assaults; 256 women reported being physically forced, and 651 reported being incapacitated. This suggests that 125 reported both physically forced assaults and incapacitated assaults (an overlap of 16% of the total number).

Similarly, it is reasonable to deduce that 391 women reported both attempted (I.A) and completed (I.B) assaults.

Since only senior women were surveyed, the report is presumed to be over four years. (In Table 1 above, the CSAS figures are divided by four to give a per-year risk.)

A particularly interesting result is that the authors frequently considered the women to have been raped, when the women themselves did not (p.5-20):

When subsetting to victims who were raped, 64.6% of physically forced rape victims and 37.8% of incapacitated rape victims considered the incident to be rape.

Exhibit 5-8 (p.5-22) describes whether students reported the assault. 12.9% of the victims of forced sexual assault reported the assault to law enforcement as compared to only 2.1% of the victims of incapacitated sexual assault. Unfortunately, this table does not distinguish between "sexual battery" versus rape.

Limitations

Because CSAS is the primary source of the 1-in-5 statistic that has been wielded to such political advantage, the limitations of the study deserve in-depth analysis.

A recurring problem is that CSAS does not generally break out rape figures; it considers all sexual assaults together. Moreover, there is some confusion because the authors use the term "sexual battery" for acts that others commonly refer to as "sexual assault." By contrast, CSAS broadly defines "sexual assault" and includes rape within the definition. But the term also includes forced kissing, grabbing, and "rubbing up against you in a sexual way." (p.A-1) This has implications for the reporting statistics. For example, how many women would call the police if a breast had been groped through clothing?

The study also does not generally count attempted rapes. It seems likely, however, that respondents would report an attempted and uncompleted rape as a sexual assault.

Cathy Young pinpointed another limitation in a *Minding the Campus* article, "The White House Overreaches on Campus Rape." [26]

> The vast majority of the incidents counted as assault involved what the study termed "incapacitation" by alcohol (or, rarely, drugs). But 'incapacitation' is a misleading term, since the question used in the study also measured far lower degrees of intoxication: 'Has someone had sexual contact with you when you were unable to provide consent or stop what was happening because you were passed out, drugged, drunk, incapacitated, or asleep?' This wording does not differentiate between someone who is unconscious or barely conscious and someone who is just drunk enough to go along with something he or she wouldn't do when sober. The questions related to sexual assault by physical force–particularly attempted sexual assault–are also worded so ambiguously that they

could refer to a clumsy attempt to initiate sex, even if the 'attacker' stops at once when rebuffed.

Three quarters of the female students who were classified as victims of sexual assault by incapacitation did not believe they had been raped; even when only incidents involving penetration were counted, nearly two-thirds did not call it rape. Two-thirds did not report the incident to the authorities because they didn't think it was serious enough.

Libby Nelson at *Vox* commented on the discrepancy between the researchers' view of rape and that of the the victims [27]. One interpretation is that the victims were lacking awareness; another is that the authors over-counted rapes:

> Studies of college women find that a large proportion don't define what happened to them as a crime. In Krebs' survey of women at two large public universities, 56 percent of the victims of forced sexual assault who didn't report their assaults to the police, and 67 percent of victims of incapacitated sexual assault who did not do so, said it was at least partly because it was not 'serious enough to report'. Slightly more than one-third of women in both categories said it was 'unclear if a crime or harm was intended'.

Nelson referred to an earlier study:

> A national survey from the Medical University of South Carolina [28] found that 15 percent of college women who were victims of forcible rape would describe what happened to them as 'unpleasant, but not a crime'. An additional 32 percent called it a crime, but not rape. For incapacitated rape, the proportions were even higher: 31 percent called it an unpleasant experience, and 40 percent a crime other than rape.

The authors of CSAS themselves openly noted another limitation, which has been resoundingly ignored ever since. In the aforementioned *Time* magazine article, researchers Christopher Krebs and Christine Lindquist stated [29],

> First and foremost, the 1-in-5 statistic is not a nationally representative estimate of the prevalence of sexual assault, and we have never presented it as being representative of anything other than the population of senior undergraduate women at the two universities where data were collected– two large public universities, one in the South and one in the Midwest.

Second, the 1-in-5 statistic includes victims of both rape and other forms of sexual assault, such as forced kissing or unwanted groping of sexual body parts– acts that can legally constitute sexual battery and are crimes. To limit the statistic to include rape only, meaning unwanted sexual penetration, the prevalence for senior undergraduate women drops to 14.3%, or 1 in 7 (again, limited to the two universities we studied).

Third, despite what has been said in some media reports, the 1-in-5 statistic does not include victims who experienced only sexual-assault incidents that were attempted but not completed. The survey does attempt to measure attempted sexual assaults, but only victims of completed incidents are included in the 1-in-5 statistic.

Fourth, another limitation of our study– inherent to web-based surveys– is that the response rate was relatively low (42%). We conducted an analysis of this nonresponse rate and found that respondents were not significantly different from nonrespondents in terms of age, race/ethnicity or year of study. Even so, it is possible that nonresponse bias had an impact on our prevalence estimates, positive or negative. We simply have no way of knowing whether sexual-assault victims were more or less likely to participate in our study.

The authors suggested that the low response rate (42%) could bias the study toward either higher or lower rates. There is reason to believe the bias would tend toward higher. If a $10 gift card did not motivate 58% of the solicited population to participate, then it seems plausible that those with additional motivation – for example, those who were victims of sexual assault or politically invested in victims' rights – would participate in disproportionate numbers. The authors stated, "the anonymity and privacy we afforded respondents may have made women comfortable with responding honestly" – that is, more likely to report. Respondents who experienced violence or were acutely sensitive to the rape culture may well have been disproportionately represented.

Yet another criticism leveled against CSAS is that only two universities were surveyed, which means the results cannot be generalized. In 2015, however, the *Washington Post* and the Kaiser Family Foundation conducted a nationwide poll to duplicate the CSAS survey, and found nearly identical results [30]:

Twenty percent of young women who attended college during the past four years say they were sexually assaulted, according to a

Washington Post-Kaiser Family Foundation poll. But the circle of victims on the nation's campuses is probably even larger.

Many others endured attempted attacks, the poll found, or suspect that someone violated them while they were unable to consent. Some say they were coerced into sex through verbal threats or promises.

In all, the poll found, 25 percent of young women and 7 percent of young men say they suffered unwanted sexual incidents in college....

Most notably, two-thirds of victims say they had been drinking alcohol just before the incidents.

Many victims were not clear on whether to categorize the incident as "sexual assault":

Forty-six percent said it's unclear whether sexual activity when both people have not given clear agreement is sexual assault. Forty-seven percent called that scenario sexual assault.

While the methodology was more random than CSAS, the definitions remained essentially the same:

Conducted by telephone from January through March [2015], the poll surveyed a random national sample of 1,053 women and men ages 17 to 26 who were undergraduates at a four-year college – living on campus or nearby – or had been at some point since 2011. They attended more than 500 colleges and universities, public and private, large and small, elite and obscure, located in every state and the District of Columbia.

The Post-Kaiser poll used questions and definitions similar to those in the 2007 [CSAS] study.

The *Washington Post* did not report any statistics for rape, just "sexual assault" (including rape).

In conclusion: The biggest problem with CSAS is an overbroad definition of "sexual assault," which produces the inflated statistic that 1-in-5 women will be sexually assaulted during four years of college. A major problem is that there is no adequate distinction between rape and sexual assault. If a distinction is attempted, then the most aggressive interpretation of the data is that the odds of being raped during college are 1-in-7.9. A more likely result would be 1-in-9.2. And, depending on the significance of the non-responses, the results could be registered as low as 1-in-21. In addition, almost 1/3 of "forcible rapes" and almost 2/3 of "incapacitated rapes" were not considered "rape" by their victims.

A fourth significant and frequently-quoted source of rape statistics is the Uniform Crime Reporting Program.

4. UCR: Uniform Crime Reporting Program, FBI (2013)

The Federal Bureau of Investigation's Uniform Crime Reporting Program [31]

> is a nationwide, cooperative statistical effort of more than 18,000 city, university and college, county, state, tribal, and federal law enforcement agencies voluntarily reporting data on crimes brought to their attention. Since 1930, the FBI has administered the UCR Program and has continued to assess and monitor the nature and type of crime in the nation.

A UCR is issued every year, with a break-down on different kinds of crime. Information presented here is from the online 2013 UCR "Rape" report. [32]

Methodology

The FBI receives reports of violent crime and property crime from most of the law enforcement agencies in the U.S. [33]:

> In 2013, law enforcement agencies active in the UCR Program represented more than 309 million United States inhabitants (98.0 percent of the total population). The coverage amounted to 98.8 percent of the population in Metropolitan Statistical Areas, 92.9 percent of the population in cities outside metropolitan areas, and 93.5 percent of the population in nonmetropolitan counties.

This represents a larger sample size than any randomized or focused survey. However, by the nature of its collection, the UCR can only count those assaults which are reported to law enforcement.

Definitions

The FBI has recently revised its definition of rape [34]:

> In 2013, the FBI UCR Program initiated collection of rape data under a revised definition within the Summary Reporting System. Previously, offense data for forcible rape was collected under the legacy UCR definition: the carnal knowledge of a female forcibly and against her will. Beginning with the 2013 data year, the term

"forcible" was removed from the offense title, and the definition was changed. The revised UCR definition of rape is: Penetration, no matter how slight, of the vagina or anus with any body part or object, or oral penetration by a sex organ of another person, without the consent of the victim. Attempts or assaults to commit rape are also included; however, statutory rape and incest are excluded.

Furthermore,

The UCR Program counts one offense for each victim of a rape, attempted rape, or assault with intent to rape, regardless of the victim's age. Sexual relations without the victim's consent which involves a familial offender is counted as a rape and not an act of incest. All other crimes of a sexual nature are considered to be Part II offenses; as such, the UCR Program collects only arrest data for those crimes. The offense of statutory rape, in which no force is used but the female victim is under the age of consent, is included in the arrest total for the sex offenses category.

Part II offenses are lesser offenses, including [35]:

Other assaults (simple) — Assaults and attempted assaults where no weapon was used or no serious or aggravated injury resulted to the victim. Stalking, intimidation, coercion, and hazing are included.

Sex offenses (except forcible rape, prostitution, and commercialized vice)– Offenses against chastity, common decency, morals, and the like. Incest, indecent exposure, and statutory rape are included. Attempts are included.

Since the Part II definitions include many crimes that are not considered sexual assault, the UCR statistics are of limited value. Only the UCR statistics for attempted and completed rape are considered here.

Results

The Rape Overview states [36]:

There were an estimated 79,770 rapes (older definition) reported to law enforcement in 2013. This estimate was 6.3 percent lower than the 2012 estimate, and 10.6 percent and 16.1 percent lower than the 2009 and 2004 estimates, respectively. (See Tables 1 and 1A.)

The rate of rapes (older definition) in 2013 was estimated at 25.2 per 100,000 females.

Some confusion exists, however. Table 1 [37] gives the rate of rape (older definition) as 25.2 per 100,000 inhabitants or 79,770 rapes over a population of 316,128,839. This renders the rate of rape at approximately 25.2 per 50,000 females, assuming that the majority of rapes reported to the FBI involve female victims. (The UCR does not seem to collect data on prison rape.)

No summary report is available for the new rape definition. Per Table 16 [38], for "All Agencies," a total of 53,621 rapes were reported using the new definition, over a population of 134,788,319, for a rate of 39.8 per 100,000 inhabitants. A total of 36,209 rapes were reported from agencies using the older definition, over a population of 156,887,921, for a rate of 23.1 per 100,000 persons. (It is not clear how to reconcile this number with that reported in Table 1.) The higher rate may result from the changes to the definition of rape. For example, the crime now includes penetration with an object and counts male victims.

Assuming, again, that rapes reported to law enforcement overwhelmingly involve female victims, and that 50% of the population is female, the "new-definition rapes" are occurring at a rate of 79.6 per 100,000 females, or 0.8 per thousand.

From reports that used the the new definition, 4.7% were for attempted rape or assaults to commit rape, and 95.1% were for "rape by force." In short, FBI statistics overwhelmingly deal with completed rapes.

Prosecution

The "Clearances" report [39] indicates that "40.6 percent of rape offenses (new definition), 40.0 percent of rape offenses (old definition), ... were cleared."

> The three conditions [for clearance] are that at least one person has been:
>
> • Arrested.
>
> • Charged with the commission of the offense.
>
> • Turned over to the court for prosecution (whether following arrest, court summons, or police notice).
>
> In its clearance calculations, the UCR Program counts the number of offenses that are cleared, not the number of persons arrested.

The arrest of one person may clear several crimes, and the arrest of many persons may clear only one offense.

40 percent of reported rapes are prosecuted. The UCR does not collect information on how many prosecutions returned a guilty verdict.

Limitations

UCR counts only crimes reported to law enforcement and so underestimates the total number of rapes. In short, unreported rapes are not counted. Also, sexual assaults are not included in FBI statistics.

Attempted rapes are included, though not separated from forcible rape or (under the new definition) incapacitated rape. The earlier 2011 report did state [40]

> The rate of forcible rapes in 2011 was estimated at 52.7 per 100,000 female inhabitants. Rapes by force comprised 93.0 percent of reported rape offenses in 2011, and attempts or assaults to commit rape accounted for 7.0 percent of reported rapes.

Unfortunately, the UCR offers no breakdown by age groups.

The UCR by itself cannot estimate the rate of rape among college-age women. From other surveys, for example, NCVS, it is possible to form a rough idea of how many rapes are *not* reported to police, and how many rapes happen to college-age women v. women of all ages. A broad estimate is offered in Table 1, presented earlier.

5. DOE Department of Education "Clery Act" Report, (2013)

The Department of Education, Office of Postsecondary Education collects data on crimes committed on or near campuses as required by the "Higher Education Opportunity Act" and the "Jeanne Clery Disclosure of Campus Security Policy and Campus Crime Statistics Act" (commonly known as the Clery Act). [41]

Methodology

The Clery Act requires the following compilation of statistics for all universities that participate in federal financial aid programs. The data is to be published by by October 1 of each year. The crime statistics must be sent to the Department of Education each year.

Crimes are categorized as occurring [42]:

(1) on campus, (2) on public property within or immediately adjacent to the campus, and (3) in or on noncampus buildings or property that your institution owns or controls.

Note that the "on campus student housing" report is a subset of "on campus."

The Data Analysis website [43] further cautions:

The crime statistics found on this website represent alleged criminal offenses reported to campus security authorities and/or local law enforcement agencies. Therefore, the data collected do not necessarily reflect prosecutions or convictions for crimes. Because some statistics are provided by non-police authorities, the data are not directly comparable to data from the FBI's Uniform Crime Reporting System which only collects statistics from police authorities.

Definitions

According to the Clery Center [44],

"When not in conflict with the Clery Act, the standards of the FBI's Uniform Crime Reporting program are to be used."

The U.S. Department of Education "Handbook for Campus Safety and Security Reporting" is more specific [45]:

The FBI's National Incident-Based Reporting System (NIBRS) edition of the UCR defines a sex offense as any sexual act directed against another person, forcibly and/or against that person's will; or not forcibly or against the person's will where the victim is incapable of giving consent.

And [46]:

Per the *Clery Act*, you must classify crimes based on the Federal Bureau of Investigation's (FBI's) *Uniform Crime Reporting Handbook (UCR)*. For sex offenses only, use definitions from the FBI's *National Incident-Based Reporting System (NIBRS)* edition of the UCR.

And in greater detail [47],

2. Sex offenses. Sex offenses are separated into two categories: forcible and non-forcible. Include attempted sex offenses, but do not include in your Clery statistical disclosures any sex offenses other than the four types of Forcible Sex Offenses and the two types of Non-forcible Sex Offenses described in this chapter.

a) Sex Offenses– Forcible is defined as any sexual act directed against another person, forcibly and/or against that person's will; or not forcibly or against the person's will where the victim is incapable of giving consent. Count one offense per victim. In cases where several offenders commit a Forcible Sex Offense against one person, count one Forcible Sex Offense. Do not count the number of offenders.

There are four types of Forcible Sex Offenses:

> • Forcible Rape is the carnal knowledge of a person, forcibly and/or against that person's will; or not forcibly or against the person's will where the victim is incapable of giving consent because of his/her temporary or permanent mental or physical incapacity (or because of his/her youth). This offense includes the forcible rape of both males and females. Count one offense per victim.

If force was used or threatened, classify the crime as forcible rape regardless of the age of the victim. If no force or threat of force was used and the victim was under the statutory age of consent, classify the crime as statutory rape. The ability of the victim to give consent must be a professional determination by a law enforcement agency.

> • Forcible Sodomy is oral or anal sexual intercourse with another person, forcibly and/or against that person's will; or not forcibly or against the person's will where the victim is incapable of giving consent because of his/her youth or because of his/her temporary or permanent mental or physical incapacity. Count one offense per victim.

> • Sexual Assault With an Object is the use of an object or instrument to unlawfully penetrate, however slightly, the genital or anal opening of the body of another person, forcibly and/or against that person's will; or not forcibly or against the person's will where the victim is incapable of giving consent because of his/her youth or because of his/her temporary or permanent mental or physical incapacity. An object or instrument is anything used by the offender other than the offender's genitalia. Examples are a finger, bottle, handgun, stick, etc. Count one offense per victim.

• Forcible Fondling is the touching of the private body parts of another person for the purpose of sexual gratification, forcibly and/or against that person's will; or, not forcibly or against the person's will where the victim is incapable of giving consent because of his/her youth or because of his/her temporary or permanent mental incapacity. Count one offense per victim.

b) Sex Offenses– Non-forcible is defined as unlawful, non-forcible sexual intercourse.

There are two types of Non-forcible Sex Offenses:

• Incest is non-forcible sexual intercourse between persons who are related to each other within the degrees wherein marriage is prohibited by law. Count one offense per victim.

• Statutory Rape is non-forcible sexual intercourse with a person who is under the statutory age of consent. Count one offense per victim.

In summary: under the Clery Act, "forcible" sexual assault includes the use of force, threat of force, or incapacity. Note that e.g. in the case of incapacity, the perpetrator's intent (sexual gratification) must be established. [48]

Results

For the 2013 reporting year, the totals reported for all campuses are [49]:

On campus

Sex offenses - forcible: 5,050

Sex offenses – non-forcible: 46

Non campus

Sex offenses - forcible: 588

Sex offenses – non-forcible: 9

Public Property

Sex offenses – forcible: 377

Sex offenses – non-forcible: 2

Reported by Local & State Police

Sex offenses – forcible: 0

Sex offenses – non-forcible: 0

Total all offenses 6,072

To explain the "Reported by Local & State Police" category [50]:

> In addition to collecting crime reports from campus security authorities, Clery requires that every institution make a "reasonable, good-faith effort" to obtain Clery crime statistics from local law enforcement agencies that have jurisdiction over the school's Clery geography. Local law enforcement agencies do not include your campus police or security department (if you have one). Those are campus security authorities.

All "Reported by Local and State Police" numbers for all crimes – not just sex offenses – are suspiciously low. Either students are reporting crimes only to campus police, or the schools aren't diligent about getting statistics from local police. For example, in 2013 there were a reported 24 instances of murder/manslaughter on campus, but 0 reported to local police. How is that possible?

The rate of sexual assault is also suspiciously small. Assume all female victims. The projected enrollment [51] for the year 2013 is 11,612,000 female college students (and 8,985,000 male). 6,069 victims in 11,612,000 is a rate of 0.52 per 1,000 per year. This is a total for forcible rape, incapacitated rape, and sexual assault other than rape.

Limitations

Universities are accused of deliberately under-reporting crimes, since this information must be published and could alienate prospective students. In September 2014, the *Columbus Dispatch* reported [52],

> The crime statistics being released by colleges nationwide on Wednesday are so misleading that they give students and parents a false sense of security.

> Even the U.S. Department of Education official who oversees compliance with a federal law requiring that the statistics be posted on Oct. 1 each year admits that they are inaccurate. Jim Moore said that a vast majority of schools comply with the law but some purposely under-report crimes to protect their images; others have made honest mistakes in attempting to comply.

In addition, weaknesses in the law allow for thousands of off-campus crimes involving students to go unreported, and the Education Department does little to monitor or enforce compliance with the law – even when colleges report numbers that seem questionable.

Phrases, such as "for the purpose of sexual gratification" in defining sexual assault, may tempt campus authorities to reclassify some sexual assaults as "ordinary" assaults if the intent is uncertain. But additional "loopholes" also allow under-reporting [53]:

One is geographic. If a reported sexual assault took place in an off-campus building that isn't owned by an officially recognized student group, a school doesn't have to publish it. So, off-campus parties, like those thrown by fraternities, tend to be left out of the published statistics entirely. And fraternity brothers are more likely to rape than men who do not join a frat – three times as likely in their first year in college.

Of the 12 reported sexual assaults in Yale University's Clery report, for example, none took place off campus. How many are they missing? There's finally a clue. Starting in 2012, Yale became the only college to voluntarily publish data on all its reports of sexual assault. In 2013, that number was 19, or 58 percent more than its Clery figure.

Another Clery booby trap is where schools collect their numbers. Under the law, a university must gather its stats from campus and local police, as well as school officials with "significant responsibility for student and campus activities," such as deans, coaches and academic advisers.

In 2003, Princeton University decided to go above and beyond the Clery law, including sex offense reports made to confidential counselors – inflating its own numbers in the interest of accuracy....

If Princeton had included confidential counselor reports again this past year, its total would have been 23, according to Mbugua. But the university's Clery report posted only six.

The bottom line: Clery Act reports are probably best viewed as a "lower bound" for the real numbers.

6. SVCW: Sexual Victimization of College Women, National Institute of Justice (2000)

Two older reports deserve brief mention. The more recent is "Sexual Victimization of College Women," published in December 2000 by the National Institute of Justice [54]. This is the same organization that commissioned the December 2007 Campus Sexual Assault Study, described above. (Page numbers below refer to the SVCW.)

Methodology

SVCW was a telephone survey of 4,446 randomly selected college women, conducted at schools with a minimum of 1,000 students. Participants were contacted between February and May 1997, and asked about assaults during the previous school year (starting in the fall of 1996). The response rate was 85.6%.

Definitions

"Rape" was defined as (p.8):

> ...penetration by force or the threat of force. Penetration includes: penile-vaginal, mouth on your genitals, mouth on someone else's genitals, penile-anal, digital-vaginal, digital-anal, object-vaginal, and object-anal.

"Sexual coercion" included (p.6):

> [someone made or tried to make you have] sexual contact when you did not want to by making threats of nonphysical punishment, such as lowering a grade, being demoted or fired from a job, damaging your reputation, or being excluded from a group...

> ...by making promises of rewards, such as raising a grade, being hired or promoted, being given a ride or class notes, or getting help with coursework...

> ...by simply being overwhelmed by someone's continual pestering and verbal pressure.

"Sexual contact" included (p.8):

> ...touching; grabbing or fondling of breasts, buttocks, or genitals, either under or over your clothes; kissing; licking or sucking; or some other form of unwanted sexual contact.

Results

Exhibit 3 (p.11) reports a prevalence of completed rape of 16.6 per 1,000 women for the preceding year. The prevalence of attempted rape was 11.0 per 1,000.

Exhibit 5 (p.16) reports the prevalence of sexual coercion was 16.6 per 1,000 completed, and 13.5 per thousand attempted.

The prevalence of completed sexual contact was 19.1 per thousand with force or threat of force, and 18.0 per thousand without force. Attempted sexual contact was 20.0 per 1,000 with force or threat of force, and 29.0 per thousand without force. It is not clear how much overlap there is between these groups.

Limitations

The survey uses broad definitions of sexual contact and sexual coercion. It does not seem to record intoxicated/incapacitated rape.

7. NVAWS: National Violence Against Women Survey, National Institute of Justice (1998)

The NIJ, in conjunction with the CDC, conducted an all-ages study from November 1995 to May 1996, which was reported in November 1998. [55] (Page numbers below refer to the report.)

Methodology

A telephone survey of 8,000 women and 8,005 men, 18 years and older, was conducted by the Center for Policy Research.

Definitions

The questions (p.13) employed a fairly standard definition of rape: vaginal, oral, or anal sex, by force, threat of force, or threatening to harm someone close to the victim. There were no specific questions about sexual assault other than rape.

Results

Exhibit 1 (p.3) reports that 17.6% of women surveyed experienced an attempted or completed rape during her lifetime. Exhibit 2 (p.4) reports that 0.3% of women surveyed (3 per 1,000) experienced an attempted or completed rape during the previous year. The statistics reported for physical assault refer to non-sexual assault, and so are not relevant here.

Exhibit 6 (p.6) indicates that 54.0% of female rape victims were under 18 years old when first raped; 29.4% were age 18-24. (The age distribution of the respondents was not mentioned in this report; the omission may skew these statistics. As an extreme example, if half the respondents were 24 years old or younger, none of those respondents would have reported a first rape after the age of 25.)

Limitations

As noted, this survey measured the prevalence and incidence only of rape and attempted rape. Other kinds of sexual assault were not included.

Conclusion

The data is a onslaught of confusion. The best statistics probably come from the NCVS, which has sound methodology and is repeated consistently on an annual basis. NCVS provides information that other studies do not, such as the rate of sexual assault for students v. non-students, and the rate of non-reporting. It is perhaps unique in that the Bureau of Justice Statistics convened a panel of experts to evaluate and improve its methods. Its main weaknesses: Being an all-crime survey, it has only a few questions about rape and sexual assault, and it does not address being assaulted while incapacitated. Other studies point to the latter as the most frequent form of sexual assault.

It would be incredibly helpful if researchers converged on a common set of definitions. As it is, some studies are very liberal in their definitions and others are conservative, which strips value and precision from comparisons.

It is clear, however, that statements like the one by Vice President Biden [56] are misleading and unnecessarily alarmist. He declared, "We know the numbers: one in five of every one of those young women who is dropped off for that first day of school, before they finish school, will be assaulted, will be assaulted in her college years."

More accurate and useful advice might sound like this:

> In any given year, there is something like a one percent chance that you will be raped. That's true whether or not you go to college – in fact, college is slightly safer for you. If you are raped, the most likely scenario will be that you are incapacitated by alcohol. So be careful around men who want to ply you with liquor. It is more likely – maybe a 5 percent chance per year – that someone will try to fondle you or kiss you against your will or pester you into having sex. Plan right now on how to handle these situations.

On the bright side, in any given year, 95 percent of you are statistically likely to encounter only men who – even if they cannot be described as well-behaved – are men who want your willing and active consent to sexual activity.

Notes

[1] As quoted in "Beware the bad survey: Science literacy isn't as bad as the statistics make it look," *PLOS blog*, May 12, 2015. http://blogs.plos.org/scicomm/2015/05/12/beware-the-bad-survey-science-literacy-isnt-as-bad-as-the-statistics-make-it-look/ Retrieved Sept. 27, 2015.

[2] Jennifer L. Truman and Michael Planty, *Criminal Victimization, 2011,* Oct. 2012, NCJ 239437. http://www.bjs.gov/content/pub/pdf/cv11.pdf Retrieved Sept. 27, 2015.

[3] "Prevalence and Characteristics of Sexual Violence, Stalking, and Intimate Partner Violence Victimization – National Intimate Partner and Sexual Violence Survey, United States, 2011," Centers for Disease Control. http://www.cdc.gov/mmwr/preview/mmwrhtml/ss6308a1.htm? s_cid=ss6308a1_e Retrieved Sept. 27, 2015.

[4] Claire Groden, "Why is it so Hard to Determine Exactly How Many Women are Raped Each Year?" *New Republic,* Sept. 8, 2014. http://www.newrepublic.com/article/119364/cdcs-report-one-five-women-raped-other-statistics-disagree Retrieved Sept. 27, 2015.

[5] Cathy Young, "The CDC's Rape Numbers Are Misleading," *Time*, Sept. 17, 2014. http://time.com/3393442/cdc-rape-numbers/ Retrieved Sept. 27, 2015.

[6] Sofi Sinozich and Lynn Langton, "Rape and Sexual Assault Victimization Among College-Age Females, 1995–2013 ", U.S. Department of Justice, Bureau of Justice Statistics, Dec. 2014. http://www.bjs.gov/content/pub/pdf/rsavcaf9513.pdf Retrieved Sept. 27, 2015.

[7] M.J. Breiding, S.G. Smith, K.C. Basile, M.L. Walters, J. Chen and M.T. Merrick, "Prevalence and characteristics of sexual violence, stalking, and intimate partner violence victimization – National Intimate Partner and Sexual Violence Survey, United States, 2011. Morbidity and Mortality Weekly Report, Surveillance Summaries, 63(8), 1–18. http://www.cdc.gov/mmwr/preview/mmwrhtml/ss6308a1.htm Retrieved Sept. 27, 2015.

[8] C.P. Krebs, C.H. Lindquist, T.D. Warner, B.S. Fisher and S.L. Martin, S.L. (2007), "The Campus Sexual Assault (CSA) study. Final report to the National Institute of Justice, grant number 2004-WG-BX-0010, document number 221153." https://www.ncjrs.gov/pdffiles1/nij/grants/221153.pdf Retrieved Sept. 27, 2015.

[9] "Crime in the United States, 2013," U.S. Department of Justice, Federal Bureau of Investigation, Uniform Crime Reporting (UCR) Program, Rape. http://www.fbi.gov/about-us/cjis/ucr/crime-in-the-u.s/2013/crime-in-the-u.s.-2013/violent-crime/rape Retrieved Sept. 27, 2015.

[10] Bonnie S. Fisher, Francis T. Cullen, Michael G. Turner, (Dec. 2000). "Sexual Victimization of College Women". National Institute of Justice. http://www.ncjrs.gov/pdffiles1/nij/182369.pdf Retrieved Sept. 27, 2015.

[11] "Prevalence, Incidence, and Consequences of Violence Against Women: Findings of the National Violence Against Women Survey". National Institute of Justice. November 1998. https://www.ncjrs.gov/pdffiles/172837.pdf Retrieved Sept. 27, 2015.

[12] The U.S. Department of Education, Office of Postsecondary Education collects data required by the "Jeanne Clery Disclosure of Campus Security Policy and Campus Crime Statistics Act" (a.k.a. the Clery act) and the "Higher Education Opportunity Act". http://ope.ed.gov/security/ Retrieved Sept. 27, 2015.

[13] For example, if in one year a woman was assaulted once, and another woman was assaulted twice, then the incidence for that year would be 3 (assaults) but the prevalence would be 2 (victims).

[14] Calculated as follows: let P be the population of women of all ages. Then the number of college-age women is 0.1P, and the number of other women is 0.9P. If the college-age rate of rape is 0.0043 (4.3 per thousand), and the non-college rate 0.0014 (1.4 per thousand), then the total number of rapes for all women is $R = (0.1P)(0.0043) + (0.9P)(0.0014)$. The per-capita rate of rape for all women, r, is calculated as R/P; dividing R by P gives $r = R/P = (0.1)(0.0043) + (0.9)(0.0014) = 0.00169$. That is a rate of 1.69 per thousand. The college rate, 4.3 per thousand, is about 2.5 times the all-women rate.

[15] Candace Kruttschnitt, William D. Kalsbeek, and Carol C. House, eds., "Estimating the Incidence of Rape and Sexual Assault," Panel on Measuring Rape and Sexual Assault in Bureau of Justice Statistics Household Surveys, National Research Council, 2014. Committee on National Statistics, Division of Behavioral and Social Sciences and Education. Washington, DC:

The National Academies Press, pp. 3-4. http://www.nap.edu/catalog.php? record_id=18605 Retrieved Sept. 27, 2015.

[16] National Research Council, op. cit., p.2.

[17] "Rape and Sexual Assault Victimization Among College-Age Females, 1995–2013," U.S. Department of Justice, Bureau of Justice Statistics, Dec. 2014. http://www.bjs.gov/content/pub/pdf/rsavcaf9513.pdf Retrieved Sept. 28, 2015.

[18] Libby Nelson, "Why some studies make campus rape look like an epidemic while others say it's rare," *Vox*, Dec. 11, 2014. http://www.vox.com/2014/12/11/7378271/why-some-studies-make-campus-rape-look-like-an-epidemic-while-others Retrieved Sept. 28, 2015.

[19] Op.cit., Breiding, "Prevalence and characteristics of sexual violence."

[20] "National Intimate Partner and Sexual Violence Survey (NISVS) 2011 victimization questions," National Center for Injury Prevention and Control (U.S.), Division of Violence Prevention. pp. 3-4. http://stacks.cdc.gov/view/cdc/24726 Retrieved Sept. 28, 2015.

[21] Ibid., p.4.

[22] "Age and Sex Composition: 2010," U.S. Department of Commerce , Economics and Statistics Administration, U.S. Census Bureau. http://www.census.gov/prod/cen2010/briefs/c2010br-03.pdf Retrieved Sept. 28, 2015.

[23] "Telescoping" refers to the tendency to include events that happened more than a year ago, when asked about events during the past year. If this is happening, it would tend to inflate the numbers.

[24] Op.cit., Krebs, "The Campus Sexual Assault (CSA) study."

[25] Christopher Krebs and Christine Lindquist, "Setting the Record Straight on '1 in 5'," *Time*, Dec. 15, 2014. http://time.com/3633903/campus-rape-1-in-5-sexual-assault-setting-record-straight/ Retrieved Sept. 28, 2015.

[26] Cathy Young, "The White House Overreaches on Campus Rape," *Minding the Campus*, Jan. 23, 2014. http://www.mindingthecampus.com/2014/01/the_white_house_overreaches_on/ Retrieved Sept. 28, 2015.

[27] Op.cit., Libby Nelson.

[28] Dean G. Kilpatrick, Heidi S. Resnick, Kenneth J. Ruggiero, Lauren M. Conoscenti, and Jenna McCauley, "Drug-facilitated, Incapacitated, and Forcible Rape: A National Study ," Medical University of South Carolina, Feb. 1, 2007. https://www.ncjrs.gov/pdffiles1/nij/grants/219181.pdf Retrieved Sept. 28, 2015.

[29] Op.cit., Krebs, *Time*.

[30] Nick Anderson and Scott Clement, Scott, "1 in 5 college women say they were violated," *Washington Post*, June 12, 2015. http://www.washingtonpost.com/sf/local/2015/06/12/1-in-5-women-say-they-were-violated/ Retrieved Sept. 28, 2015.

[31] "Crime in the United States, 2013: Summary of the Uniform Crime Reporting Program," U.S. Department of Justice, Federal Bureau of Investigation. https://www.fbi.gov/about-us/cjis/ucr/crime-in-the-u.s/2013/crime-in-the-u.s.-2013/about-ucr/aboutucrmain_final.pdf Retrieved Sept. 28, 2015.

[32] "Crime in the United States 2013: Rape," U.S. Department of Justice, Federal Bureau of Investigation. http://www.fbi.gov/about-us/cjis/ucr/crime-in-the-u.s/2013/crime-in-the-u.s.-2013/violent-crime/rape Retrieved Sept. 28, 2015.

[33] Op.cit., "Crime in the United States 2013: Summary of the Uniform Crime Reporting Program."

[34] Op.cit., "Crime in the United States 2013: Rape."

[35] "Crime in the United States 2011: Offense Definitions," U.S. Department of Justice, Federal Bureau of Investigation. https://www.fbi.gov/about-us/cjis/ucr/crime-in-the-u.s/2011/crime-in-the-u.s.-2011/11offensedefinitions_final.pdf Retrieved Sept. 28, 2015.

[36] Op.cit., "Crime in the United States 2013: Rape."

[37] "Crime in the United States 2013: Table 1," U.S. Department of Justice, Federal Bureau of Investigation. https://www.fbi.gov/about-us/cjis/ucr/crime-in-the-u.s/2013/crime-in-the-u.s.-2013/tables/1tabledatadecoverviewpdf/table_1_crime_in_the_united_states_by_volume_and_rate_per_100000_inhabitants_1994-2013.xls Retrieved Sept. 28, 2015.

[38] "Crime in the United States 2013: Table 16," U.S. Department of Justice, Federal Bureau of Investigation. https://www.fbi.gov/about-us/cjis/ucr/crime-in-the-u.s/2013/crime-in-the-u.s.-2013/tables/table-16/table_16_rate_by_population_group_2013.xls Retrieved Sept. 28, 2015.

[39] "Crime in the United States 2013: Clearances," U.S. Department of Justice, Federal Bureau of Investigation. http://www.fbi.gov/about-us/cjis/ucr/crime-in-the-u.s/2013/crime-in-the-u.s.-2013/offenses-known-to-law-enforcement/clearances/clearancetopic_final Retrieved Sept. 28, 2015.

[40] "Crime in the United States 2011: Forcible Rape," U.S. Department of Justice, Federal Bureau of Investigation. https://www.fbi.gov/about-us/cjis/ucr/crime-in-the-u.s/2011/crime-in-the-u.s.-2011/violent-crime/forcible-rape Retrieved Sept. 28, 2015.

[41] "The Campus Safety and Security Data Analysis Cutting Tool," U.S. Department of Education, Office of Postsecondary Education. http://ope.ed.gov/security/ Retrieved Sept. 28, 2015.

[42] "Handbook for Campus Safety and Security Reporting," U.S. Department of Education, p.11. http://rems.ed.gov/docs/ED_CampusSafetyAndSecurityReportingHandbook.pdf Retrieved Sept. 28, 2015.

[43] Op.cit., "The Campus Safety and Security Data Analysis Cutting Tool," U.S. Department of Education, Office of Postsecondary Education.

[44] Clery Act Compliance Resources, Clery Center. http://clerycenter.org/clery-act-compliance-resources Retrieved Sept. 28, 2015.

[45] "Handbook for Campus Safety and Security Reporting," U.S. Department of Education, p.141.

[46] Ibid., p. 34.

[47] Ibid., pp.37-39.

[48] Ibid., p. 39.

[49] "The Campus Safety and Security Data Analysis Cutting Tool: Aggregated Data," U.S. Department of Education, Office of Postsecondary Education. (Using the link "Get aggregated data for a group of campuses".) http://ope.ed.gov/security/GetAggregatedData.aspx http://ope.ed.gov/security/ Retrieved Sept. 28, 2015.

[50] "Handbook for Campus Safety and Security Reporting," U.S. Department of Education, p.82.

[51] "Digest of Education Statistics, 2013, Table 303.10, National Center for Education Statistics. "Total fall enrollment in degree-granting postsecondary institutions, by attendance status, sex of student, and control

of institution: Selected years, 1947 through 2023."
http://nces.ed.gov/programs/digest/d13/tables/dt13_303.10.asp See also
http://nces.ed.gov/fastfacts/display.asp?id=98 Both retrieved Sept. 28,
2015.

[52] Collin Binkley, Jill Riepenhoff, Mike Wagner and Sara Gregory,
"Reports on college crime are deceptively inaccurate," *The Columbus Dispatch*, Sept. 30, 2014.
http://www.dispatch.com/content/stories/local/2014/09/30/campus-insecurity.html Retrieved Sept. 28, 2015.

[53] Clair Gordon, "Sexual assault reports jump 61 percent at top colleges
in two years," *Al-Jazeera America*, Oct. 7, 2014.
http://america.aljazeera.com/watch/shows/america-tonight/articles/2014/10/7/colleges-clery-sexualassault1.html Retrieved
Sept. 28, 2015.

[54] "Sexual Victimization of College Women," National Institute of Justice.
http://www.ncjrs.gov/pdffiles1/nij/182369.pdf Retrieved Sept. 28, 2015.

[55] "Prevalence, Incidence, and Consequences of Violence Against
Women: Findings of the National Violence Against Women Survey,"
National Institute of Justice, Nov. 1998.
https://www.ncjrs.gov/pdffiles/172837.pdf Retrieved Sept. 28, 2015.

[56] Joseph Biden as quoted by Glenn Kessler, "One in five women in
college sexually assaulted: the source of this statistic," *Washington Post*,
May 1, 2014. http://www.washingtonpost.com/blogs/fact-checker/wp/2014/05/01/one-in-five-women-in-college-sexually-assaulted-the-source-of-this-statistic/ Retrieved Sept. 28, 2015.

Chapter Six: Harms of the Rape Culture

> Harvard's policy [on sexual assault] was written by people who think sexual assault is so heinous a crime that even innocence is not a defense. –Alan Dershowitz [1]

During the Q&A of the rape culture debate I had with PC feminist Jessica Valenti at Brown University in November 2014, an audience member wondered aloud whether phrasing the debate as a conflict between supporting the accuser or the accused made the exchange more adversarial than necessary. Valenti answered, "[I]n the society we live in now, we need to side with the survivors. That might not be a fair and equal thing, but that's how I think it has to be." [2]

On one level, the questioner was correct. When a crime is alleged, it is inappropriate for third parties to divide immediately into cheerleading teams and take sides. The appropriate response is to remain impartial while trying to ascertain the truth.

On another level, the questioner was *in*correct. Valenti and other rape culture proponents define the debate in terms of women versus men, accusers versus the accused and their demand to believe the woman becomes an automatic presumption of the man's guilt.

But I define the debate differently. I want to weigh the evidence in every case. My insistence on due process for an accused is *not* a defense of men at the expense of women; it does not endorse one side or the other. Instead, it refuses to abandon the principles of fairness for *any* and *every* human being, male or female. Just as I would never chant, "always believe the man," neither would I repeat, "always believe the woman." What should be believed is the evidence as it is revealed through an unbiased investigation.

It is true. Those who deny the rape culture dwell on the rights of accused men and on the harm of false or unfounded accusations. The reason is because rape culture adherents have effectively blocked the possibility of a fair hearing for an accused, which is necessary for an unbiased investigation. If a man were found "guilty" by an unbiased court, however, I would not defend him anymore than I would defend a female found "guilty." The debate is not men versus women but evidence versus ideology.

Valenti's comment on abandoning fairness may seem outrageous but it is typical of rape culture zealots. "The end justifies the means." In other words, fairness should be sacrificed to achieve the greater good of protecting women and encouraging them to report sexual assault. And, so, women who make an accusation must be reflexively believed because the harm of *not* doing so is immense. The harm done to the innocently accused is trivial by comparison. Or it may not even exist.

> [T]he costs of wrongly disbelieving a survivor far outweigh the costs of calling someone a rapist. Even if Jackie [the rape victim depicted by *Rolling Stone*] fabricated her account, U-Va. should have taken her word for it during the period while they endeavored to prove or disprove the accusation. This is not a legal argument about what standards we should use in the courts; it's a moral one, about what happens *outside* the legal system. –Zerlina Maxwell [3]

False Claims That Encourage Harms

Questioning any aspect of rape culture ideology or statistics is seen as an attack on raped women, even if the questioner is female or a rape victim herself. Valenti explained this point in an article, entitled "If you can't talk about rape without blaming victims, don't talk about rape." She wrote, "The worst offense is...[the] apparent belief that there is a 'debate' to be had – as if there are two equal sides, both with reasonable and legitimate points. There are not. On the one side, there are the 20% of college women who can expect to be victimized by rapists and would-be rapists; on the other side is a bunch of adult men (and a few women) worrying themselves to death that a few college-aged men might have to find a new college to attend." [4]

There is most definitely a debate to be had, and a vigorous one. But PC feminists prefer acquiescent silence from the "adult men" and the *many* women who disagree. Dissenting women receive slurs rather than counter-arguments. A current smear tactic is to accuse them of being the products of white privilege, which makes them patriarchal collaborators and co-oppressors. When Christina Hoff Sommers spoke on rape at Oberlin College in April, 2015, for example, her mere presence was denounced as an act of violence. One protest sign read, "Rape Culture is Real and You are a Participant." Many audience members taped their mouths shut to imply that Sommers was silencing them when the truth was they were trying to silence Sommers through a campaign to disinvite her. [5]

Questioning the rape culture is not remotely similar to denying the existence of rape or its importance. I have interacted with hundreds of rape culture skeptics. They grasp the evil of rape and want to confront it as effectively as possible. In fact, a main point of disagreement with rape culture ideologues is over how to best confront a crucial issue. Solutions must be rooted in reality, with a valid view of what rape is and its impact on individuals and society. The dynamics of rape must be taken seriously enough to be judged on facts and evidence, not ideology. This benefits not only the falsely accused but also victims who deserve the justice of an unbiased hearing.

The cry immediately arises: if we do not believe the women, then victims will not report sexual assault. This is a red herring. The demand to believe every accusation *without* evidence or despite the evidence is more likely to discourage victims from filing reports. When blanket validity is extended to *all* reports of a crime, false accusers multiply and dilute the credibility of honest ones. When accounts of rape are revealed as lies, then reasonable people wonder about every other accusation. They become less sympathetic and more skeptical toward real victims.

The debacle surrounding *Rolling Stone*'s fictional account of the U-Va. gang rape may have chilled reports of sexual assault on campus, but the chill cannot be blamed on people who sought the truth. Truth is not the enemy of justice. Hysteria is. Rape culture proponents created a hysterical environment that buoyed a blatantly false accusation. Even after *Rolling Stone* publicly apologized, campus zealots crusaded against the wrongly-accused fraternity. They did so despite indications that "Jackie" herself felt traumatized by their spotlight. If U-Va. rape victims remain silent in the future, then campus feminists should examine their own behavior.

The way to encourage honest reports is to return justice to the process. An important step in restoring public confidence is for rape culture adherents to admit they make mistakes. They should acknowledge the U-Va. was a fiasco and witch hunt, apologize and ask the university to remove the sanctions imposed on fraternities. If they did so, then people might take their accusations seriously.

Another rape culture claim is 100% false: namely, that their politics and ideology inflict no deep harm. Both are devastating to rape victims, to women in general, to men, to universities and to society.

The least discussed harms of rape culture are those inflicted upon rape victims and women themselves. Most of the book so far has highlighted damage done by the rape culture to men. Thus, the bulk of discussion in this chapter focuses on the harm to women.

The Harms Inflicted on Rape Victims and on Women

Second Wave Feminism had a profoundly salutary impact on the issue of rape and on the ability of victims to heal. Chapter One acknowledged my obligation of gratitude but I will restate it here. An essay in my book *Sexual Correctness: The Gender-Feminist Attack on Women* stated, "I owe a debt to '60s feminism. I emerged from the experience [of rape] in one piece largely because of the groundwork feminism had already laid for rape victims....From feminism I learned an irreplaceable and healing lesson: it was not my fault." [6] An individual man had committed a crime against me, and I was not to blame.

But PC feminism redefined rape as a gender crime. It became a politically motivated act that every woman experiences in some form and to some degree whether or not she is ever physically assaulted. It became an act from which every man benefited whether or not he attacked a woman. In the rape culture, woman as a class were victims; men (sometimes expressed as "white men") as a class were victimizers. Relationships devolved to gender warfare. The core of the redefinition was captured by Liz Kelly, Professor of Sexualised Violence at London Metropolitan University, in her book *Surviving Sexual Violence* (1988). "Sexual violence includes any physical, visual, verbal or sexual act that is experienced by the woman or girl, at the time or later, as a threat, invasion or assault, that has the effect of hurting her or degrading her and/or takes away her ability to control intimate contact." [7]

Contrast Kelly's definition with the one offered a decade earlier by Dr. A. Nicholas Groth in his book *Men Who Rape: The Psychology of the Offender* (1979). Groth, with assistance from H. Jean Birnbaum Groth, drew a sharp distinction between sexual oppression and sex that occurs because of persuasion, seduction or other non-violent circumstances – that is, "pressured assault." Groth wrote, "The defining characteristic of forced assault is the risk of bodily harm to the woman should she refuse to participate in sexual activity. All non consenting sex is assault. In the pressured assault, the victim is sexually harassed or exploited. In forced assaults, she is a victim of rape." [8]

By blurring the line between force and pressure, important sexual and legal distinctions are erased, such as the difference between rape and seduction. When sexual assault is defined as a "visual, verbal or sexual act that is experienced... as...degrading her and/or takes away her ability to control intimate contact," then anything can be sexual violence. Sexual attack becomes an amorphous thing against which females should guard at every minute. It is impossible to measure the harm such sexual paranoia does to women's sense of well-being or their ability to relate to men in a healthy manner.

I don't have to imagine the harm sexual paranoia inflicts on victims of rape because, like most victims, I have dealt with it. I healed by gaining perspective and by realizing there were individuals – both male and female – whom I could trust and with whom I was safe. Defining society as sexual violence and men as oppressors would have been a huge hurdle to my healing.

The injury the rape culture inflicts on rape victims and women in general is six-fold, at least.

It prevents healthy sexual relationships

The **first** and most obvious harm has been mentioned: rape culture proponents advance an irrational view of sex and men that make healthy relationships unnecessarily difficult.

The disconnect from reality is embodied by the current "yes means yes" campaign. What is that campaign? A pioneering work is the 2008 book by Jaclyn Friedman and Jessica Valenti, *Yes Means Yes: Visions of Female Sexual Power and A World Without Rape*. [9] (Friedman was well-known for her Fucking While Feminist podcast.) The introduction explains, "So often it seems as if the discourse is focused solely on the 'no means no' model – which, while of course useful, stops short of truly envisioning how suppressing female agency is a key element of rape culture, and therefore how fostering genuine female sexual autonomy is necessary in fighting back against it. We wanted to talk about how to make the world safer for women to say no *and* yes to sex as we please." [10]

The "yes means yes" campaign is a proposed replacement for the "no means no" one that preceded it. "No means no" hinges on a key concept: if a person verbally or physically rejects sexual activity and the other person continues, then the activity becomes assault. But significant gray areas exist. A particularly controversial one is when consent is present at the beginning but is withdrawn at some point, and perhaps with subtlety. If the male assumes sustained consent and continues, is he guilty of rape?

"Yes means yes" attempts to erase the gray areas by requiring an explicit "yes" at every stage of sexual activity; the absence of an explicit "yes" is deemed to be a "no." In other words, in moving from a consensual kiss to hugging or fondling, the male must pause to renew the female's consent. A "yes" at every stage literally means at *every* stage.

What does "yes means yes" look like in practice as a policy or law? The California law reads,

> The policy shall include all of the following: (1) An affirmative consent standard in the determination of whether consent was given by both parties to sexual activity. 'Affirmative consent' means affirmative, conscious, and voluntary agreement to engage in sexual activity. It is the responsibility of each person involved in the sexual activity to ensure that he or she has the affirmative consent of the other or others to engage in the sexual activity. Lack of protest or resistance does not mean consent, nor does silence mean consent. Affirmative consent must be ongoing throughout a sexual activity and can be revoked at any time. The existence of a dating relationship between the persons involved, or the fact of past sexual relations between them, should never by itself be assumed to be an indicator of consent. [11]

The concept may seem innocuous. After all, shouldn't sex be clearly consensual? Yet, in real life, how many people explicitly and repeatedly consent to be touched on the cheek, then to be kissed, then to be hugged, and so on? In the throes of passion, people do not negotiate which piece of clothing comes off next. Explicitly vetting an ongoing contract of sex is more appropriate to a lawyer's office than it is to a bedroom, especially for an established couple who have consented to each other on many occasions.

There is no dispute: a "no" must always be respected and it should cause an immediate cessation of sex at any stage. But legally requiring a constant "yes" runs counter to real world experience.

The situation worsens as "yes means yes" is further defined. [12] Anyone who is drunk or on drugs is deemed incapable of rendering consent even if a "yes" is being screamed in rapid succession. Or, rather, in practice, the woman is viewed as being incapable of consenting while the man is held responsible. Again this runs counter to real world experience. Engaging in sex after having a few is extremely common, especially for young people who may be nervous or partying hard. Now a natural part of dating and relationships is being criminalized.

In fairness, some rape culture activists concede that a "yes" can be rendered non-verbally through active participation in sex. But others maintain the rigid standard of requiring an explicit and repeated "yes" at every stage. Assemblywoman Bonnie Lowenthal, who co-authored the California measure, has "said affirmative consent means an individual 'must say "yes,"'" and 'if an individual says nothing, that doesn't imply consent.'" [13] When Lowenthal was asked precisely how an innocent man could prove consent to a hearing or court, she replied, "Your guess is as good as mine." [14]

In a *Time* article, Cathy Young explained just one problem with Lowenthal's flip response.

> Nonverbal cues indicating consent are almost certainly present in most consensual sexual encounters. But as a legal standard, nonverbal affirmative consent leaves campus tribunals in the position of trying to answer murky and confusing questions – for instance, whether a passionate response to a kiss was just a kiss, or an expression of 'voluntary agreement' to have sexual intercourse. Faced with such ambiguities, administrators are likely to err on the side of caution and treat only explicit verbal agreement as sufficient proof of consent. In fact, many affirmative-consent-based student codes of sexual conduct today either discourage reliance on nonverbal communication as leaving too much room for mistakes... [15]

By contrast, a "no means no" standard does not encourage such massive intrusion into people's sexual lives by institutions and legislatures.

It increases skepticism about rape claims

A **second** harm inflicted on rape victims deserves repetition. As rape culture policies become more unrealistic, as more accusations are revealed to be false, reasonable people become suspicious of victims who come forward. This discourages and stigmatizes reporting.

Some recent cases of false accusations are presented below to indicate why doubt about rape claims is increasing, especially about campus assault.

In February 2013, Morgan Triplett claimed to have been raped at the University of California, Santa Cruz. The *Daily Caller* later revealed, "Turns out, though, Morgan Triplett's story was a hoax. According to police, the bizarre truth is that she successfully used Craigslist to locate a stranger who agreed to beat her up in exchange for sex." [16]

In April 2013, Meg Lanker Simons, a University of Wyoming student, received an anonymous post through Facebook. "I want to hatefuck Meg Lanker Simons so hard. That chick runs her liberal mouth all the time and doesn't care who knows it. I think its so hot and makes me angry. One night with me and shes gonna be a good Republican bitch." As it turned out, Simons had sent the post to herself. Nevertheless, campus feminists held rallies in her support. Simons' motive was apparently to call attention to the rape culture. [17]

Also in April, 2013, a former University of Florida student, Tanya Borachi, reported being bound and gagged in the Campus Lodge apartment's parking lot. She later recanted, defending the lie by calling it "a lesson to women in the area that an attack could happen to them." [18]

In September 2014, Columbia University student Emma Sulkowicz launched a piece of performance art called "Carry That Weight" as her senior thesis. Sulkowicz vowed to carry a mattress around campus until the male student she accused of rape was expelled or otherwise departed. A university inquiry found him "not responsible." Sulkowicz's accusation fell apart after a February 2015 article by Cathy Young called the accusation into question, to say the least. [19] Sulkowicz's motive seemed to be attention-seeking.

In December 2014, a *Rolling Stone* account of gang rape at a U-Va. frat party collapsed spectacularly in the face of facts. (See Chapter Three for extensive discussion of the case.) The motive of the accuser is unknown. Some view her as a disturbed young woman who was exploited by an unethical reporter.

On March 5, 2015, a *Huffington Post* headline read, "Brown University Shuts Down Date Rape Investigation After Botched Lab Results." Two lab tests procured by Brown agreed that two female students had been dosed with a rape drug at a frat party but no results were released. The accused fraternity did separate testing which disputed the original results. In an open letter, the fraternity declared the second test to be "conclusively negative." [20] Brown eventually dropped the charges.

An April 27, 2015 *Breitbart* headline stated "After Falsely Accusing an Innocent Man, Lena Dunham Is Celebrated as a Rape Role Model." The alleged campus rape occurred years earlier when Dunham was a student. *Breitbart* continued, "In the autobiography, which was labeled as non-fiction, Dunham described her rapist using seven completely unnecessary details that immediately identified him..." For months, the falsely-accused man fought to clear his name. Only after the *Breitbart* article did Dunham and Random House admit that the details about her alleged rapist were fictional. Nevertheless, as *Breitbart* observed, "[Dunham] is still being celebrated and honored as a sexual assault role model at events like...*Variety*'s Power of Women New York Luncheon, and throughout the mainstream media." [21]

On May 6, 2015, the website Community of the Wrongly Accused reported on an apparently sober female student at Claremont McKenna College who had sex with a young man after he obtained explicit consent. Nevertheless, the woman described being "raped by rape culture." By this, she meant a type of rape by which a woman's consent has been "coerced by the culture that had raised us and the systems of power that worked on us." She later stated, "consent is a privilege, and it was built for wealthy, heterosexual, cis, white, western, able-bodied masculinity." [22]

On April 8, 2015, the website Save Our Sons announced, "Student cleared of false accusation files lawsuit against Kenyon College." The background: Former Kenyon student Stephen Zingarelli was acquitted of rape and gross sexual imposition by a Common Pleas court in June 2013. He filed suit against Kenyon, a college Sexual Misconduct Advisor, and his accuser. The College is accused of violating Title IX of the Education Amendments by discriminating against him based on gender. Zingarelli suggested the accuser's motivation was malice. [23]

An April 10, 2015 headline in *The Wall Street Journal* read, "In Campus Rape Tribunals, Some Men See Injustice." Lewis McLeod, a senior student, was accused of raping a freshman. A police investigation did not find sufficient evidence to proceed. *The Wall Street Journal* described what happened next. "A Duke University disciplinary panel didn't find he gave her alcohol or used force. But the panel concluded it was 'more likely than not' the woman didn't agree to sex and was too intoxicated to consent. Regarding a degree, Duke lawyers later said, 'Mr. McLeod is not entitled to that honor'." He was expelled two weeks before graduation. The accuser's motive is unknown. [24]

The foregoing cases do not indicate that most accusations are either false or unfounded. What the cases *do* indicate, however, is the need to weigh allegations and evidence for both the accuser and the accused. Otherwise, victims who come forward will be increasingly dismissed rather than heard.

It can prevent healing

The **third** injury the rape culture inflicts on traumatized victims is by acting as a barrier to psychological healing. Here, I speak for myself. I will never tell another human being how to recover from sexual assault. There is no single solution for all rape victims because the trauma is too personal, too individual. But I believe the way I recovered is common, and I know that embracing a rape culture ideology would have prevented it.

One reason: Rape culture adherents push for attacks to be reported even though a woman might not wish to do so. There can be good reasons for silence. A sex worker might want to conceal her profession or she might not trust the police. A deeply religious woman could refuse to discuss such an intimate matter with strangers. A married woman may not want her spouse to know she had been "stepping out." If drugs or alcohol were involved, then the woman could be confused.

I did not report my rape. I did not discuss it for years afterward. It happened when I was a teenager on the street, sleeping in a church in order to keep warm. When a minor chooses to live in the street rather than in a shelter, it means she or he does not trust authority. The teen-aged me viewed authority as a form of psychological rape. To a large extent, I still do. If I were attacked today, however, I would report the crime because I now enjoy far, far greater control over who I am and my circumstances. But, on a visceral level, I know why victims do *not* speak out, and I cannot criticize anyone who chooses silence.

When a woman has been raped, it is her right to decide on whether to make a report. Just as a victim of theft can choose not to press charges so, too, should a victim of rape be free to choose silence without being pressured by PC feminists. And, yet, victims are pressed to disclose their assaults in public venues or to authorities. Even if the pressure is well intentioned, victims can be harmed.

For example, a victim may be told to make a report so that the same rapist does not attack others. This line of argument seems logical but it can damage a suffering victim whose first concern should be to heal herself. It is never clear whether a rape victim will be able to bear the emotional ordeal of a public process that keeps her rape alive inside her for years. Moreover, the argument contains an insidious assumption; namely, the victim is in some way responsible for the actions her rapist may take tomorrow. But, just as she was not responsible for her own rape, she cannot be blamed for the future actions of another person. It is his choice and his responsibility, not hers. To instill additional guilt into a traumatized person is vicious.

Some people argue that confronting a rapist has a healing impact but every human being reacts differently. Years ago, an "expert" counseled a friend of mine to confront her rapist who was then in prison. She did so several times. The confrontations were so agonizing that she broke off an otherwise solid relationship with a good, decent man. She became so enraged and confused that she could not distinguish between hitting out at the rapist and attacking a man she loved. After a few years, the two were lucky enough to find each other again and to marry.

Another way in which rape culture ideology hinders recovery is its insistence that rape is an expression of patriarchy. To PC feminists, even intensely personal acts reduce to political terms. In her essay, "The Personal is Political," the path-breaking Carol Hanisch famously remarked of consciousness-raising sessions, "There are no personal solutions at this time. There is only collective action for a collective solution." Although she acknowledged the therapeutic aspects of shared experience, Hanisch called the process "'political therapy' as opposed to personal therapy." The problem was the system, which women needed to change rather than focusing on "personal solutionary." [25]

I know differently. I was not raped by men as a class, by the patriarchy or by society. One man was responsible. Most men I know would have defended me, even if it had endangered them, because they are decent human beings. An essential step in my healing was to direct my rage at the individual who had harmed me and to *not* to blame men who would have protected me. If I had generalized my fury, then I doubt if I could have fallen in love with my husband. I would have missed the greatest emotional fulfillment I've ever found.

I rejected another common assertion of rape culture ideologues; namely, rape is the worst thing that can happen to a woman, and she never really recovers. Rape is far from the worst thing that has happened to me; it cannot compare to the death of people I've loved. And I have recovered from the attack. I refused to define myself by a brutal act that was done *to* me; it was not done *by* me.

A feeling has haunted me since I began to read rape culture analysis. I don't merely disagree with the politics but also with the psychology that jumps off the page. There is a macabre celebration of victimhood that is chilling.

The competition to be the most oppressed and most victimized–
the 'Victim Olympics'– led to a view of people's class oppressions as
the central organizing principle of their lives. They are holders of
the Progressive 'special knowledge', and with the sword of
righteousness they go out to correct the culture. –Jeb Kinnison [26]

PC feminists honor abused women as though their rapes were a source of
special worth or value. But there is neither honor nor shame in being raped.
And rape victims must stop defining themselves by one awful incident and,
instead, move on to become survivors.

Sociologist Frank Furedi wrote of a "society that celebrates victimhood
rather than heroism. We are all expected to compete, like guests on a
television programme, to prove that we are the most put-upon and pathetic
people in the house, the most deserving of counseling and compensation.
The virtues held up are passivity rather than activism, safety rather than
boldness. And the rather diminished individual that emerges is indulged on
the grounds that, in a world awash with conditions and crises and
impending catastrophes, he or she is doing a good job just by surviving."
[27]

It endangers women's safety

A **fourth** way in which rape culture policies harm women and create
victims is by discouraging the art of self-defense. It used to be a matter of
common sense. People avoided walking down alleys at midnight in high-
crime areas. They bolted the door behind them at night. They tried not to
conspicuously wave hundred dollar bills in bars. They locked up Porsches
parked on the street and did not pass out drunk in a stranger's apartment.
These practices greatly reduced their chances of being victimized in a
dangerous world. The advice applies whether a person is male or female,
white or black.

Learning self-defense, which includes tactics of prevention, used to be a
sign that a person took responsibility for her own safety. Advising someone
to act defensively used to be an expression of concern for the person's well-
being. Arguing for self-defense today, however, is called victim-blaming and
it is viewed as a form of rape facilitation. Victim-blaming is the process of
holding the victim of a crime fully or partly responsible for the crime itself.

PC feminists conflate crime prevention with victim-blaming and deny the
fundamental difference between them. In fact, the two are opposites of
each other; one is a display of concern and the other is an expression of
contempt. But when a concerned person gives a female student cab fare as

she heads out the door to bar-hop, that person is accused of victim-blaming. Why? As bizarre as it sounds, it is because PC feminists believe a woman should be able to walk naked through a bikers' bar and *never* be attacked or threatened.

In one sense, they are correct. In an ideal world, everyone should be able to proceed peacefully through their lives without experiencing violence. They are also correct in demanding that moral and legal liability fall entirely upon the aggressor. But the world is not ideal. It is filled with danger, as rape culture adherents constantly remind us. In a less than perfect world, it is prudent for people to act in a manner that minimizes the possibility of harm. Why is this such a controversial position?

A book by psychologist William Ryan, *Blaming the Victim* (1971), pioneered the conflation of crime prevention and victim-blaming. [28] Ryan claimed that "blaming the victim" was based on a fallacious hypothesis known as "Just World" – that is, a world in which individuals get what they deserve. People of good character and habits achieve good things; those with bad character and habits "achieve" the opposite. An example is health. Those who watch their diet and exercise are more healthy than those who chow down on junk food and are inactive. Ryan believed this hypothesis led to a logical but false conclusion: if a person is not being rewarded, then he or she should look within themselves for the reason and change behaviors.

When it came to racism and other social injustices, however, Ryan argued that the social environment needed to be changed, not the individual. Centuries of slavery and discrimination were responsible for the disadvantages experienced by blacks, not the content of their characters. Returning to the health analogy, a black should not be blamed for ill-health; instead, the cause should be located in outside factors, such as poverty, which may limit the person's choice in food or access to medical care. When a doctor looked only to the lifestyle of a disadvantaged patient for explanations of poor health, he was engaged in "victim-blaming." Instead, the social disadvantages should be addressed.

Consciously or not, PC feminists have adapted Ryan's argument to apply to the danger experienced by women. Namely, the violence against them is located in patriarchy and the rape culture. To suggest that women change their own behavior in response to the injustice is to victim-blame.

The logic to this argument quickly breaks down. There is no contradiction in advising a person to take reasonable steps to avoid danger while also trying to change the social factors that create those dangers. The positions are not mutually exclusive.

Rape culture ideologues are establishing an either-or situation that does not exist. If someone suggests a woman refrain from drinking to extreme in public, the outraged PC response is "a woman doesn't deserve to be raped because she is drunk!" But that's not what the person is saying. She is merely identifying one of the risk factors for being raped and suggesting a behavior that could reduce the danger.

Camille Paglia elicited fury from PC feminists because of a passage in her book, *Sex, Art and American Culture: Essays* (1992). The text was quoted earlier in Chapter One but it deserves to be restated in this altered context.

> These girls say, 'Well, I should be able to get drunk at a fraternity party and go upstairs to a guy's room without anything happening.' And I say, 'Oh, really? And when you drive your car into New York City, do you leave your keys on the hood?' My point is that if your car is stolen after you do something like that, yes, the police should pursue the thief and he should be punished. But at the same time, the police – and I – have the right to say to you, 'You stupid idiot, what the hell were you thinking?' [29]

Paglia's tone is harsher than my own but I agree with her basic point. Women should learn how to protect themselves and take common sense measures to do so. When a female student agrees to "go upstairs to a guy's room," she is not asking for it. She does not deserve whatever she gets. What she *does* deserve, however, is to know which behaviors on her part will increase or decrease the risk of harm.

In 2014, Katherine Timpf published an article in *National Review* entitled "Apparently, anything that helps women protect themselves is offensive." [30] The proximate cause was the PC response to a new product from a start-up company, *Undercover Colors*, which describes itself as "the first fashion company empowering women to prevent sexual assault." Its new nail polish changed color when it came into contact with a date-rape drug in a drink. A woman could dip in a finger to make sure her glass had not been tampered with.

The college-student inventors were blasted for contributing to the rape culture. (Their maleness may have contributed to the negative response.) Some critics called the men "well-meaning but ultimately misguided" – misguided because their product placed responsibility for prevention on the women, not the men. A *Think Progress* article by Health Editor Tara Culp-Ressler was much harsher. "Women are already expected to work hard to prevent themselves from becoming the victims of sexual assault. They're told to avoid wearing revealing clothing, travel in groups, make sure they don't get too drunk, and always keep a close eye on their drink. Now, remembering to put on anti-rape nail polish and discreetly slip a finger into each drink might be added to that ever-growing checklist – something that actually reinforces a pervasive rape culture in our society." [31]

The *Think Progress* article quoted Rebecca Nagle, a co-director of the activist group FORCE: Upsetting Rape Culture. "I'm told not to go out alone at night, to watch my drink, to do all of these things. That way, rape isn't just controlling me while I'm actually being assaulted – it controls me 24/7 because it limits my behavior. Solutions like these actually just recreate that. I don't want to fucking test my drink when I'm at the bar. That's not the world I want to live in." [32]

Nagle's position is odd because no one is forcing her to test drinks. The nail polish is just another choice for the women who want to use it. And the choice might save them from violence.

> Every time I see a post on how women don't need self-defense and men should be taught not to rape, I always wonder if the people who write this kind of shit ever realize they're making women even bigger targets. –Karen Straughan [33]

The popular PC site *Feministing* [34] added its own critique of the nail polish by asking a series of questions. "Is your product free? Will if be universally available in bars and on college campuses? What if I'm interested in ensuring not only *my* safety but also the safety of all the other women who have not heard about – or cannot afford to buy – your nail polish? Do you recommend that I just purchase a bulk order and set up a nail-painting table outside my local bar? Can you provide some advice for how to discreetly ask strangers if they'd like me to stir their drinks as well?" Apparently, a business is morally complicit in assault if its anti-rape product is not provided gratis and to everyone. Of course, this practice would convert the business into a charity or non-profit. The standards reflected by the questions are so unrealistic as to preclude *any* anti-rape product from being viewed as pro-woman and not pro-rape.

It infantilizes women

A **fifth** way in which rape culture policies damage victims and women is by infantilizing them. Women need the opposite; they need empowerment.

Before the Brown University debate with Valenti, the on-campus Sexual Assault Task Force issued a "trigger warning" because I was a rape culture denier who might upset some students.

What is a trigger warning? The Monash Women's Department explained the mechanism. "Trigger warnings are....designed to prevent people who have an extremely strong and damaging emotional response (for example, post-traumatic flashbacks or urges to harm themselves) to certain subjects from encountering them unaware." The material against which students need to be warned include "descriptions of war, like the Vietnam war, or the US operations in Afghanistan" and "discussion of eating-disordered behavior." The Media Fan area of the Geek Feminism Wiki recommended trigger warnings for the following:

- depiction or discussion of violence

- depiction or discussion of particular kinds of consensual sexual activity (BDSM, homosexual encounters, heterosexual encounters...)

- depiction or discussion of any consensual sexual activity

- depiction or discussion of discriminatory attitudes or actions, such as sexism or racism

If trigger warnings are attached to an event, such as a lecture or debate, the Wiki suggested, "Where possible, have self-comfort places and objects available to your participants such as things they can play with with [sic] their hands, and a self-comfort area available such as a quiet room." [35]

Volunteers at Brown provided a safe space as a sanctuary for those who were traumatized by ideas and needed to recuperate from hearing them. In a *New York Times* article, "In College and Hiding From Scary Ideas," columnist Judith Shulevitz described Brown's safe space.

> The room was equipped with cookies, coloring books, bubbles, Play-Doh, calming music, pillows, blankets and a video of frolicking puppies, as well as students and staff members trained to deal with trauma. Emma Hall, a junior, rape survivor and 'sexual assault peer educator' who helped set up the room and worked in it during the debate, estimates that a couple of dozen people used it. At one point she went to the lecture hall – it was packed – but after a while, she had to return to the safe space. 'I was feeling bombarded by a lot of viewpoints that really go against my dearly and closely held beliefs', Ms. Hall said. [36]

Safe spaces became popular in the '90s. Geek Feminism Wiki described how it evolved into a political framework. "Safe space is a term for an area or forum where either a marginalised group are [sic] not supposed to face standard mainstream stereotypes and marginalisation, or in which a shared political or social viewpoint is required to participate in the space." [37]

The first safe spaces on campus seemed designed to allow vulnerable students to meet in a manner that would not be threatening. But the concept has expanded into a demand to control free speech on a university-wide level. Policies, events, curriculum, class discussion, out-of-class discussion...all have been subjected to the shrill demand to exclude ideas, words or attitudes that could "trigger" and cause distress. Instructors have been pressured to convert classrooms into safe spaces by censoring ideas and even by rewriting history.

Columbia University's student newspaper, *Columbia Spectator*, recently made the sort of demand that has become commonplace. Four members of the student Multicultural Affairs Advisory Board (MAAB) called out to professors of literature to be sensitive when presenting "trigger material." They explained, "[d]uring the week spent on Ovid's 'Metamorphoses', the class was instructed to read the myths of Persephone and Daphne, both of which include vivid depictions of rape and sexual assault." A student who was a sexual assault survivor had been "triggered" and "completely disengaged from the class discussion as a means of self-preservation." Apparently, the professor ignored her expressed "concerns."

Such texts, MAAB declared, were "narratives of exclusion and oppression" that could be difficult for "a survivor, a person of color, or a student from a low-income background" to read and discuss. Calling for "possible interventions" (read, the shutting down of classroom discussion), the authors criticized professors for not being "effective facilitators in the classroom." What would they facilitate? "[A] space to hold a safe and open dialogue about experiences in the classroom that all too often traumatize and silence students." [38]

The SJWs claimed they did not wish to infringe academic freedom. But requiring instructors to use "effective strategies" in presenting ideas *is* an infringement. For one thing, what is an "effective strategy" and for whom? An approach that makes a marginalized group feel safe may destroy the educational value for the majority of students. The two approaches could be in direct conflict. MAAB's demand converts the classroom from a forum for knowledge into a therapy center.

A bright spot in the *Columbia Spectator* article was the comment section. It brimmed with calls for free speech and uncensored education, interspersed with cynicism directed at MAAB. Comments included:

- You people sound like 1980s Christian mothers talking about their kids being exposed to the evil influence of Madonna. Grow up, open up....Such an insufferable breed of self-centered Care Bears.

- Millennial leftists blathering about "social justice" and pretending to be "progressive"; when really, they're all acting like the worst right wing social conservatives. Hey snowflakes. Hey. Listen up. You're not Rosa Parks. You're Anita Bryant. Get a clue.

- [A]s a gay man who grew up in the south I don't have any sympathy for these melting little snowflakes. Life is a difficult, unfair journey. You will encounter...individuals who think or act in ways that make you upset or uncomfortable....Grow up. Deal with your problems. Go to therapy. But stop acting as if you are owed gentleness and understanding by dint of being born....The syllabus no doubt made it clear Ovid would be...in the course. No surprises, plenty of time to drop early and pick something gentler on these students' precious psyches. I'd suggest childhood literature.

- Your statements and actions have consequences. Real ones like not getting a job - or losing it - because you can't handle reality. Honestly, you've been screwed over by the system which has turned you into this mush who believes his identity is what matters more than anything else. It's sad, really.

Safe spaces prevent students from acquiring the art of critical thinking which requires ideas to be examined, challenged, and defended. The "dumbing down" hits so-called marginalized students, like women, the hardest because they are the ones most vulnerable to believing they need safe spaces. A person protected from information will join the ranks of what has been called the "intellectually swaddled generation" who are intellectually infantilized. This leaves them unprepared for life in the real world.

It short-circuits critical thinking and polarizes women

This is the **sixth** harm inflicted by the rape culture policies. Law student Alex Kasnetz described the dynamic of short-circuiting the ability to reason. "Young liberals aren't being taught how to argue. Derision, rather than refutation, seems to be the norm of discourse in mainstream politics as well. Accordingly, opposing views are seen as a sign of some moral defect, not genuine disagreement.... Progressives think their vitriolic name-calling undermines their opponents. But Munger [Duke professor Michael Munger] has it right: 'The absence of [dissent] is harmful, not so much to those who would agree with the dissenting voice, but to those who are thus denied the chance to collide with error'." [39] The left is committing intellectual suicide and impoverishing society in the process.

PC feminists are also polarizing women, and needlessly so. Dissident feminist Maria Maltseva wrote,

> I am a gender traitor, and I stand in solidarity with other gender traitors like me. We have a rich history, you see. During the holocaust, gay men were labeled gender traitors by the Nazis and then cruelly exterminated, and today I stand in solidarity with gay men (and with people of all sexual orientations and genders). In the 50s in the US, white supremacists called white liberals who believed in racial equality "race traitors," a term analogous to gender traitors, and I stand in solidarity with people of all races. This very day, a subset of vocal and powerful feminists...is labeling all other women – including liberal, libertarian, and equity feminists – as gender traitors, and I stand in solidarity with all women labeled as such. Further, I stand in solidarity with every man who has been unfairly accused of misogyny for simply being born male and daring to question feminist ideology or the wrong woman's ideas. [40]

Rape culture ideologues are even turning on each other over minor disputes. The PC feminist site *Jezebel* outlined [41] a protest that confronted Northwestern University professor Laura Kipnis.

Kipnis's sin? She wrote an article that objected to sexual paranoia on college campuses. Kipnis stated, "Women have spent the past century and a half demanding to be treated as consenting adults, now a cohort on campuses [is] demanding to relinquish those rights, which I believe is a disastrous move for feminism." She objected specifically to a proposed new code for sexual assault hearings, which she believed gave bureaucrats too much control over the personal lives of students.

In response, two female students filed Title IX complaints against Kipnis despite her sterling reputation for feminism. Kipnis was plunged into a bureaucratic hell from whence she protested her innocence. "I wrote back to the Title IX coordinator asking for clarification: When would I learn the specifics of these complaints, which, I pointed out, appeared to violate my academic freedom? And what about my rights – was I entitled to a lawyer? I received a polite response with a link to another website. No, I could not have an attorney present during the investigation, unless I'd been charged with sexual violence. I was, however, allowed to have a 'support person' from the university community there, though that person couldn't speak. I wouldn't be informed about the substance of the complaints until I met with the investigators."

Rape culture zealots will not tolerate deviation even from the Founding Mothers of their own movement. A September 2015 headline in *The American Interest* read   [42], "The revolution devours its own. Susan Brownmiller, Heretic." The article described how the author of the "enormously influential *Against Our Will*" had become a feminist outcast.

> In an interview with *New York* magazine last week, the 80-year-old Brownmiller suggested that the campus rape movement is narrow, elitist, and 'doesn't accept reality'. Asked what advice she would give activists, Brownmiller said, 'extend your focus to the larger percentage of women and girls who are in danger of being raped. They are more important than the college kids'. She also violated the well-known taboo against drawing a connection between sexual assault and the campus culture of binge drinking: 'If you drink you lose your sense of judgment. Everybody knows that. You should know that when you are going into a fraternity party, something can happen'.

The backlash was predictable but shocking nevertheless. It confirmed the willingness of SJWs to throw *anyone* under the bus over a deviation. *The American Interest* continued,

> The rape crisis crusaders contemptuously brushed Brownmiller's views aside. Downgrading her to a "former feminist hero," Amanda Marcotte wrote in *Slate* that Brownmiller is "downright victim-blame-y, sneering at girls today with their booze and their clothes and their asking-for-it," a line echoed by writers at *Salon* and elsewhere. Jessica Valenti wrote in the *Guardian* that 'the movement will go on without' outdated thinkers like Brownmiller. According to one feminist writer, Brownmiller's views 'seem to be straight from a 1970s chauvinist'.

The Harm PC Feminism Inflicts on Universities

> [The aim of public education is not] to fill the young of the species with knowledge and awaken their intelligence....Nothing could be further from the truth. The aim...is simply to reduce as many individuals as possible to the same safe level, to breed and train a standardized citizenry, to put down dissent and originality. That is its aim in the United States.... –H.L. Mencken

The quality of higher education in North America is declining. One factor is the political correctness that permeates campuses, especially in fields described as the humanities or the soft sciences or liberal arts.

How dramatic is the PC impact? Some law schools now balk at teaching classes on rape law. Jeannie Suk, a professor at Harvard Law School, described the environment on her campus.

> Student organizations representing women's interests now routinely advise students that they should not feel pressured to attend or participate in class sessions that focus on the law of sexual violence, and which might therefore be traumatic. These organizations also ask criminal-law teachers to warn their classes that the rape-law unit might 'trigger' traumatic memories. Individual students often ask teachers not to include the law of rape on exams for fear that the material would cause them to perform less well. One teacher I know was recently asked by a student not to use the word "violate" in class– as in "Does this conduct violate the law?"– because the word was triggering. Some students have even suggested that rape law should not be taught because of its potential to cause distress. [43]

Another triggering aspect seems to be the traditional law class approach of having students argue the merits of opposing positions. The process allows students to understand the best arguments on both sides. Now it is viewed as a source of trauma, not enlightenment.

Exploring legal gray areas is also a trigger. Consider a scenario: An accused rapist did not realize there was absence of consent because the partner appeared to cooperate and there was a history of prior sex. The instructor might ask, "does a reasonable assumption of consent mitigate the man's legal responsibility?" The very question is a slap at rape culture theory. And, so, difficult legal questions are being raised less frequently even though they will arise in the practice of law.

Real world criminal cases often reflect the horrors of life, including rape. Part of a criminal lawyer's job is to dispassionately represent the best interests of a client, which requires the lawyer to have distance from personal reactions. If law schools cease to teach "trigger issues," then sexual victims will be denied the solid representation they so desperately need. Law students who prioritize their own triggers above information are harming rape victims.

Nevertheless, some professors have dropped instruction on rape law and other areas of sexuality. More are considering the option. After all, careers can be damaged or ruined by student complaints.

The intellectual gaps at law schools are a tiny aspect of how political correctness devastates universities. The dumbing-down policies within classrooms have spilled over and become campus-wide policies of social control that regulate innocuous interactions.

Another reason rape culture ideology reduces educational quality is because it diverts funds away from instruction and into the expensive administration of PC policies. A *National Review* article entitled "The Decline of College. The four-year campus experience is becoming a thing of the past" examined the California State University system, which is the largest university complex in the world. The article stated, "Administrators used to come from among the top faculty, who rotated a few years from teaching and scholarship to do the unenviable nuts-and-bolts work of running the university. Now, administrators rarely, if ever, teach. Instead, they became part of a high-paid, careerist professional caste – one that has grown exponentially. In the CSU system, their numbers have exploded in recent years – a 221 percent increase from 1975 to 2008. There are now more administrators in that system than full-time faculty." What happened? "[P]rofessors of the traditional arts and sciences could or would not effectively defend their disciplines or the classical university system, [and so] agenda-driven politicians, partisan ideologues, and careerist technocrats absorbed them." [44]

The increase in bureaucracy is picking up pace. After an analysis of federal statistics, the New England Center for Investigative Reporting and the American Institutes for Research issued their findings. From 1987 to 2011-12, "universities and colleges collectively added 517,636 administrators and professional employees, or an average of 87 every working day." [45]

How much do the administrators cost? The Higher Eds Job site reported results from "the 2012-13 Administrators in Higher Education Salary Survey conducted by The College and University Professional Association for Human Resources (CUPA-HR)." The findings reflected "the salaries of 55,017 job incumbents in public and private institutions nationwide. Salaries were reported by 1,251 institutions for 190 selected positions, mostly at the director level and above." The median salary for a "Chief Diversity Officer" was $112,000. [46]

Meanwhile, tuition continues to soar. The College Board Advocacy & Policy Center tracks the cost of higher education. The Center recently stated,

"Average published tuition and fees at public four-year colleges and universities increased by 19 [percent] beyond the rate of inflation over the five years from 2003-04 to 2008-09, and by another 27 [percent] between 2008-09 and 2013-14." [47] The increase is higher than in virtually any other sector of the economy.

It is not possible to ascertain with accuracy how much the jump in costs comes from non-educational programs, administrators, staff, and paperwork. Dan King, president of the American Association of University Administrators, claimed that thousands of regulations governed the distribution of financial aid alone. It is fair to claim, however, that government policies are instrumental in turning American universities into bankrupt social experiments.

Yet another non-educational cost is increasing dramatically; lawsuits are resulting from campus sexual assault investigations and hearings. The suits fall into two rough categories: An accused claims the university acted with legal malfeasance, especially regarding due process; and, an accuser claims the university mishandled her complaint. The most common lawsuits are brought by accused male students. [48]

It is impossible to ascertain how much the lawsuits and settlements have cost universities because many are wrapped in confidentiality agreements. But some arrangements are public. For example, in July 2014, the University of Connecticut paid nearly $1.3 million to five plaintiffs in order to settle a federal lawsuit. [49] In February 2015, the University of Colorado paid a suspended male student $15,000 and agreed to keep his disciplinary record confidential; the student withdrew from the university. [50] The wide swing from $1.3 million to $15,000 undoubtedly reflects significant differences in the circumstances and, perhaps, in the merits of the cases. But it also reflects the confusion of an ever-changing legal context for sexual assault complaints.

The battle and the costs will continue. Rape culture ideologues on campus are immovably hostile to lawsuits by accused male students. Caroline Heldman, a professor at Occidental College, called such suits, "an incredible display of entitlement, the same entitlement that drove them [the litigants] to rape." [51] No compromise seems possible.

The Harm PC Feminism Inflicts on Men

Below is a list of policies and procedures that may discourage victims from disclosing and reporting assaults at some schools.... 1. Disclosure of offender's rights in the adjudication process.... –From a survey about sexual assault that was circulated to 350 college and university presidents by Senator Claire McCaskill. [52]

On April 4, 2011, the Department of Education's Office for Civil Rights (OCR) circulated a letter. It instructed every college and university that accepted federal funds – virtually every institution of higher learning – to change the standards by which complaints of "sexual assault" were adjudicated. Administrators were to determine the guilt of students accused of rape – a felony assault. It did not matter if the adjudicators had no investigative or judicial background. It did not matter if the rape had not been reported to the police or had been dismissed by them. The university process was to be independent of traditional criminal and judicial procedures. Indeed, the campus procedures departed sharply from Western judicial standards that have been safeguards of justice for centuries. It was a call to suspend due process for those who were accused.

The 19-page set of instructions, called the "Dear Colleague" letter, was an attempt to address both a genuine problem and a manufactured one. The genuine problem is that sexual assault occurs on campus. The manufactured problem is the rape culture contention that there is an epidemic of rape which requires extraordinary political and legal remedies.

The Dear Colleague letter had precedent. Some universities already treated an accusation as though it were proof of guilt. A 2006 case from Brown University illustrates the manner in which accused men were being increasingly treated. William McCormick III was a freshman when Marcella "Beth" Dresdale accused him of rape. She reportedly did so with reluctance and due to pressure from university administrators. At the time, McCormick was a straight A student and a star wrestler with a full financial aid scholarship.

According to a 2012 report in the student newspaper, *Brown Spectator*, "Brown's reaction to the allegation was swift. [The original complaint of sexual harassment was filed on September 7.] On Sept. 8, McCormick was ordered to move all his belongings across campus without assistance from the University. He was also forced to drop two of his courses because they were in the same building as some of Dresdale's classes. He was restricted to only eating at dining halls and participating in clubs located on Pambroke Campus. During this time, however, Dresdale did not file an official report with the Providence Police Department."

The *Spectator* provided insight into the swiftness of Brown's response. "Richard Dresdale's influence over Brown stems from his significant donations to the University. He has a medical school scholarship named after him. He and three other donors were lauded for their 'extraordinary generosity' in building the Brown Rugby field. He is one of only 54 members of the Brown Annual Fund Leadership Council. He is on the board of directors for the Brown University Sports Foundation. He is a past recipient of the H. Anthony Ittleson '60 Cup, which is given to extraordinary donors to the Brown Annual Fund." [53] Dresdale was also a business partner with then-President of Brown, Ruth Simmons.

Dresdale began emailing Brown officials about McCormick on September 6 – a day before his daughter filed the first complaint. On learning the name of the administrator handling the matter, Dresdale traveled to Brown and took the man to dinner. On September 11, the same administrator reported to Dresdale that Beth had said her father would "help straighten out a path for [the administrator's] future." The man expressed gratitude to Dresdale for becoming a mentor. Two days later, on September 13, a second complaint was filed against McCormick; it alleged rape. The original complaint was retroactively altered to reflect the rape accusation and to include brutal attacks on McCormick's character from fellow students. By contrast, statements in the original complaint had painted him as an average freshman whose nature evinced no violence.

On October 3, Richard Dresdale emailed the following message to President Simmons. "Ruth … I am working to resolve the matter with the student who attacked Beth – the goal is to have him withdraw from Brown and not have a University hearing. This will enable Beth and the other students to avoid having to come in contact with the student and face questioning from his advocate."

With no investigation, no police report or hearing, the university gave McCormick a one-way ticket home to Wisconsin. Shortly thereafter, and allegedly under pressure from his attorney, McCormick agreed to withdraw from Brown in exchange for a promise that criminal charges would not be pursued. McCormick subsequently sued Brown, Beth and Richard Dresdale. The case was settled in 2011 but it is now sealed. McCormick's university advocate attended the negotiations and did not sign a release, however. According to his account, the case was settled for approximately $1 million. McCormick went on to graduate from Bucknell University, Pennsylvania. [54]

It is tempting to dismiss McCormick's experience as a fluke that resulted from a wealthy man's influence. There are two reasons not to do so.

First, even if the case devolves to the influence of money and power, this indicates how universities respond to money and power; that is, they pander. The most powerful force in the funding of and authority over academia is the federal government. If a venerated Ivy League university would destroy an innocent student at the behest of one man, then what would it do to comply with a much more commanding force? And why would other universities act differently?

Second, the *Spectator* article immediately mentioned a second and similar case at Brown. In other words, McCormick was not a fluke. Coverage in *The New York Times* noted a third case. "The McCormick case is not the first time Brown has been sued over a sexual misconduct case. In 1998, the university settled a lawsuit with Adam Lack, a student who was suspended for a semester after another student accused him of having sex with her without her permission. His accuser later acknowledged she was drunk and did not remember the incident." [55]

Clearly, the Dear Colleague letter did not introduce the suspension of due process for males onto American campuses. Many campuses already expressed an overzealous approach that often included:

- refusing to reveal the exact charges to an accused

- demanding confidentiality that only the accuser seemed able to breach without consequence

- discouraging or prohibiting the accused from consulting a lawyer

- the placing of immediate restrictions upon an accused

The Dear Colleague letter did something new, however. It *mandated* measures, such as the suspension of due process for an accused; it required campuses across America to adopt the approach, even if they strenuously objected. Sexual assault hearings *had* to proceed in the prescribed manner if the university wished federal funds. Heavy fines were threatened against any university that received funds but did not comply. Virtually every campus in America became Brown in how it proceeded on sexual misconduct charges. Males became second class students as a matter of university policy.

The OCR drew on at least three powerful sources of strength.

First, the federal government and many liberal politicians have declared a "War on Women." A key battleground is the sexual abuse of women, especially young women on campus. The highly inflated statistic of "1-in-5 female students will be raped" has been broadcast by the White House, Democratic Senators and other politicians with a vested interest in promoting the crisis. No wonder the elimination of the rape epidemic on campus is a trademark cause for the Obama Administration.

Second, it draws heavily upon Title IX. This provision within the Education Amendments of 1972 is a federal law with sharp teeth. It reads, in part, "No person in the United States shall, on the basis of sex, be excluded from participation in, be denied the benefits of, or be subjected to discrimination under any education program or activity receiving federal financial assistance." [56] The Dear Colleague letter was referring to Title IX when it stated, "The sexual harassment of students, including sexual violence, interferes with students' right to receive an education free from discrimination and, in the case of sexual violence, is a crime." Universities were "to take immediate and effective steps to end sexual harassment and sexual violence." [57] Not doing so is deemed to be discrimination because females are assumed to be the ones who are sexually assaulted.

Third, with the support of Women's Study Departments and other PC outlets on campuses, left-leaning activists have organized along ideological lines for decades. Sexual violence has been a particular focus. A favored tactic is to file reports or complaints with the federal government against universities, accusing them of Title IX violations.

Support for the Dear Colleague letter continues unabated. "Not Alone: The First Report of the White House Task Force to Protect Students From Sexual Assault" was published in April 2014. It is a set of recommended actions from the White House to universities for handling sexual assault on campuses. "Today, the Department of Education's Office for Civil Rights (OCR) is releasing a 52-point guidance document," it announced, "that answers many frequently asked questions about a student's rights, and a school's obligations, under Title IX." [58]

What are the specifics of the 2011 letter that cemented suspension of due process into campus hearings?

In a *Slate* article, Emily Yoffe explained [59], "Schools that hold hearings to adjudicate claims of sexual misconduct allow the accuser and the accused to be accompanied by legal counsel [or advocate]. But...many schools ban lawyers from speaking to their clients (only notes can be passed). During these proceedings, the two parties are not supposed to question or cross examine each other, a prohibition recommended by the federal government in order to protect the accuser. And by federal requirement, students can be found guilty under the lowest standard of proof: Preponderance of the evidence, meaning just a 51 percent certainty is all that's needed for a finding that can permanently alter the life of the accused." There is no meaningful legal representation, if it is allowed at all. There is no right of cross examination by which an accused can face his accuser. There is no presumption of innocence. The criminal standard of "beyond a reasonable doubt" is replaced by the lowest possible requirement of proof: "a preponderance of the evidence," or a 50.1% likelihood.

In what resembles double jeopardy, it is common for the police to be involved during or after the hearing. Information divulged to the university can be used by a prosecutor to pursue a case in court against the male student. Of course, an accused can refuse to answer questions from campus law enforcement or speak at the hearing. But if he does so, he will almost automatically be found "guilty" and probably expelled.

Yoffe described a protest that had been signed by more than two dozen Harvard Law School professors. It read, in part, "Harvard has adopted procedures for deciding cases of alleged sexual misconduct which lack the most basic elements of fairness and due process." Yoffe cited the law professors' concern about the federally-mandated Title IX officer who would be in charge of "investigation, prosecution, fact-finding, and appellate review." Yoffe commented "this means there will be no real hearing for an accused student and no ability for him to offer a defense. The Harvard law professors accused the administration of 'jettisoning balance and fairness in the rush to appease certain federal administrative officials'." Yoffe incisively concluded, "But to push back against Department of Education edicts means potentially putting a school's federal funding in jeopardy, and no college, not even Harvard, the country's richest, is willing to do that."

Critics of the OCR policy predicted the flood of false accusations that have resulted from taking an allegation as proof of guilt while scrapping judicial fairness for the accused.

The treatment of accused males on campus has worsened dramatically in recent years but rape culture warriors have always dismissed the harm inflicted on men. In 2001, Catherine Comins, assistant dean of student life at Vassar College, was quoted in a *Time* magazine article, "When Is It Rape?" Unjustly accused men could profit from the experience, Comins claimed. "They have a lot of pain, but it is not a pain that I would necessarily have spared them. I think it ideally initiates a process of self-exploration. 'How do I see women?' 'If I didn't violate her, could I have?' 'Do I have the potential to do to her what they say I did?' Those are good questions." [60]

Then and now, SJWs dismiss the pain of men and trivialize the damage done to them. To do so, they must consider fairness, truth and reputation to be of no importance to a person's well-being. They must consider slander, career destruction, stigma, malice, discrimination and a lifelong sense of injustice to be character builders. Of course, when such misfortune befalls a woman, there are howls of outrage. But innocent men can be devastated without hesitation or regret.

For years, I have been loosely associated with what has been called "the men's movement," which is more accurately known as "the equity movement." I've lost count of how many heart-wrenching emails I've received from men whose lives were destroyed by false accusations and unjust laws. I have read hundreds of similar online accounts.

The suspension of due process and the stigma of being branded as a sex criminal are far from the only damages done to males on campus. The following harms are a brief sampling of other injuries being inflicted under the guise of justice.

There is a continuing violation of men's space. Chapter Three addressed the treatment of fraternities by administrations and feminists. Frats are far from the only male space being demonized and deconstructed, however. Even as female-only spaces expand, male-dominated sports and clubs are attacked as being discriminatory. The lack of male space is particularly disturbing when it comes to sexually assaulted men. Women who have been assaulted or fear violence have safe places into which men are not admitted. Male students have no similar sanctuary.

Men are on the brunt end of a double standard. Rape culture adherents make hate-filled statements about males. The popular slogan, "I bathe in male tears," has been printed on T-shirts, coffee cups and the like, with scathing ridicule directed toward anyone who objects. The vicious slander is called humor or retributive justice, even though similar language would not be tolerated about blacks, gays or other protected categories.

The most significant double standards, however, are those embedded into policy and law because they are imposed and inescapable. An example: When two students drink beyond reason and engage in apparently consensual sex, it is the male and not the female who is prosecuted as a rapist. When Sue Wasiolek, Dean of Students for Duke University, was asked about that specific situation, she confirmed that double standard. "Assuming it is a male and female, it is the responsibility in the case of the male to gain consent before proceeding with sex." [61] Logically speaking, there are only two outcomes that do *not* reflect a double standard. The two drunken students can be seen as equally *not* responsible. Or they can both be seen as rapists and both suffer the consequences. But neither option fits the rape culture narrative.

Young men are shamed because they are male. There is a constant insistence that males, especially white males, are guilty of a political crime simply by being born. The crime is *privilege,* and it is a condition from which no white male can escape no matter how marked his poverty, infirmity, or other misfortune. In the case of William McCormick III, detailed above, the female accuser came from a billionaire family. McCormick was from a modest background. She bought justice; he was expelled. No sane society would consider McCormick to be the privileged one. Doing so shatters men's sense of fair play and can make them callous toward the suffering of women.

Accused male students lose all privacy. The sexual history, character, and activities of an accused become fair game for everyone on campus. University policy may guarantee confidentiality but, in practice, the policy protects only the accuser. The male is often named, stigmatized, and prohibited from specific areas of the campus. He is advised to stay silent rather than defend himself. Meanwhile, accusers who speak out, as Emma Sulkowicz did by carrying a mattress around campus, are not punished. Indeed, Sulkowicz carried the mattress onto the stage when she received her degree.

The university breaches its contract with male students. When a student enrolls and pays tuition, the university's acceptance of money establishes a contract. Upon fulfillment of academic requirements, it promises to provide a degree that may be necessary for future employment. Nothing in the contract says "upon unsubstantiated reports of bad behavior, we will throw you to the curb. No due process. No degree. And there will be a permanent black mark on your record that could bar you from other universities and your profession of choice." By contrast, even if a female accuser lies, she suffers no real punishment.

Men who are expelled suffer negative economic consequences. The permanent notation in a student's records can haunt him for life. It becomes difficult or impossible for him to pursue careers such as law enforcement, to enter the military, to run for public office, or to receive security clearance. Even jobs to which he has access are threatened because he may need to explain the notation to potential employers.

An expelled student must also absorb the cost of enrolling at another university – that is, if one will accept him. Even if the credits are transferred, there is a break in continuity in terms of his classes, contacts, time and geography. All of these factors have economic consequences.

Falsely accused male students suffer devastating emotional consequences. Nothing conveys the damage as dramatically as an accused male who speaks for himself.

"Kevin Parisi is 5 feet, 5 inches tall and barely weighs 120 pounds" are the words with which Ashe Schow began [62] an August 2014 article in the *Washington Examiner*. "He's hunched over and walking with a cane after back surgery earlier this year. He suffers from severe anxiety and digestive disorders, along with extreme allergies and panic attacks." Nevertheless, Parisi was accused of raping a student who went on to become a professional athlete. He was banned from campus for the three months.... [A] disciplinary proceeding...[found] him 'not responsible'."

Schow explained, "Being accused, however, was enough to cause his world to collapse." Parisi told her, "The whole world seems hopeless and like, your heart pounds and the world – the walls – kind of close in on you." He was subject to frequent panic attacks. Parisi described the ordeal of the accusation, "It's just, it's … If you haven't experienced one, I don't know how you could understand. It's just really – dread. A sense of dread. Nothing's ever going to be better. "

Parisi sued the university.

Conclusion

Real rape needs to be addressed. The manner in which PC feminism approaches rape, however, moves away from solutions. It harms innocent people while destroying the structure of justice itself. It is a bitter irony that victims of sexual assault, whom rape culture campaigners claim to champion, are among the people most devastated by their crusade.

Notes

[1] "Prof. Alan Dershowitz: 'Harvard's policy was written by people who think sexual assault is so heinous a crime that even innocence is not a defense'," Community of the Wrongly Accused (COTWA), Oct. 25, 2014. http://www.cotwa.info/2014/10/prof-alan-dershowitz-harvards-policy.html Retrieved Oct. 1, 2015.

[2] "As between 'survivors' and accusers, Jessica Valenti says we need to side with the survivors," COTWA, Nov. 24, 2014.

http://www.cotwa.info/2014/11/as-between-survivors-and-accusers.html
Retrieved Oct. 1, 2015.

[3] Zerlina Maxwell, "No matter what Jackie said, we should generally
believe rape claims," *Washington Post*, Dec. 6, 2014.
http://www.washingtonpost.com/posteverything/wp/2014/12/06/no-
matter-what-jackie-said-we-should-automatically-believe-rape-claims/
Retrieved Oct. 1, 2015.

[4] Jessica Valenti, "If you can't talk about rape without blaming victims,
don't talk about rape," *The Guardian,* Nov. 17, 2014.
http://www.theguardian.com/commentisfree/2014/nov/17/rape-blaming-
victims-talk Retrieved Oct. 1, 2015.

[5] Nick [sic], "Oberlin 'feminists' accuse Christina Hoff Sommers of
supporting rapists," Third Base Politics, April 20, 2015.
http://www.thirdbasepolitics.com/oberlin-feminists-accuse-christina-hoff-
sommers-of-supporting-racists/ Retrieved Oct. 1, 2015.

[6] Wendy McElroy, *Sexual Correctness: The Gender-Feminist Attack on
Women* (Jefferson, N. Carolina: McFarland, 2001).
https://books.google.ca/books?isbn=0786411449 Retrieved Oct. 1, 2015.

[7] Liz Kelly, *Surviving Sexual Violence,* (University of Minnesota, 1988),
p.41

[8] A. Nicholas Groth, *Men Who Rape: The Psychology of the Offender* (New
York, Plenum Press, 1979), p.3.

[9] "Yes Means Yes," Wikipedia.
http://en.wikipedia.org/wiki/Yes_Means_Yes Retrieved Oct. 1, 2015.

[10] Jaclyn Friedman, Jessica Valenti, *Yes Means Yes!: Visions of Female
Sexual Power and A World Without Rape* (Berkley, Ca.: Seal Press, 2008),
p.6. http://www.amazon.ca/Yes-Means-Visions-Female-
Without/dp/1580052576 Retrieved Oct. 1, 2015.

[11] Senate Bill No. 967, California Legislative Information.
https://leginfo.legislature.ca.gov/faces/billNavClient.xhtml?
bill_id=201320140SB967 Retrieved Oct. 1, 2015.

[12] "California Adopts 'Yes Means Yes' Sexual Assault Rule," *Huffington
Post*, Sept. 9, 2014.
http://www.huffingtonpost.com/2014/09/28/california-yes-means-
yes_n_5897828.html Retrieved Oct. 1, 2015.

[13] As quoted by Josh Dulaney, "Students question 'affirmative consent' bill designed to combat sexual assaults," *San Gabriel Valley Tribune*, Aug. 6, 2014. http://www.sgvtribune.com/government-and-politics/20140608/students-question-affirmative-consent-bill-designed-to-combat-sexual-assaults Retrieved Oct. 1, 2015.

[14] "How can a student prove consent to sexual activity under California's proposed 'affirmative consent' law? The bill's co-author says: 'Your guess is as good as mine'," COTWA, June 12, 2014. http://www.cotwa.info/2014/06/how-can-student-prove-consent-to-sexual.html Retrieved Oct. 1, 2015.

[15] Cathy Young, "Campus Rape: The Problem With 'Yes Means Yes'," *Time*, Aug. 29, 2014. http://time.com/3222176/campus-rape-the-problem-with-yes-means-yes/ Retrieved Oct. 1, 2015.

[16] Eric Owens, "Student sought man on Craigslist to beat her up and have sex with her, then reported it as rape," *Daily Caller*, April 2, 2014. http://dailycaller.com/2013/04/02/student-sought-man-on-craigslist-to-beat-her-up-and-have-sex-with-her-then-reported-it-as-rape/ Retrieved Oct. 1, 2015.

[17] Eric Owens, "Police say 28-year-old undergrad threatened herself with rape in Facebook hoax," *Daily Caller*, Jan. 5, 2013. http://dailycaller.com/2013/05/01/police-say-28-year-old-undergrad-threatened-herself-with-rape-in-facebook-hoax/ Retrieved Oct. 1, 2015.

[18] Greg Hamilton, "Police say woman made up story of attack at Campus Lodge apartments," *Gainesville Sun*, May 2, 2013. http://www.gainesville.com/article/20130502/ARTICLES/130509895/1109/sports?p=1&tc=pg Retrieved Oct. 1, 2015.

[19] Cathy Young, "Columbia Student: I Didn't Rape Her," *The Daily Beast*, March, 2, 2015. http://www.thedailybeast.com/articles/2015/02/03/columbia-student-i-didn-t-rape-her.html Retrieved Oct. 1, 2015.

[20] The Brothers of Phi Kappa Psi, "Message to the Community," undated. https://docs.google.com/document/d/1URd0k1oo4Q9lm0xU-KaACPusA66KA5rB3AlXzOcxFdI/edit Retrieved Oct. 1, 2015.

[21] John Nolte, "After Falsely Accusing an Innocent Man, Lena Dunham Is Celebrated as a Rape Role Model," *Breitbart*, April 27, 2015. http://www.breitbart.com/big-hollywood/2015/04/27/after-falsely-accusing-an-innocent-man-lena-dunham-is-celebrated-as-a-rape-role-model/ Retrieved Oct. 1, 2015.

[22] "Woman who consented to sex claims she was 'raped by rape culture'," COTWA, May 6, 2015. http://www.cotwa.info/2015/05/woman-who-consented-to-sex-claims-she.html Retrieved Oct. 1, 2015.

[23] "Student cleared of false accusation files lawsuit against Kenyon College," Save Our Sons, April 8, 2015. http://helpsaveoursons.com/student-sues-college-after-being-cleared-of-false-accusation/ Retrieved Oct. 1, 2015.

[24] "In Campus Rape Tribunals, Some Men See Injustice," Instapundit, April 11, 2015. Reproduction of *Wall Street Journal* article because the original is unavailable without a subscription. http://pjmedia.com/instapundit/204941/ Retrieved Oct. 1, 2015.

[25] Carol Hanisch, "The Personal Is Political," Feb. 1969, (published 1970) http://www.carolhanisch.org/CHwritings/PIP.html Retrieved Oct. 1, 2015.

[26] Jeb Kinnison, "Feminism's heritage: Equity vs. victim feminism," A Voice for Men, Aug. 21, 2014. http://www.avoiceformen.com/feminism/feminisms-heritage-equity-vs-victim-feminism/ Retrieved Oct. 1, 2015.

[27] Frank Furedi, *Culture of Fear* (London: Continuum, 2002, first published April 1997). http://www.amazon.com/Culture-Fear-Frank-Furedi/dp/0826459307 Retrieved Oct. 1, 2015.

[28] William Ryan, *Blaming the Victim* (New York: Vintage, 1976.) http://www.amazon.ca/Blaming-Victim-William-Ryan/dp/0394722264 Retrieved Oct. 1, 2015.

[29] Camille Paglia, *Sex, Art and American Culture: Essays* (New York: Vintage, 1992), p.57. http://www.amazon.ca/Sex-Art-American-Culture-Essays/dp/0679741011 Retrieved Oct. 1, 2015.

[30] Katherine Timpf, "Feminists Say Roofie-Detecting Nail Polish Is Actually Also Rape Culture," *National Review*, Aug. 25, 2014. http://www.nationalreview.com/article/386267/feminists-say-roofie-detecting-nail-polish-actually-also-rape-culture-katherine-timpf Retrieved Oct. 1, 2015.

[31] Tara Culp-Ressler, "Why Rape Prevention Activists Don't Like The New Nail Polish That Can Detect Roofies," *Think Progress*, Aug. 25, 2014. http://thinkprogress.org/health/2014/08/25/3475190/date-rape-nail-polish/ Retrieved Oct. 1, 2015.

[32] op.cit., *Think Progress.*

[33] Karen Straughan, "How some feminist shaming tactics discredit feminist theory," A Voice for Men, June 24, 2014. http://www.avoiceformen.com/feminism/how-some-feminist-shaming-tactics-discredit-feminist-theory/ Retrieved Oct. 1, 2015.

[34] Maya Dunesbery, "Some questions about Undercover Colors anti-rape nail polish," Feministing, Aug. 25, 2014. http://feministing.com/2014/08/25/some-questions-about-undercover-colors-anti-rape-nail-polish/ Retrieved Oct. 1, 2015.

[35] Trigger warning, Geek Feminism Wiki. http://geekfeminism.wikia.com/wiki/Trigger_warning Retrieved Oct. 1, 2015.

[36] Judith Shulevitz, "In College and Hiding From Scary Ideas, *New York Times*, March 21, 2015. http://www.nytimes.com/2015/03/22/opinion/sunday/judith-shulevitz-hiding-from-scary-ideas.html?_r=0 Retrieved Oct. 1, 2015.

[37] Safe space, Geek Feminism Wiki. http://geekfeminism.wikia.com/wiki/Safe_space Retrieved Oct. 1, 2015.

[38] Kai Johnson, Tanika Lynch, Elizabeth Monroe and Tracey Wang, "Our identities matter in Core classrooms," *Columbia Spectator*, April 30, 2015. http://columbiaspectator.com/opinion/2015/04/30/our-identities-matter-core-classrooms Retrieved Oct. 1, 2015.

[39] Alex Kasnetz, "Young American liberals are losing the ability to argue," *Spiked,* May 23, 2015. http://www.spiked-online.com/newsite/article/young-american-liberals-are-losing-the-ability-to-argue/17007#.VWN42Yam1Ss Retrieved Oct. 1, 2015.

[40] Maria Maltseva, "Gender Traitor Solidarity," *Skepticink*, Nov. 1, 2012. http://www.skepticink.com/skepticallyleft/2012/11/01/gender-traitor-solidarity/ Retrieved Oct. 1, 2015.

[41] Natasha Vargas-Cooper, "Feminist Students Protest Feminist Prof for Writing About Feminism," *Jezebel*, May 29, 2015. http://jezebel.com/feminist-students-protest-feminist-prof-for-writing-abo-1707714321 Retrieved Oct. 1, 2015.

[42] "The revolution devours its own. Susan Brownmiller, Heretic," *The American Interest*, Sept. 21, 2015. http://www.the-american-interest.com/2015/09/21/susan-brownmiller-heretic/ Retrieved Oct. 1, 2015.

[43] Jeannie Suk, "The Trouble with Teaching Rape Law," *The New Yorker,* Dec. 15, 2014. http://www.newyorker.com/news/news-desk/trouble-teaching-rape-law Retrieved Oct. 1, 2015.

[44] Victor Davis Hanson, "The Decline of College," *National Review*, Sept. 19, 2013. http://www.nationalreview.com/article/358841/decline-college-victor-davis-hanson Retrieved Oct. 1, 2015.

[45] Jon Marcus, "New Analysis Shows Problematic Boom In Higher Ed Administrators," *Huffington Post*, June 2, 2014. http://www.huffingtonpost.com/2014/02/06/higher-ed-administrators-growth_n_4738584.html Retrieved Oct. 1, 2015.

[46] "Administrators in Higher Education Salaries," *Higher Ed Jobs*. https://www.higheredjobs.com/salary/salaryDisplay.cfm?SurveyID=22 Retrieved Oct. 1, 2015.

[47] J.D. Tucille, "Expect Soaring College Costs From the President's Price-Subsidizing Student Loan Scheme," *Reason*, June 13, 2014. http://reason.com/archives/2014/06/13/expect-soaring-college-costs-from-the-pr Retrieved Oct. 1, 2015.

[48] Ashe Schow, "More evidence colleges are bad at adjudicating sexual assault: Accuser lawsuits," *Washington Examiner*, Jan. 12, 2015. http://www.washingtonexaminer.com/more-evidence-colleges-are-bad-at-adjudicating-sexual-assault-accuser-lawsuits/article/2558514 Retrieved Oct. 1, 2015.

[49] Jake New, "Major Sexual Assault Settlement," *Inside Higher Education*, July 21, 2014. https://www.insidehighered.com/news/2014/07/21/u-connecticut-pay-13-million-settle-sexual-assault-lawsuit Retrieved Oct. 1, 2015.

[50] Sarah Kuta, "CU-Boulder paying 'John Doe' $15K to settle Title IX lawsuit stemming from sexual assault case," *Daily Camera*, Feb. 20, 2015. http://www.dailycamera.com/cu-news/ci_27566071/cu-boulder-paying-john-doe-15k-settle-title Retrieved Oct. 1, 2015.

[51] As quoted in Emily Shugerman, "Men Sue in Campus Sexual Assault Cases," *Ms Blog*, June 18, 2014. http://msmagazine.com/blog/2014/06/18/men-sue-in-campus-sexual-assault-cases Retrieved Oct. 1, 2015.

[52] As quoted in "Sen. Clare McCaskill's nationwide survey to colleges suggests that affording students accused of sex offenses due process might discourage accusers from reporting," COTWA, April 16, 2014.

http://www.cotwa.info/2014/04/sen-clare-mccaskills-nationwide-survey.html Oct. 1, 2015.

[53] Ryan Fleming, "A University's Shame: How Brown betrayed one of its students," *Brown Spectator,* May 26, 2012. http://brown-spectator.com/2012/05/a-universitys-shame-how-brown-betrayed-one-of-its-students/ Retrieved Oct. 1, 2015.

[54] Greg Berman, "Secret Recording in Brown Rape Case," *GoLocalProv.,* Jan. 20, 2012. http://www.golocalprov.com/news/brown-mccormick/ Retrieved Oct. 2015.

[55] Katie Thomas, "Ex-Student Sues Brown Over Rape Accusation," *New York Times,* April 14, 2010. http://www.nytimes.com/2010/04/15/us/15student.html Retrieved Oct. 1, 2015.

[56] 20 U.S.C. §1681(a). https://www.law.cornell.edu/uscode/text/20/1681 Retrieved Oct. 1, 2015.

[57] Dear Colleague Letter, U.S. Department of Education, April 4, 2011. http://www2.ed.gov/about/offices/list/ocr/letters/colleague-201104.html Retrieved Oct. 1, 2015.

[58] NOT ALONE : The First Report of the White House Task Force to Protect Students From Sexual Assault, White House, April 2014. http://www.whitehouse.gov/sites/default/files/docs/report_0.pdf Retrieved Oct. 1, 2015.

[59] Emily Yoffe, "The College Rape Overcorrection," *Slate,* Dec. 7 2014. http://www.slate.com/articles/double_x/doublex/2014/12/college_rape_campus_sexual_assault_is_a_serious_problem_but_the_efforts.html Retrieved Oct. 1, 2015.

[60] As quoted by Nancy Gibbs, "When Is It Rape?" *Time,* June 24, 2001. http://content.time.com/time/magazine/article/0,9171,157165,00.html Retrieved Oct. 1, 2015.

[61] As quoted by Trey Sanchez, "Duke Dean on Drunken Student Sex: Consent is the Male's Responsibility," *Truth Revolt,* May 29, 2014. http://www.truthrevolt.org/news/duke-dean-drunken-student-sex-consent-males-responsibility Retrieved Oct. 1, 2015.

[62] Ashe Schow, "Backlash: College men challenge 'guilty until proven innocent' standard for sex assault cases," *Washington Examiner,* Aug. 11, 2014. http://www.washingtonexaminer.com/article/2551863 Retrieved Oct. 1, 2015.

Chapter Seven: Solutions to Rape Culture Hysteria

Institutionalization of the Rape Culture

The rape culture myth will continue for years despite a growing awareness of the damage it wreaks upon freedom, academia, the justice system and innocent people. For one thing, it has been institutionalized through law and embedded into government policies; it is deeply rooted into some of the most important institutions of society, which makes it difficult to remove. (The word "institution" is used here to mean "an established structure, practice, or custom that defines a society in whole or in significant part.") Rape culture ideology is particularly entrenched at public universities but it is also powerful in other schools that are dependent upon federal funds. Funding is control.

In part, the entrenchment has been accomplished by repurposing laws to make them serve a PC agenda. A primary example is Title IX of the Education Amendments of 1972. [1] Subsequent legislation and court decisions have revised the provision but its basics remain the same. Title IX prohibits gender discrimination in public education as well as at private universities or educational programs that receive federal funds. In 1987, the provision was broadened to cover almost every operation of such schools. Health services, counseling, admissions, financial assistance, academic programs, athletics, recreation, housing and residential life programs – virtually every campus activity was included.

241

In its early implementation, Title IX was used to make schools rectify gender imbalances in their sports activities or spending because an imbalance was assumed to be discrimination against females. Even privately-financed sports fell under Title IX if any other part of the school received federal funds. More recently, Title IX has become a popular vehicle through which rape culture warriors file complaints alleging that a campus policy or activity is violating their civil rights. Sexual misconduct is usually cited, and the term's definition is elastic enough to range from uttering an "improper" word to committing a brutal rape. Ari Cohn, a lawyer at the Foundation for Individual Rights in Education (FIRE), astutely observed, "Title IX is being turned into a Swiss army knife that can be used by colleges and universities to justify (and provide political cover for) virtually any academic or institutional policy even tangentially related to sex or gender." [2]

Since 2011, sexual misconduct has been the focus of Title IX investigations. 2011 is the same year that the Department of Education's Office of Civil Rights (OCR) sent out its Dear Colleague letter, mandating the suspension of due process for an accused. The Dear Colleague letter was examined in Chapter Six but the OCR was only touched upon. The OCR aggressively supports the complaints of accusers by conducting a massive campaign through which its interpretation of Title IX is enforced and universities suspected of violations are punished.

Robby Soave, an advocate of such old-fashioned civil rights as freedom of speech, described the dynamics between the OCR and Title IX in a *Daily Beast* article, "Campus Censorship is the Feds' Fault: How obscure federal bureaucrats are squashing free expression on college campuses." [3] The OCR is "a massive, bureaucratic agency staffed with 650 lawyers....[with] one job: punish universities that don't sufficiently police campuses for harassment and discrimination." It does so by wielding Title IX. "Harassment, according to OCR's confusing and ever-mutating guidance, is ill-defined and largely subjective," Soave continued. "And since universities risk losing millions of dollars in funds if OCR deems them out of sync with Title IX, administrators have understandably decided they are better off airing [sic] on the side of censorship."

Soave offered [4] a concrete example of how far preemptive compliance has gone. At the beginning of 2015, City University of New York's (CUNY) Graduate Center instructed its faculty to cease addressing students in person or in writing as "Mr" or "Ms" because the gendered terms might cause offense. The policy was to be "encouraged 'as broadly as possible'."

According to CUNY's Provost Louise Lennihan, the change was necessary for the university to conform with Title IX.

The OCR is deadly serious about compliance. On January 7, 2015, the *Huffington Post* announced [5], "Barnard College Joins List Of 94 Colleges Under Title IX Investigations" for violation of the provision. Amy Zavadil, associate dean for equity and Title IX coordinator at the private women's college, offered a response that is typical of university bureaucrats. "Barnard does not tolerate violence or discrimination of any kind....Senior administrators are carefully reviewing the OCR inquiry and will respond in accordance with applicable law, and in a manner consistent with our own core values as an institution." In short, Barnard will snap to. [6] Almost every university does. The few that do resist, as Harvard Law School did, eventually capitulate. [7]

According to *Inside Higher Education* [8], the OCR has not only expanded its staff dramatically but also its pervasive involvement at universities. Bureaucratic growth has not made the agency more efficient. *Inside Higher Education* observed that it took the OCR "on average, 1,469 days to complete campus sexual assault investigations in 2014....The average time it took to resolve a complaint in 2009 was 379 days." And, yet, the dominant cry is to *increase* the OCR's staff and funding.

Rape culture ideology drives that cry. Together with campus activists, Gender and Women's Studies Departments have been instrumental in creating what is called the "New Campus Anti-Rape Movement." [9] The movement focuses on higher education's compliance with federal sexual assault laws, including Title IX, Title IV (regulating the administration of federal financial aid programs for students), and the Clery Act. The movement emphasizes the need for correct bureaucratic responses to complaints of sexual violence, such as "always believe the woman."

You would expect a backlash but dissident voices usually self-censor because careers can be destroyed by contrarian views, especially ones described as sexually harassing or triggering. Professors have been terminated due to a single complaint by a student who felt uncomfortable in class. Other types of intimidation are common. Greg Lukianoff, President of FIRE, explained a new sexual harassment policy at the University of Montana (UM). Training on UM's new policy was mandatory, with non-attendees being reported to the federal government. Since the policy was jointly drafted by the DOE and the Department of Justice, presumably the lists would be turned over to those two agencies, at the very least. No one wants to be on a DOJ list.

Lukianoff continued, "Worse still, students and faculty may face discipline even if they are cleared of harassment and discrimination charges. Couple these flaws with broad, vague definitions, and the result is that UM has vast discretion to silence students and faculty members, to the detriment of fairness, clarity, and free speech." [10]

Poignant stories of students and professors being suppressed are plentiful. One account is particularly interesting because it highlights the change in campus policies since Obama's presidency, which began in 2009.

In a June 2015 article, "I'm a liberal professor, and my liberal students terrify me," [11] Edward Schlosser (a pseudonym) described himself as "a professor at a midsize state school" who has been "teaching college classes for nine years" and "almost always score(s) highly on...student evaluations." Schlosser offered a snapshot of how the university atmosphere transformed during his nine years on campus.

In 2009, a student complained about a classroom video and discussion, in which he said Schlosser was "communistical [sic]...and everyone knows that communisticism [sic] is wrong." The university administrator knew the complaint was bogus and, after Schlosser filled out some stock paperwork, she dismissed the student's report "with prejudice."

In 2015, Schlosser wrote, "boat-rocking isn't just dangerous – it's suicidal." He now carefully restricts the ideas and words he uses in class. "I have intentionally adjusted my teaching materials as the political winds have shifted. (I also make sure all my remotely offensive or challenging opinions, such as this article, are expressed either anonymously or pseudonymously). Most of my colleagues who still have jobs have done the same. We've seen bad things happen to too many good teachers – adjuncts getting axed because their evaluations dipped below a 3.0, grad students being removed from classes after a single student complaint, and so on."

When an adjunct was dropped because a student objected to reading Mark Twain, Schlosser purged his own syllabi of anything that could be remotely "upsetting" to a "coddled undergrad." Among the discards was the ultra-liberal Upton Sinclair.

Schlosser captured the difference between 2009 and 2015. The earlier complaint was directed at his ideology. "And as I was allowed to rebut it, I didn't hesitate to reuse that same video in later semesters, and the student's complaint had no impact on my performance evaluations." Today, a complaint takes a different form. "Instead of focusing on the rightness or wrongness (or even acceptability) of the materials we reviewed in class, the complaint would center solely on how my teaching affected the student's emotional state. As I cannot speak to the emotions of my students, I could not mount a defense about the acceptability of my instruction. And if I responded in any way other than apologizing and changing the materials we reviewed in class, professional consequences would likely follow." He concluded, "The real problem: a simplistic, unworkable, and ultimately stifling conception of social justice."

Lukianoff added insight into why institutions themselves have become so intimidated by their own students. "One thing you quickly learn is universities are terrified of Title IX investigations and lawsuits. The investigations themselves are really onerous, the lawsuits are expensive, and given the climate on campus, they are really afraid just to be accused of discrimination....We need cultural pushback but we also need to understand that there is a structural governmental reason for why this stuff is so out of control." [12]

The "structural governmental reason" identified by Lukianoff is key. Social control on campus exists only because it is supported by government law and tax dollars. The most direct and effective way to prevent the damage of the rape culture is to remove its main sponsorship.

Political Fixes: Abolish the Department of Education

> Our attitude towards ourselves should be 'to be satiable in learning' and towards others 'to be tireless in teaching.' – Mao Zedong quoted on the DOE's site "Kids Zone" [13]

The way to stop rape culture hysteria in its tracks is to abolish the DOE. The suggestion is not meant to be glib nor to deny the difficulty of abolishing any government agency. But there are practical reasons to assume the goal can be achieved. And there are sound political arguments. Indeed, such arguments *have* been made in the past, and they seem to be enjoying a revival.

The Cabinet-level department is a comparatively new creation; it was signed into law in 1980 by President Jimmy Carter. [14] A DOE had been established in the 1860s but the Cabinet-level agency was quickly demoted to an Office and stripped of Presidential prestige. Responsibility for education was scattered across various government departments and agencies with the Office of Education eventually falling under the auspices of the Department of Health, Education, and Welfare.

When Carter proposed reinstating the agency within the Cabinet, the proposal met stiff political resistance from Republicans and vested interests. The bill only narrowly passed the House of Representatives by a vote of 210 to 206. Even then, it was not clear whether the widely disparate House and Senate versions of the bill could be reconciled.

The *Spokesman-Review* newspaper (July 12, 1979) explained [15], "as it emerged from the House, the bill had been amended to permit voluntary prayer in public schools, to ban busing of students to achieve racial desegregation, to prohibit use of racial or sexual quotas for admission to colleges and to bar abortions in the proposed new department's medical facilities for employees." The newspaper continued, "Opposing creation of the department was a coalition that seldom before had ever joined forces. These included a majority of House Republicans, who feared the bill would lead to federal control of local education, as well as creation of another giant bureaucracy; and a large number of liberal Democrats who feared creation of the single-issue department would crumble the education-labor-health-civil rights block that has wielded power over social legislation."

A main argument *against* creating the DOE was that the federal government had no constitutional authority to do so. In short, the word "education" did not appear in the U.S. Constitution. Federal intrusion into education would be an executive overreach.

Supporters argued that the DOE was constitutionally justified by the Commerce Clause, which allows Congress to regulate anything with an impact on the national economy. The relevant passage reads, "To regulate Commerce with foreign Nations, and among the several States, and with the Indian tribes." This was interpreted as assigning authority to the federal government over any matter influencing national commerce. An educated populace was of national concern, advocates claimed. Thus, funding authority for the DOE was drawn from the Taxing and Spending Clause, which reads, "The Congress shall have Power To lay and collect Taxes, Duties, Imposts and Excises, to pay the Debts and provide for the common Defence and general Welfare of the United States; but all Duties, Imposts and Excises shall be uniform throughout the United States."

Republicans countered with the Tenth Amendment to the Bill of Rights: "The powers not delegated to the United States by the Constitution, nor prohibited by it to the States, are reserved to the States respectively, or to the people." Education was a state's rights matter, not the business of the federal government.

Opposition to a DOE was not restricted to bipartisan politics in Congress nor to Democrats' concern about weakening their influence over social legislation. The *Spokesman-Review* commented [16] on the reaction of unions and the general labor movement, which wielded immense political influence. "Strong backing came from the National Education Association (NEA) with its 1.8 million membership of teachers and educators. Opposing the new department were the American Federal of Teachers (AFT) and a number of other educational groups and individuals." The two organizations were rivals. In her book, *Jimmy Carter as Educational Policymaker: Equal Opportunity and Efficiency,* Deanna L. Michael observed [17], "Albert Shanker, President of the American Federation of Teachers, opposed the creation of the department of education and lived in New York....[H]is opposition may have influenced the *New York Times.*"

Maurice R. Berube's book, *American Presidents and Education,* noted [18], "A strong critic of the proposed Department of Education was teacher [and NEA] union rival, Albert Shanker...Shanker lambasted the idea as adding another bureaucratic layer to education mainly for the reason of 'prestige', which he felt was 'not a good reason'. Others perceived Shanker's opposition on the grounds that he feared the NEA would dominate a new education department." History generally views the DOE's creation as Carter's quid pro quo for the NEA's endorsement of his 1976 Presidential campaign. Thus, Shanker's concerns seem legitimate although self-interested. (Note: some sources claim the AFL also supported the creation of the DOE but this appears to be inaccurate.)

The constitutionality and legitimacy of the DOE have been questioned ever since its establishment. In the 1980 presidential election campaign, for example, Ronald Reagan pledged to eliminate the DOE from his cabinet and reduce federal spending in education. During Reagan's Presidency (1981-1989), however, the DOE remained a cabinet agency and federal spending on education expanded. Some blame obstruction by Democrats for Reagan's failure to deliver on election promises; others claim he back-burnered the issue. Whatever dynamics were in play, as a candidate, Reagan obviously believed that weakening federal authority over education would appeal to the American voting public.

The DOE re-emerged as an election issue in 1996. Sitting President William Clinton promised to strengthen education, making it a top priority. Meanwhile, Republican nominee Bob Dole pledged to "cut out" the DOE. At that time, the official GOP platform stated [19], "The Federal government has no constitutional authority to be involved in school curricula or to control jobs in the market place. This is why we will abolish the Department of Education."

But eliminating the DOE seems to have fallen off the official Republican agenda. Instead, DOE growth has been steady under both Democrat and Republican administrations. A *National Review* article observed [20], "According to the National Center for Education Statistics, DE's [Department of Education's] original budget, in 1980, was $13.1 billion (in 2007 dollars), and it employed 450 people. By 2000, it had increased to $34.1 billion, and by 2007 it had more than doubled to $73 billion. The budget request for fiscal 2011-2012 is $77.8 billion, and the department employs 4,800." Under President George W. Bush, federal authority over American education dramatically increased through the No Child Left Behind program.

Backlash against the American education system has surged. Perhaps the most visible manifestation is the riveting rise in homeschooling. According to both the DOE's National Center for Education Statistics and the Home School Legal Defense Association [21], the total number of homeschooled students rose 17% from 2007 to 2013. Widespread discontent with the federal Common Core program is likely to hike those numbers.

In the last few years, Constitutional arguments against the DOE have become more frequent. A 2011 article from Cato Institute [22], "Yes, the Department of Education Is Unconstitutional," is an example. Adjunct scholar Adam B. Schaeffer quoted then-Congresswoman Michele Bachmann as stating, "[T]he Constitution does not specifically enumerate nor does it give to the federal government the role and duty to superintend over education that historically has been held by the parents and by local communities and by state governments."

That same year, Neal McCluskey commented in the *Washington Times* on Obama's proposed budget for the DOE. In "End Fed Ed," he wrote [23], "[E]xcept for granting jurisdiction over the District of Columbia and empowering the feds to prohibit schooling discrimination by states, the Constitution gives Washington zero authority to meddle in education. That means every federal education program, and the department itself, is unconstitutional....The Founders gave the feds no education power for good reason. They knew that a national government couldn't effectively govern education or anything else that works best when tailored to the unique needs of individual people and communities....History has borne their wisdom out."

Eliminating the DOE is the most effective and long-term solution to the damage wrought by rape culture hysteria on campus. The solution could take years to achieve, however. Is there a speedier step in the right direction?

Four come immediately to mind:

- drastically reduce the DOE's budget
- repeal specific measures such as Title IX
- return more control to the state level
- encourage the privatization of higher education

Drastically reduce the DOE's budget

In an article entitled "Put Department of Education in a Timeout," Richard W. Rahn, a senior fellow with Cato Institute, acknowledged a strong objective case for abolishing the DOE. Nevertheless, teachers' unions would probably would block the effort, especially if union-backed Democrats were politically dominant. Rahn suggested the more moderate step of slashing the DOE's budget.

The current political atmosphere may be favorable to budget-slashing. The increase in DOE power and arrogance under Obama has created a rebellious mood. Obama's FY 2015 budget included $131 million request for the OCR, which was an increase of $30.7 million for an additional 200 full-time employees. Cutting off the glut of money is attractive on several levels. For example, it would be far easier to accomplish than abolishing the DOE. But it is not clear how the funding cut would affect OCR's budget. It could lead to slashing K-12's budget, instead.

The next strategy could produce more predictable results.

Repeal Title IX

Title IX is the key legislation from which the OCR draws authority. Short of abolishing the DOE, repealing the provision would be the most effective way to halt the damage of rape culture policies on campus. Title IX and its associated measures are vulnerable because they are used in a manner that badly oversteps their original purpose and authority.

Title IX is part of the United States Education Amendments of 1972. It reads, "No person in the United States shall, on the basis of sex, be excluded from participation in, be denied the benefits of, or be subjected to discrimination under any education program or activity receiving federal financial assistance." The provision's purpose was to end gender discrimination in education; specifically, it aimed at eliminating discrimination against women. With females now constituting over half of the student population, few people would argue that such discrimination still exists. The need for Title IX protection seems to be in the past.

Regulations and court decisions have strengthened the interpretation of the provision, however. Constitutional attorney David A. French wrote [24], "The statute has been dramatically amplified by voluminous regulations, passed through the typical notice-and-comment process, which is less democratic (obviously) than statutory enactment but still formally allows for public input."

But the Obama administration is notorious for expanding Title IX without going through the mandated process for doing so. French explained, "the Obama administration abandoned both the statutory and the regulatory rule-making processes" when it "unilaterally" issued the 2011 Dear Colleague letter, which greatly expanded the reach of Title IX. The letter also created constitutional problems by requiring procedures that violated privacy rights, restrained freedom of speech and suspended due process for students accused of sexual misconduct. Thus, the letter's mandate can be opposed on either a statutory or a constitutional basis. There is reason to believe such opposition would succeed. French observed, "Multiple Title IX regulations have been challenged in court, with the cases often resulting in significant changes to the regulations as well as the statute itself."

The mood on campus is becoming more favorable to change. In early 2015, the *Washington Post* reprinted an open letter from 16 faculty members of the University of Pennsylvania Law School. It protested the Dear Colleague letter as well as the expansion of Title IX and the mishandling of sexual misconduct complaints. Without diminishing the seriousness of rape, the law professors declared [25],

> [I]n addressing the issue of sexual assault, the federal government has sidestepped the usual procedures for making law. Congress has passed no statute requiring universities to reform their campus disciplinary procedures. OCR has not gone through the notice-and-comment rule required to promulgate a new regulation. Instead, OCR has issued several guidance letters whose legal status is questionable....
>
> [T]his lawmaking process has sacrificed the traditional safeguards that accompany traditional lawmaking procedures. Both the

legislative process and notice-and-comment rule making are transparent, participatory processes that afford the opportunity for input from a diversity of viewpoints. That range of views is critical because this area implicates competing values, including privacy, safety, the functioning of the academic community, and the integrity of the educational process for both the victim and the accused, as well as the fundamental fairness of the disciplinary process. A formal lawmaking process would have required the federal government to deliberate, strike reasonable balances, and offer an explicit justification for its policy judgments. Formal lawmaking would have required the federal government...to consider explicitly the costs of its proposed policies as well as the benefits.

A year before the Penn Law protest, the *Boston Globe* published a similar open letter from 28 current and retired Harvard Law School professors. It rejected the Dear Colleague letter as legally inappropriate. The professors accused the OCR of expanding "the scope of forbidden conduct," including sexual harassment, by adopting definitions that went "significantly beyond Title IX and Title VII law." The wording of Title IX, they insisted, did not contain or imply the definition of sexual harassment imposed by the Dear Colleague letter.

Additionally, the investigation process being mandated was deemed unfair from its inception through to its adjudication. The process began with "[t]he lodging of the functions of investigation, prosecution, fact-finding, and appellate review in one office," which was "a Title IX compliance office rather than an entity that could be considered structurally impartial." The universities chose who presided over investigations and hearings. The choice(s) came from administrators, faculty or students – all of whom were prone to bias. Administrators and faculty were likely to act to benefit the institution that signed their paychecks. Student participants who offered time and effort were likely to be activists with a built-in bias. In other words, the structure of the process violated the right of an accused to be objectively judged.

The Dear Colleague letter also encouraged a double standard. For example, when a female and a male student engaged in sex while both were drunk or on drugs, the female was presumed to be a victim and the male was presumed to be an aggressor. This presumption was only one way in which an accused was stripped of due process rights. Other violations included:

- lowering the standard of evidence to "a preponderance of the evidence"

- a lack of legal representation for the accused

- no disclosure of the charges prior to a hearing

- anonymous testimony

- testimony that is not under oath

- refusal to consider testimony from the accused

- an inability to question an accuser or witnesses

- a permanent mark being placed in college records

- no discipline for false accusers or accusers who breached confidentiality

- the possible provision of hearing evidence to the police

- no right of appeal

University officials   routinely deflect criticism by pointing to the federal government as the dictating authority. There are problems with claiming "it's not our fault," however. For one thing, universities do *not* have to abide by DOE instructions. They choose to do so rather than to refuse and endanger tax-dollars. Ultimately, the decision to betray due process, free speech and academic freedom rests on their shoulders. Universities are ideologically complicit in the harms imposed by the Dear Colleague letter because most campus administrators and bureaucrats eagerly embrace its policies.

Like abolishing the DOE, repealing Title IX would profoundly weaken the impact of the rape culture on campus. Merely rolling the provision back to the status it enjoyed before the Dear Colleague letter (pre-2011) would be a sharp turn toward sanity. But it is not the only possible step in that direction.

Devolve Educational Authority to State Level

> Instead of using centralized decrees to turn mediocre institutions into excellent ones, as they [the federal government] have been trying but failing to do for the last several decades, the state and federal governments should be empowering individual families to "vote with their feet" by transferring to the schools of their own choice. The key locus for such revolutionary reforms is the states.

The best contribution the national government can make to educational improvement is to avoid educational policymaking and allow states to experiment with school choice programs. –Lawrence A. Uzzell [26]

Although far from ideal, returning authority over education to the state level would be a positive step. It is not ideal because a state government might not show more respect for individual rights than the federal one. Nevertheless, state-level authority offers at least seven advantages.

First, educational standards, content and policies would vary from state to state and, perhaps, widely so. This would offer parents and students a true choice between options about which they may feel strongly. Just as some choose a religious school over a secular one, those who prefer a PC environment could select an appropriate campus; those who disagree could "vote with their feet." The decentralization of education offers greater consumer choice.

Second, states are more responsive to local pressure. The Founders left education in the hands of the states because they doubted that a centralized power would be responsive to the concerns of individuals. In *The Cato Handbook for Congress,* David Boaz observed [27], "[T]he Founders were right to reserve most subjects to state, local, or private endeavor. The Founders feared the concentration of power. They believed that the best way to protect individual freedom and civil society was to limit and divide power."

Third, states are more likely to bump up the quality of education because they would compete for customers whom they could not take for granted. Instead of income coming from compliance with federal regulations, universities would need to produce the solid educational results. Moreover, small local governments are better able to adapt than distant behemoths. Boaz explained, "Thus [for the Founders] it was much better to have decisions made independently by 13–or 50–states, each able to innovate and to observe and copy successful innovations in other states, than to have one decision made for the entire country."

Fourth, states are less able to mask problems in their own backyards. Government bureaucracies are notorious for falsifying, interpreting or not reporting data that harms their interests. State bureaucracy is no exception. But the larger the bureaucracy or the more remote it is from public feedback, the more likely it is that cover-ups will succeed. Proximity promotes accountability.

Fifth, returning education to the states is an end run around the DOE's worst policies. Without repealing those policies, it would render them ineffective.

Sixth, bureaucracy would shrink. National control means administrators must ensure an homogenized application of policy across the states. This creates hordes of bureaucrats at the federal level. The enforcement does little or nothing to improve the academic quality of education. Arguably, they reduce it.

Seventh, variation in schools reflects the pluralism of America. Uzzell observed [28], "[S]chooling inescapably involves judgments about truth and virtue, about what kind of person a youngster should aspire to be. In an increasingly pluralistic society, Americans are inevitably going to disagree with each other about those judgments. Which historical figures should children be encouraged to revere as heroes? What should they be taught about ancient belief systems such as Christianity and Islam– and about modern ideologies such as feminism and environmentalism? ... Americans...have no more chance of reaching consensus on those questions than of agreeing on what church (if any) we should all attend. That is why we keep the state out of controlling churches, just as we keep it out of other value-forming institutions such as publishing and journalism."

Returning education to the state also has strategic advantages for those who oppose the concept of a rape culture. There is powerful historical precedent in state control of schooling, which makes it easier to accomplish. The constitution grants specific authority to the federal government only over the duties for which states are ill-suited. The duty to provide a common defense against invasion is an example. All other responsibilities are supposed to devolve to the states.

Moreover, the issue of states' rights appeals to many politicians as well as to large sectors of the public. State-level politicians are generally sympathetic because it increases their own power and prestige. The public is sympathetic because their feedback gives them greater control.

The downside: Returning education to the states may require an appeal to the United States Supreme Court. If so, the states face a hurdle. Federal control is not exercised through legislation so much as it is through funding. A school that forgoes federal tax-dollars can avoid some of the worst federal policies. If they voluntarily accept the funding, however, they are deemed to have agreed with the attached policies. This makes it difficult for schools to claim the injury that is necessary if they are to have standing before the court.

Happily, another strategy has the pronounced charm of avoiding lawyers and courts.

Privatize Higher Education

> Originally, the primary goal of the federal student-aid programs was to improve access to college for lower-income persons. Here, the record is one of total failure: *A smaller percentage of recent college graduates come from the bottom quartile of the income distribution today than was the case in 1970*, when federal student-assistance programs were in their infancy. –Richard Vedder [29]

Free market competition is the most effective counter to bureaucracy. Education, as a consumer good, is in short supply and in high demand. No one can fill the void better than entrepreneurs who offer an competitive service for an honest dollar; no one can make a more informed decision about which service is best than the person who pays for it. The current situation embodies the opposite of the foregoing scenario. A shortage in education is created by the quasi-monopoly of government and by tax-funding that drives up the prices through waste and social experiments that have nothing to do with academic excellence. Ideally, higher education should be 100% privatized.

An immediate hue and cry will arise and predict a flood of illiteracy. Such critics should look to the example of homeschooling, which has a track record of providing children with a sounder education than public schools, and doing so without burdening taxpayers. Literacy does not require public education.

Indeed, after many decades of public education, the literacy rate is not impressive. In 2002, the National Center for Education Statistics released a report, *Adult Literacy in America. A First Look at the Findings of the National Adult Literacy Survey.* [30] Its findings:

- "Twenty-one to 23 percent – or some 40 to 44 million of the 191 million adults in this country – demonstrated skills in the lowest level of prose, document, and quantitative proficiencies (Level 1)." They can read well enough to fill out a bank deposit or find basic information in a brief news article. The 23 percent included "others" who were unable "to respond to much of the survey." In fairness, some within the lowest level of literacy may have been disadvantaged by age or another contributing factor.

- "Some 25 to 28 percent of the respondents, representing about 50 million adults nationwide, demonstrated skills in the next higher level of proficiency (Level 2) on each of the literacy scales." They were "quite limited" but able "to locate information in text, to make low-level inferences using printed materials, and to integrate [information] easily." Many of the 90+ million within Level 1 or 2 reported receiving assistance from others in order to read necessary material.

- "Nearly one-third..., or about 61 million adults nationwide, demonstrated performance in Level 3 on each of the literacy scales. Respondents performing in this level on the prose and document scales were able to integrate information from relatively long or dense text or from documents."

- "Eighteen to 21 percent of the respondents, or 34 to 40 million adults, performed in the two highest levels of prose, document, and quantitative literacy (Levels 4 and 5)."

In his book, *The Transformation of the American Economy* [31], historian Robert Higgs gave a glimpse of historical literacy rates and how the ability to read evolved outside of public education. He wrote, "In 1870 about 90 percent of adult white Americans could read and write; by 1910, 95 percent possessed these basic skills. For obvious reasons, literacy was much less prevalent among the nonwhite population - predominately blacks - but improvement was rapid. In 1870 only about 20 percent of the adult nonwhite population was literate; by 1910 the proportion had increased to 70 percent." It is not clear that the National Center for Education Statistics and Higgs use the same definition. Nevertheless, Higgs's reference to "basic skills" suggest that the rates are comparable.

Higgs ascribes much of the rise in literacy rates to economic factors. "Workers oftentimes went on their own to learn certain intellectual skills required for different jobs, and it is important to remember that gains in productivity allow for increased leisure time, which includes providing parents the opportunity to teach their children (whereas earlier the opportunity cost of taking the time to teach your child how to read included the loss of necessary wages). There was also a lot of on-the-job training, where employers were more than willing to provide workers the tools necessary for employment." In short, the free market and individual initiative caused a dramatic increase in literacy quite apart from governmental efforts. [32]

Another objection to privatizing education comes from those to whom competition resembles chaos. But free market education would be no more disorderly than other goods and services delivered by the market. A good example is the provision of food by grocery stores.

A rebellious trend toward privatization may be emerging. An April 2015 *New York Times* headline [33] read, "To Keep Free of Federal Reins, Wyoming Catholic College Rejects Student Aid." The article explained, "the school decided this winter to join a handful of other religious colleges in refusing to participate in the federal student-aid programs that help about two-thirds of students afford college. For students here, the decision means no federal loans, work-study money or grants to finance their annual $28,000 tuition, which includes housing in gender-segregated dorms and three meals in the school's lone dining hall." Instead, the College intends to focus on raising money through private programs and donations.

The reason for refusing federal money? The College does not wish to comply with certain government policies, such as the demand to provide birth control. Obamacare requires most employers to provide coverage of contraceptives, sterilization and some abortion-inducing drugs free of charge, even if the employer morally objects.

The *National Catholic Reporter* pointed to a long-standing precedent apart from the religious community [34]. "Hillsdale College in Michigan, the first American college to prohibit...discrimination based on race, religion or sex, had a similar experience in the 1970s regarding affirmative action." The Department of Health, Education and Welfare insisted that Hillsdale "count its students by race, which the college asserted was against its charter." After losing a U.S. Supreme Court decision in 1984, Hillsdale refused to accept students who accessed federal grants or loans.

Privatization gives universities more autonomy. It also means students are treated as consumers who must be satisfied in order to induce them to pay tuition on a continuing basis. Privatization also encourages schools to prevent waste in the form of bureaucracy. That's part of operating for a profit.

Politicians, bureaucrats and academia will vigorously resist privatization because their livelihoods are on the line. They go so far as to propose free tuition – read, tax-paid tuition – for community colleges across America. [35]

The political thrust is to embed government ever more deeply into academic policy. But the opposite direction is the only sane one to pursue.

Return Constitutional Rights to the Campus

> Our concerns about fundamental fairness are not academic or theoretical in nature. There are documented cases of a rush to judgment on charges of sexual misconduct at universities, including the Duke Lacrosse case and the recent events at the University of Virginia. In the criminal justice system, there have been a large number of post-conviction exonerations of persons convicted of serious crimes, including many sexual assault cases. Due process of law is not window dressing; it is the distillation of centuries of experience, and we ignore the lessons of history at our peril. –Open letter from 16 Penn Law School Professors. [36]

Envision the following scenario. The DOE continues to exist. Title IX is not repealed. States' rights flounder before an intransigent U.S. Supreme Court. The privatization of education proceeds at a snail's pace because most universities cannot resist the lure of federal funds.

It is still possible to counter rape culture hysteria on campuses. How?

1. Discard the unconstitutional and illegal requirements of the Dear Colleague letter and demand respect for the due process rights of an accused; and,

2. Treat sexual violence as a criminal matter by turning accusations over to the police for investigation and to the courts for adjudication.

1. Discard the unconstitutional and illegal requirements of the Dear Colleague letter and demand respect for the due process rights of an accused.

The procedures spelled out in the Dear Colleague letter should be discarded or, at least, made optional.

Prior to the Obama administration, the OCR recognized the need for universities to adopt differing policies. In its 1997 Sexual Harassment Guidance, the OCR stated [37], "Procedures adopted by schools will vary considerably in detail, specificity, and components, reflecting differences in audiences, school sizes and administrative structures, State or local legal requirements, and past experience." Now one policy fits all. That policy discards the constitutional rights of an accused student. It requires universities to be the first line of investigation and adjudication in criminal matters such as rape.

Yet administrators argue that campus hearings are **not** criminal proceedings because they cannot   impose a prison sentence or similar sanctions. The statement has some validity but it is blunted by the increasingly common practice of turning hearing records and evidence over to police departments. In a *Washington Examiner* article, "Police officer brags about circumventing due process in sexual assault cases," Ashe Schow described [38] the practice with specific reference to a case at the University of Wisconsin-Madison (UW). Schow wrote:

> The UW guide states that "If the student does not respond to the [university] investigating officer's offer to discuss the matter, the investigating officer may proceed to make a determination on the basis of the available information." That is, the investigating officer will only have the accuser's side of the story and is under no obligation to investigate on behalf of the accused.

> This presents an impossible situation for accused students, who must waive their 5th Amendment rights in their only chance to avoid expulsion. Of course, with the way the system is rigged now, that won't help. The student is also at the mercy of the investigating officer, who may take inaccurate or twisted notes and withhold information he or she deems 'irrelevant'. These same investigators work for the Title IX office, which is predisposed to support the accuser.

> Police using information gathered from this Kafkaesque procedure may have an easier time arresting someone based on a sexual assault accusation, but would the charges hold up in court?

Criminal courts often throw out a case based on sloppy police work but campus hearings routinely use tainted evidence. When dubious statements are entered into a hearing transcript, they become fair game for the police to use. Courts will entertain the evidence because it was "freely" rendered by an accused and does not violate police procedure. In a presentation to the 2015 meeting of the International Association of College Law Enforcement Administrators, Susan Riseling advised her colleagues to use information from campus investigations to pursue criminal charges against accused male students. "It's Title IX, not Miranda," Riseling said. "Use what you can."

Riseling is the campus chief of police and the associate vice chancellor at the University of Wisconsin-Madison. Her advice was not a slip of the tongue. She later told the *Washington Examiner*, "Title IX is not a police action, and Miranda only applies to in-custody arrests. Yes, in order to prosecute crimes, we should use every legal means available – it's all about using the legal resources we have to hold someone accountable for their actions."

Schow analyzed a UW case that had proceeded from a hearing to a police investigation. *Inside Higher Ed* described what happened during the police interrogation. [39] "The accused student denied the charges....In his disciplinary hearing, however, he changed his story in an apparent attempt to receive a lesser punishment by admitting he regretted what had occurred. That version of events was 'in direct conflict with what he told police', Riseling said. Police subpoenaed the Title IX records of the hearing and were able to use that as evidence against the student."

Riseling and other campus law enforcement have penned a flood of white papers on how hearings can systematically cooperate with police departments. Campus agents are urged to tailor investigations to make them as useful as possible for criminal prosecution. It is crucial, Riseling and her associates argue, to convince reluctant District Attorney offices to pursue charges in court.

The claim that campus hearings are civil proceedings is eroding quickly. For the sake of argument, however, let's grant that campus hearings straddle the fence between a criminal and a civil proceeding. This does not mitigate the need for due process protections; it increases the need. Both the federal government and the Constitution recognize this fact in the procedures they mandate for federal civil courts. Joseph Cohn of FIRE pointed [40] to how civil cases are presented in federal courts where a "preponderance of the evidence" is the legal standard. To maximize fairness in the presence of a reduced burden of proof, procedural safeguards have been embedded.

"For example, to ensure fairness, reliability, and constitutionality," Cohn explained, "[federal] civil trials are presided over by experienced, impartial, and legally educated judges. At either party's request, facts are determined by a jury of one's peers. The parties have the right to representation by counsel, and a mandatory process of 'discovery' ensures that all relevant evidence will be made available if the opposing party asks for it." This is in stark contrast to campus hearings.

Cohn continued, "And speaking of evidence, strict rules apply [in federal civil courts] that exclude hearsay, evidence of prior bad acts or crimes, and other information that is either irrelevant or unreliable. Moreover, all depositions and testimonies are given under oath or affirmation, with witnesses subject to perjury charges if they intentionally lie about material issues. The list goes on and on."

Allow me to expand the list.

The right to cross-examine witnesses is the most effective method of securing the truth in court. The right is not prohibited by the Dear Colleague letter, but it is strongly discouraged, and most hearings ban it. The stated purpose is to protect the accuser from experiencing trauma. This purpose can be served without destroying the rights of an accused, however. For example, an accuser's sexual history with other people can be ruled off-limits. Reasonable boundaries do not require the elimination of cross-examination.

Many campus hearings give the appearance of fairness by allowing an accused to submit questions that can be posed by the adjudicator(s) to the accuser or witnesses. This is inadequate for at least three reasons. *First*, questions must be submitted in advance, and this precludes examining statements made at the hearing. Because secrecy usually surrounds pre-hearing accusations, it is essential for an accused to dispute evidence as it unfolds. *Second*, asking a question is at the discretion of the hearing adjudicator(s) and cannot be viewed as a right possessed by the accused; it is a power possessed by the adjudicator(s). *Third*, the right to face an accuser derives its effectiveness from the reluctance of people to lie directly into the face of someone they are wronging. It is far easier for accusers to lie to administrators who have a vested interest in believing them.

Another item on the expanded list: An accused is found guilty not merely by "a preponderance of the evidence" standard but also by a majority vote. If 2 out of 3 members of a panel vote "guilty," then the dissenting vote is discarded. Here, again, the rules of campus hearings contradict those used by federal civil courts. Cornell University Law School offers the Federal Rules of Civil Procedure [41], "Unless the parties stipulate otherwise, the verdict must be unanimous..." Even if the campus hearing is a civil procedure, why does an accused not enjoy the same protection as in federal civil court?

Another due process violation is the lack of public access. The transparency of federal civil cases is a strong brake on arbitrary decisions, corrupt judges and procedural mistakes; transcripts are protections of justice. By contrast, campus hearings are secretive and records are usually sealed. Confidentiality agreements are common but accusers seem to speak out with impunity while those accused receive swift penalties for doing so. Only one side is heard.

Another difference: Campus hearings include no right against self-incrimination. According to a standard legal dictionary [42], "The Self-

Incrimination Clause applies to any state or federal legal proceeding, whether it is civil, criminal, administrative, or judicial in nature. This privilege is frequently invoked during the trial phase of legal proceedings, where individuals are placed under oath and asked questions on the witness stand."

Cohn is correct. The list goes on and on. Campus hearings violate almost every one of the protections embedded in federal civil court proceedings.

A massive step in the correct direction?

2. Treat sexual violence as a criminal matter by turning accusations over to the police for investigation and to the courts for adjudication.

> You know what would be really empowering? Putting rapists– real rapists, not the victims of regrettable sex– in jail. But somehow, like a nightmarish conference call that never ends, modern feminists would rather just keep talking, twisting logic, making excuses, embracing victimhood, and ignoring common-sense paths to justice for women who are actually aggrieved. –Heather Wilhelm [43]

Rape is a crime. It is an abhorrent crime that no civilized society will tolerate. Universities must take it seriously enough to hand accusations of sexual assault over to the police who are trained in criminal investigation and prosecution. If murders were committed on campus, bureaucrats and academics would not shoulder the task of forensic investigation or adjudication. The police would handle the crime.

In its 2014 letter to the White House, RAINN stressed the importance of treating sexual assaults on campus "as the felonies that they are." RAINN stated [44], "The FBI, for purposes of its Uniform Crime Reports, has a hierarchy of crimes – a ranking of violent crimes in order of seriousness. Murder, of course, ranks first. Second is rape. It would never occur to anyone to leave the adjudication of a murder in the hands of a school's internal judicial process. Why, then, is it not only common, but expected, for them to do so when it comes to sexual assault? We need to get to a point where it seems just as inappropriate to treat rape so lightly."

The police are miles away from perfect but they are more likely to be unbiased and to provide competent forensics. *Not* deferring to the police vastly increases the probability of several bad outcomes. They include:

• Sexual predators attack again

- Innocent men are found "guilty" and their lives are devastated
- Sexual assaults do not receive professional investigation
- False accusations proliferate
- Rape is trivialized as a disciplinary matter rather than the felony it is
- Rape is politicized and attached to ideological issues
- Sexual assault is tried in the court of public opinion, which encourages a circus atmosphere and further trivialization
- A hostile schism between the genders deepens

Rape culture adherents are eager to use the police as another weapon in their arsenal but they resist allowing the police role to dominate. Law enforcement is to be introduced only after campus hearings. After all, a police investigation flies in the face of PC dogma such as *always believe the woman*. Rape culture warriors may prefer imprisonment as the final scenario for those who are accused. But they want police to become primary only after campus investigations and hearings have sidestepped inconvenient obstacles like due process.

Conclusion

> Welcome to the cartoon comic book world of the modern feminist. They are the Super Victim Heroes called into battle against hordes of drooling, barbaric men who actually believe that rape is reasonable and justifiable. Back in Realityville, of course, no such belief system exists (outside of prisons, mental asylums, and the Middle East). Here, in the Land of Things That Are, we have feminists who use rape as a narrative tool to advance their agenda, and then the rest of us who are just about sick and tired of going along with the lunacy. [45]

Anyone who cares about rape victims wants to reduce the rate of assault.

The rape culture is not only a myth but also a barrier to preventing rape. Adherents show a disregard for victims whenever they excoriate crime-prevention advice and conflate it with slut-shaming. They destroy the reality of rape by substituting highly-flawed studies for facts and character assassination for arguments. By constructing unjust procedures to address reports of sexual assault on campus, they destroy public confidence in rape accusations and the women who make them. False accusations encourage a cynicism that no genuine victim should ever have to face.

The rape culture hysteria has been wildly successful within academia partly because it wears a mask of benevolence and justice. In reality, rape culture politics expresses intolerance and a dogmatic disregard for fairness. Political correctness is the opposite of what is purports to be. It does not champion human rights; it destroys them. It does not express morality; it converts morality into a mockery imposed by government. It destroys the goodwill that naturally flows between free individuals who are equal.

The rape culture does so through a war on ideas, attitudes and words.

In George Orwell's novel *1984*, a character named Syme works alongside protagonist Winston Smith at the Ministry of Truth. A language specialist, Syme is working to produce a new edition of the "Newspeak" dictionary. Newspeak is a drastically pared down version of the English language which redefines and eliminates undesirable words. In one of the most famous passages of English literature, Syme explains [46],

> It's a beautiful thing, the Destruction of words....Take 'good,' for instance. If you have a word like 'good,' what need is there for a word like 'bad'? 'Ungood' will do just as well – better, because it's an exact opposite, which the other is not. Or again, if you want a stronger version of 'good,' what sense is there in having a whole string of vague useless words like 'excellent' and 'splendid' and all the rest of them? 'Plusgood' covers the meaning or 'doubleplusgood' if you want something stronger still. Of course we use those forms already, but in the final version of Newspeak there'll be nothing else. In the end the whole notion of goodness and badness will be covered by only six words – in reality, only one word. Don't you see the beauty of that?

The purpose of Newspeak is to control the ability of people and society to think and communicate so that only correct thoughts and speech occur. Syme continues:

> Don't you see that the whole aim of Newspeak is to narrow the range of thought? In the end we shall make thoughtcrime literally impossible, because there will be no words in which to express it. Every concept that can ever be needed will be expressed by exactly one word, with its meaning rigidly defined and all its subsidiary meanings rubbed out and forgotten....By 2050, earlier, probably – all real knowledge of Oldspeak will have disappeared. The whole literature of the past will have been destroyed. Chaucer,

> Shakespeare, Milton, Byron – they'll exist only in Newspeak versions, not merely changed into something different, but actually changed into something contradictory of what they used to be....The whole climate of thought will be different. In fact there will be no thought, as we understand it now. Orthodoxy means not thinking – not needing to think. Orthodoxy is unconsciousness.

Words are vehicles of ideas; ideas feed behavior. When the language with which human beings think and communicate is regulated, then thought and action are regulated. Political correctness is the new totalitarianism.

With a bitter irony, PC feminism and the rape culture hysteria on which it thrives is destroying the basis of feminism itself. The freedom of women has always rested on one thing: the ability to say "no," the ability to say "I disagree." Without being able to dissent, there is no freedom, no justice, no color to life. There is only 1984. Welcome to the true rape culture – the rape of human freedom.

Notes

[1] Title IX of the Education Amendments of 1972 should not be confused with somewhat similar Title IX of the Civil Rights Act of 1964 which ended racial segregation in schools. http://www2.ed.gov/about/offices/list/ocr/aboutocr.html Retrieved Oct. 8, 2015.

[2] As quoted by Veronica Elliot, "School Bans Use of Gender Greetings 'Ms.' and 'Mr.'," FIRE, Jan. 30, 2015.   https://www.thefire.org/school-bans-use-gender-greetings-ms-mr/ Retrieved Oct. 9, 2015.

[3] Robby Soave, "Campus Censorship is The Feds' Fault," *The Daily Beast*, June 6, 2015. http://www.thedailybeast.com/articles/2015/06/06/campus-censorship-is-the-feds-fault.html Retrieved Oct. 8, 2015.

[4] Robby Soave, "CUNY Tells Profs Not to Say 'Mr.' or 'Ms.' Because That's Offensive and Illegal-ish (It's Not)," *Reason*, Jan. 30, 2015. http://reason.com/blog/2015/01/30/cuny-prohibits-profs-from-using-mr-or-ms Retrieved Oct. 8, 2015.

[5] Tyler Kingkade, "Barnard College Joins List Of 94 Colleges Under Title IX Investigations," *Huffington Post*, Jan. 7, 2015. http://www.huffingtonpost.com/2015/01/07/barnard-college-title-ix-investigations_n_6432596.html Retrieved Oct. 8, 2015.

[6] OCR Complaint Processing Procedures, Department of Education. http://www2.ed.gov/about/offices/list/ocr/complaints-how.html Retrieved Oct. 8, 2015.

[7] K.C. Johnson, "OCR Settles with Harvard Law," *Minding the Campus*, Jan. 2, 2015. A key disagreement between OCR and Harvard was whether the university would abandon the standard of "beyond a reasonable doubt" and adopt "preponderance of the evidence" instead. http://www.mindingthecampus.org/2015/01/ocr-settles-with-harvard-law/ Retrieved Oct. 8, 2015.

[8] Jake New, "Justice Delayed," *Inside Higher Education*, May 6, 2015. https://www.insidehighered.com/news/2015/05/06/ocr-letter-says-completed-title-ix-investigations-2014-lasted-more-4-years Retrieved Oct. 8, 2015.

[9] Note: this explanatory article is being currently considered for deletion from the Wiki. No explanation is given. http://ca.wow.com/wiki/The_New_Campus_Anti-Rape_Movement Retrieved Oct. 3, 2015.

[10] "Feds Approve University of Montana Sexual Harassment Policy That Threatens Speech; Faculty Who Refuse Training To Be Reported To Federal Government," Foundation for Individual Rights in Education, Oct. 1, 2013. https://www.thefire.org/feds-approve-university-of-montana-sexual-harassment-policy-that-threatens-speech-faculty-who-refuse-training-to-be-reported-to-federal-government/ Retrieved Oct. 8, 2015.

[11] Edward Schlosser (pseudonym), "I'm a liberal professor, and my liberal students terrify me," *Vox*, June 3, 2015. http://www.vox.com/2015/6/3/8706323/college-professor-afraid Retrieved Oct. 8, 2015.

[12] As quoted by Soave, "Campus Censorship is The Feds' Fault," op. cit.

[13] Jessica Montoya Coggins, "Outrage as Department of Education quotes notorious Chinese leader Mao Zedong on its website," *Daily Mail*, March 24, 2013. It was subsequently removed and replaced by a quote from Abraham Lincoln. http://www.dailymail.co.uk/news/article-2298282/Outrage-Department-Education-quotes-notorious-Chinese-leader-Mao-Zedong-website.html Retrieved Oct. 8, 2015.

[14] Jimmy Carter, Department of Education Organization Act Statement on Signing S. 210 Into Law, October 17, 1979, American Presidency Project. http://www.presidency.ucsb.edu/ws/?pid=31543 Retrieved Oct. 8, 2015.

[15] Spokesman-Review archives. Browse and search archived content published online. www.spokesman.com/archives/ Retrieved Oct. 8, 2015.

[16] Ibid.

[17] Deanna L. Michael, *Jimmy Carter as Educational Policymaker: Equal Opportunity and Efficiency,* (State Univ of New York, 2008), p.162.

[18] Maurice R. Berube, *American Presidents and Education: Contributions to the Study of Education,* (Westport, Ct: Praeger, 1991), p.51.

[19] Gerald M. Pomper, "The Alleged Decline of the American Parties," as quoted in *Politicians and Party Politics,* ed. John Gray Geer (Johns Hopkins University Press, 1998), p.26.

[20] Mona Charen, "Wanting to Abolish the Department of Education Is Not Radical," *National Review*, June 11, 2010. http://www.nationalreview.com/article/229936/wanting-abolish-department-education-not-radical-mona-charen Retrieved Oct. 8, 2015.

[21] J Michael Smith, "U.S. Department of Education: Homeschooling Continues to Grow!," HSLDA, September 3, 2013. http://www.hslda.org/docs/news/2013/201309030.asp Retrieved Oct. 8, 2015.

[22] Adam S. Schaeffer, "Yes, the Department of Education Is Unconstitutional," Cato Institute, Sept. 6, 2011. http://www.cato.org/blog/yes-department-education-unconstitutional Retrieved Oct. 8, 2015.

[23] Neal McCluskey, "End the Fed," Cato Institute (reprint) from the *Washington Times*, Feb. 22, 2010. http://www.cato.org/publications/commentary/end-fed-ed Retrieved Oct. 13, 2015.

[24] David French, "Title IX, the All-Purpose Leftist Excuse: It allows persecution of anyone who contravenes feminist doctrine," *National Review*, June 4, 2015. http://www.nationalreview.com/article/419344/title-ix-all-purpose-leftist-excuse-david-french Retrieved Oct. 8, 2015.

[25] Eugene Volokh, "Open letter from 16 Penn Law School professors about Title IX and sexual assault complaints," *Washington Post*, Feb. 19, 2015. http://www.washingtonpost.com/news/volokh-conspiracy/wp/2015/02/19/open-letter-from-16-penn-law-school-professors-about-title-ix-and-sexual-assault-complaints/ Retrieved Oct. 8, 2015.

[26] Lawrence A. Uzzell, "No Child Left Behind: The Dangers of Centralized Education Policy," Cato Institute, May 31, 2005. Uzzell is a former staff member of the U.S. Department of Education and the U.S. House and Senate committees on education. http://object.cato.org/sites/cato.org/files/pubs/pdf/pa544.pdf Retrieved Oct. 8, 2015.

[27] As quoted by David Boaz, "Education and the Constitution," Cato Institute, May 1, 2006. http://www.cato.org/blog/education-constitution Retrieved Oct. 8, 2015.

[28] Uzzell, op. cit.

[29] Richard Vedder, "To Improve Higher Education, Scale Back Federal Involvement," *National Review*, April 2, 2015. http://www.nationalreview.com/article/416356/improve-higher-education-scale-back-federal-involvement-richard-vedder Retrieved Oct. 8, 2015.

[30] Irwin S. Kirsch , Ann Jungeblut, Lynn Jenkins, Andrew Kolstad,"Adult Literacy in America," National Center for Education Statistics, April 2, 2002. http://nces.ed.gov/pubs93/93275.pdf Retrieved Oct. 8, 2015.

[31] Robert Higgs, *The Transformation of the American Economy: An Essay in Interpretation (American Economic History),* (Hoboken, NJ: John Wiley & Sons, 1971), p.34.

[32] As quoted by Jonathan M. Finegold, "America's Greatest Industrial Transformation," Mises Institute, Oct. 3, 2011. https://mises.org/library/americas-greatest-industrial-transformation#footnote24_gi9nrc3 Retrieved Oct. 8, 2015.

[33] Jack Healy, "To Keep Free of Federal Reins, Wyoming Catholic College Rejects Student Aid," *New York Times*, April 11, 2015. http://www.nytimes.com/2015/04/12/us/to-keep-free-of-federal-reins-wyoming-catholic-college-rejects-student-aid.html Retrieved Oct. 8, 2015.

[34] Nate Madden, "Wyoming college says declining federal funds protects Catholic identity," *National Catholic Reporter*, March 16, 2015. http://ncronline.org/news/faith-parish/wyoming-college-says-declining-federal-funds-protects-catholic-identity Retrieved Oct. 8, 2015.

[35] Philip DiSalvo, "New Directions for Higher Education: Q&A with Muriel Howard on Public Higher Ed," New England Board of Higher Education, March 31, 2014. http://www.nebhe.org/thejournal/new-

directions-for-higher-education-qa-with-muriel-howard-on-public-higher-ed/ Retrieved Oct. 8, 2015.

[36] Eugene Volokh, op. cit.

[37] "Sexual Harassment Guidance 1997," OCR, Department of Education. http://www2.ed.gov/about/offices/list/ocr/docs/sexhar01.html Retrieved Oct. 8, 2015.

[38] Ashe Schow, "Police officer brags about circumventing due process in sexual assault cases," *Washington Examiner*, July 9, 2015. http://www.washingtonexaminer.com/police-officer-brags-about-circumventing-due-process-in-sexual-assault-cases/article/2567949 Retrieved Oct. 8, 2015.

[39] Jake New, "Making Title IX Work," *Inside Higher Ed*, July 6, 2015. https://www.insidehighered.com/news/2015/07/06/college-law-enforcement-administrators-hear-approach-make-title-ix-more-effective Retrieved Oct. 8, 2015.

[40] Joseph Cohn, "Campus Is a Poor Court for Students Facing Sexual-Misconduct Charges," The Chronicle of Higher Education, Oct. 1, 2012. http://chronicle.com/article/Campus-Is-a-Poor-Court-for/134770/ Retrieved Oct. 13, 2015.

[41] "Rule 48. Number of Jurors; Verdict; Polling," Cornell University Law School Legal Information Institute. Note: on the state court level, the percentage of the vote required for a verdict varies widely. https://www.law.cornell.edu/rules/frcp/rule_48 Retrieved Oct. 8, 2015.

[42] Fifth Amendment, Free Legal Dictionary. http://legal-dictionary.thefreedictionary.com/fifth+amendment Retrieved Oct. 8, 2015.

[43] Heather Wilhelm, "The Rise of the Weak-Kneed Feminists, *Real Clear Politics*, Feb. 5, 2015. http://www.realclearpolitics.com/articles/2015/02/05/the_rise_of_the_weak-kneed_feminists.html Retrieved Oct. 8, 2015.

[44] Rape, Abuse, Incest National Network, Letter to White House Task Force to Protect Students from Sexual Assault United States Department of Justice Office on Violence Against Women, Feb. 8, 2014. Note: RAINN's letter does not advocate turning reports entirely over to the police but urges the university to partner with the police from the moment a report is filed. http://rainn.org/images/03-2014/WH-Task-Force-RAINN-Recommendations.pdf Retrieved Oct. 8, 2015.

[45] Matt Walsh, "Rape Culture Doesn't Exist And There Is No Rape Epidemic," *The Blaze*, Dec. 9, 2014. http://www.theblaze.com/contributions/rape-culture-doesnt-exist-and-there-is-no-rape-epidemic/ Retrieved Oct. 8, 2015.

[46] George Orwell, *1984*. http://msxnet.org/orwell/1984 Retrieved Oct. 8, 2015.